WORKBOOK/LAB MANUAL
TO ACCOMPANY

Invitation
au monde francophone

Invitation à écouter, à lire et à écrire

WORKBOOK/LAB MANUAL
TO ACCOMPANY

Invitation
au monde francophone

SECOND EDITION

GILBERT A. JARVIS
The Ohio State University

THÉRÈSE M. BONIN
The Ohio State University

DIANE W. BIRCKBICHLER
The Ohio State University

MELISSA M. GRUZS

ANNE LAIR
University of Northern Iowa

THOMSON

HEINLE

Australia ◆ Canada ◆ Mexico ◆ Singapore ◆ Spain ◆ United Kingdom ◆ United States

THOMSON

HEINLE

Invitation au monde francophone
Workbook / Lab Manual
Second Edition
Jarvis / Bonin / Birckbichler / Gruzs / Lair

Editor-in-Chief: *PJ Boardman*
Publisher: *Janet Dracksdorf*
Acquisitions Editor: *Lara Semones*
Senior Development Editor: *Glenn A. Wilson*
Senior Production Project Manager: *Esther Marshall*
Marketing Manager: *Lindsey Richardson*
Manufacturing Manager: *Marcia Locke*
Compositor: *Greg Johnson, Art Directions*
Illustrator: *Len Shalanski*
Cover Designer: *Diane Levy*
Printer: *Darby Printing Company*

For more information contact Thomson Heinle, 25 Thomson Place, Boston, Massachusetts 02210 USA,
or you can visit our Internet site at **http://www.thomson.com**

ISBN: 1-4130-0138-6

Table des matières

Preface

Invitation à écouter, à lire et à écrire is both a workbook and a guide to the audio program that accompanies *Invitation au monde francophone*. Each chapter is divided into two parts, a **Partie écrite** and a **Partie orale**. The **Partie écrite**—the workbook portion—is designed to improve your ability to read and write in French. The **Partie orale**—the lab manual portion—provides opportunities for out-of-class practice in speaking and listening skills. The ample use of realia (ads, charts, maps, text from websites, etc.) and contextualized activities in both parts will enhance your understanding of francophone culture.

PARTIE ÉCRITE

Each **partie écrite** begins with activities that focus on the vocabulary presented in the **Point de départ** section of the text. Exercises that correspond to the grammar presentations within each chapter follow, and the **Partie écrite** concludes with an **Intégration et perspectives** section that provides opportunities to improve your reading and writing skills and to learn more about different regions of France.

For each grammar topic, the feature **Êtes-vous prêts?** provides a series of statements that will help you assess your understanding of the topic before you begin working on the activities. You will indicate how well you think you can handle the topic by ranking each statement from 1 (least comfortable) to 5 (most comfortable). If you mark 1 to 3 for any statement, you should review the material in your textbook before beginning the activities. Next is a series of activities ranging from structured exercises to freer communication activities. The exercises provide supplementary practice of the new language structure; the more open-ended activities encourage you to use the new structure and vocabulary you know in personalized situations. All exercises and activities are situated in a real-life context that relates to the chapter theme, which requires you to pay attention to meaning as you work with a language structure.

Intégration et perspectives has three parts:

1. **Chez nous en France** presents texts written from the perspective of French people living in different areas of France such as **la Bretagne, le Périgord,** and **les Alpes.** Each **Chez nous** text is followed by an **Avez-vous compris?** section that checks the your comprehension of the reading.

2. **À vous de lire** is an authentic reading generally taken from a francophone website and is related to the theme of the **Chez nous** text. You will read and interpret these challenging but interesting readings and then complete specific tasks to develop your reading strategies and to help you determine how well you have understood the reading.

3. **À vous d'écrire** is a four-step creative process-writing activity related to the chapter theme. In **Préparation,** you brainstorm ideas to use in the writing task. In **Brouillon,** you write your first draft, incorporating both your ideas from **Préparation** and the pertinent chapter vocabulary and grammar structures. In **Révision,** you evaluate your composition based on the questions and suggestions provided. Last, in **Rédaction,** you incorporate the changes you note in **Révision** into the final version of your composition.

PARTIE ORALE

For each chapter of your textbook, the audio program for *Invitation à écouter, à lire et à écrire* begins with a listening comprehension activity based on the vocabulary presented in the chapter's **Point de départ** section.

Practice with grammar structures follows; the structures and readings of the **Situation** conversations are taken up in the same sequence as in the textbook. For each structure, you complete several oral exercises that move from simple to more complex. These exercises are taken from the **Communication et vie pratique** section of your textbook and are indicated by an asterisk (*) in the **Partie orale.** A listening comprehension activity then tests your oral comprehension of the grammar and vocabulary you have studied. All exercises are based on a meaningful context so that you will practice vocabulary and structures in lifelike situations.

The next section offers a series of activities based on the chapter's **Intégration et perspectives.** You will hear a listening comprehension passage that relates to the chapter theme and integrates the chapter grammar and vocabulary. Comprehension questions about the passage are printed in the **Partie orale.** A contextualized dictation focusing on the grammar, vocabulary, and theme of the chapter gives you an opportunity to write in French what you hear.

The **Bien prononcer** sections from your textbook are recorded. These sections allow you to practice the pronunciation of individual sounds and words.

The **Partie orale** provides space for you to complete the various listening tasks, write out dictation sentences, and answer comprehension questions based on the listening passages. The corresponding track number from the audio program appears next to each exercise in the **Partie orale.**

LA FRANCE

LE ROYAUME-UNI

LA MER DU NORD

LES PAYS-BAS (m. pl.)

LA BELGIQUE

la Wallonie

Langues maternelles

Le français langue maternelle majoritaire

Le français langue maternelle d'une minorité importante

Langues officielles

Le français est la seule langue officielle

Le français est une des langues officielles du pays ou de l'état

Le français est la langue de la culture ou des affaires pour une partie importante de la population

LE LUXEMBOURG

LA MANCHE

Dunkerque
Calais
Boulogne
Lille
NORD-PAS-DE-CALAIS
Dieppe
Amiens
PICARDIE
Cherbourg
HAUTE-NORMANDIE
Charleville-Mézières
Le Havre
Rouen
ÎLE-DE-FRANCE
Reims
Verdun
Metz
la Seine
Paris
Caen
CHAMPAGNE-ARDENNE
LORRAINE
Nancy
St. Malo
BASSE-NORMANDIE
Versailles
Strasbourg
ALSACE
L'ALSACE (f.)
Brest
le Mont-St. Michel
Chartres
Fontainebleau
Troyes
BRESSE
LES VOSGES
Rennes
Colmar
L'ALLEMAGNE (f.)
BRETAGNE
CENTRE
Le Mans
Orléans
la Loire
BOURGOGNE
FRANCHE-COMTÉ
Angers
Blois
Dijon
la Saône
Besançon
Nantes
Tours
la Loire
LIMOUSIN
Bourges
LA SUISSE
PAYS DE LA LOIRE
LA FRANCE
Poitiers
LE JURA
La Rochelle
AUVERGNE
le Val d'Aoste
POITOU-CHARENTES
Lyon
RHÔNE-ALPES
L'OCÉAN ATLANTIQUE (m.)
Limoges
Clermont-Ferrand
L'ITALIE (f.)
PÉRIGORD
Grenoble
Bordeaux
Rocamadour
LES ALPES
AQUITAINE
LE MASSIF CENTRAL
le Rhône
la Garonne
Moissac
PROVENCE-ALPES-CÔTE D'AZUR
Nice
Albi
Nîmes
Avignon
Cannes
MIDI-PYRÉNÉES
Montpellier
Arles
Aix-en-Provence
MONACO (f.)
Biarritz
Toulouse
Marseille
LE PAYS BASQUE
Lourdes
Carcassonne
LANGUEDOC-ROUSSILLON
LES PYRÉNÉES (f.pl.)
Perpignan
la CORSE
L'ANDORRE (f.)
LA MER MÉDITERRANÉE
L'ESPAGNE (f.)

| 0 | 25 | 50 | 75 | 100 MILLES |

| 0 | 50 | 100 | 150 KILOMÈTRES |

L'AMÉRIQUE DU NORD

LE GROENLAND

L'OCÉAN ARCTIQUE (m.)

l'Alaska (m.) (LES ÉTATS-UNIS)

le Yukon

les Territoires du Nord-Ouest (m. pl.)

le Nunavut

Saint-Pierre-et-Miquelon (LA FRANCE)

L'AMÉRIQUE DU NORD (f.)

Langues maternelles

- ☐ Le français langue maternelle majoritaire
- ☐ Le français et un créole français langues maternelles
- ☐ Créole français langue maternelle majoritaire
- ☐ Le français langue maternelle d'une minorité importante

Langues officielles

- ☐ Le français est la seule langue officielle
- ▨ Le français est une des langues officielles du pays ou de l'état
- ☐ Le français sert de langue administrative ou dans l'enseignement

LE CANADA

la Colombie Britannique

l'Alberta (m.)

le Manitoba

la Saskatchewan

l'Ontario (m.)

le Québec

le Maine

Terre-Neuve (f.)

l'Île du Prince-Edouard (f.)

la Nouvelle-Écosse

le New Hampshire

le Vermont

Québec

Montréal ⦿

★ Ottawa

le Nouveau-Brunswick

le Massachusetts

le Rhode Island

le Connecticut

LES ÉTATS-UNIS (m. pl.)

la Louisiane

Les Îles Hawaii (m. pl.) (LES ÉTATS-UNIS)

L'OCÉAN ATLANTIQUE (m.)

LE MEXIQUE

GOLFE DU MEXIQUE

LE BELIZE

CUBA (m.)

LES CARAÏBES (m. pl.)

LA JAMAÏQUE

HAÏTI (m.)

LA GUYANE FRANÇAISE (LA FRANCE)

L'AMÉRIQUE CENTRALE (f.)

LE GUATEMALA

LE SALVADOR

LE HONDURAS

LE NICARAGUA

LE COSTA RICA

LE PANAMA

(LA RÉPUBLIQUE DE) L'ÉQUATEUR (m.)

LE VENEZUELA

LA COLOMBIE

Cayenne ★

LA GUYANA

LE SURINAM

L'OCÉAN PACIFIQUE (m.)

L'AMÉRIQUE DU SUD (f.)

LE PÉROU

LE BRÉSIL

LA BOLIVIE

LES CARAÏBES

CUBA (m.)

LA RÉPUBLIQUE DOMINICAINE

la Guadeloupe (LA FRANCE)

PUERTO RICO (m.)

Port-au-Prince ★

LA MER DES CARAÏBES

Pointe-à-Pitre ★

DOMINIQUE (f.)

Fort-de-France ★

HAÏTI (m.)

la Martinique (LA FRANCE)

SAINTE LUCIE (f.)

MILLES	
0	300

KILOMÈTRES	
0	450

À 45° LATITUDE

	0	200	400	600	800 MILLES

	0	400	800	1.200 KILOMÈTRES

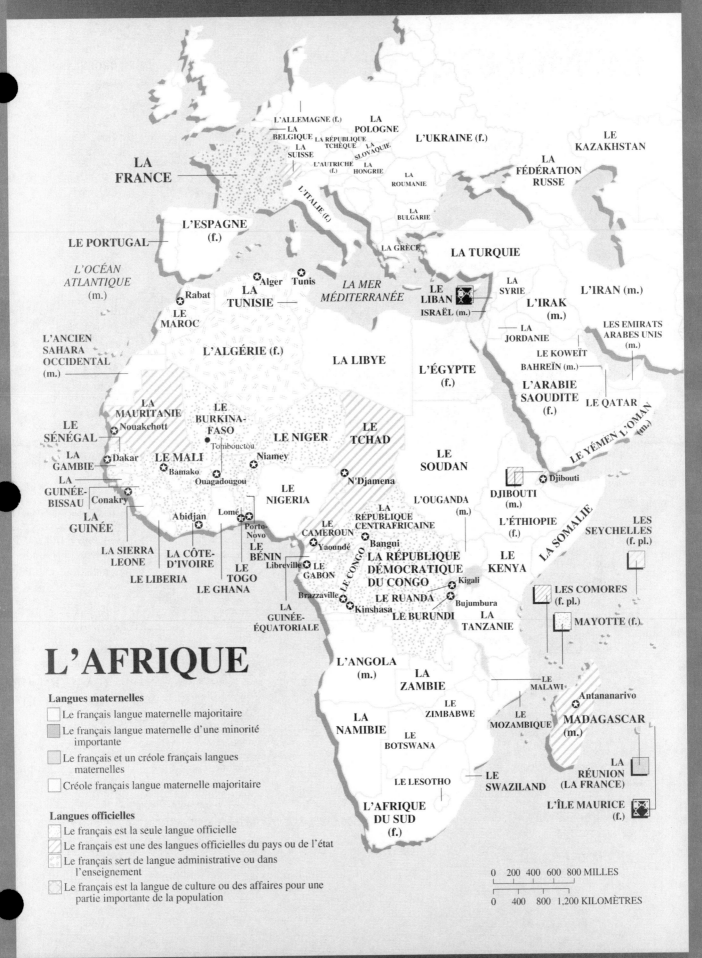

L'AFRIQUE

L'ALLEMAGNE (f.)
LA POLOGNE
L'UKRAINE (f.)
LE KAZAKHSTAN
LA BELGIQUE
LA RÉPUBLIQUE TCHÈQUE
LA SLOVAQUIE
LA SUISSE
L'AUTRICHE (f.)
LA HONGRIE
LA FÉDÉRATION RUSSE
LA FRANCE
LA ROUMANIE
LA BULGARIE
L'ESPAGNE (f.)
LA GRÈCE
LA TURQUIE
LE PORTUGAL
L'OCÉAN ATLANTIQUE (m.)
LA MER MÉDITERRANÉE
Alger Tunis
LA SYRIE
L'IRAN (m.)
LE LIBAN
ISRAËL (m.)
L'IRAK (m.)
Rabat
LA TUNISIE
LA JORDANIE
LES EMIRATS ARABES UNIS (m.)
LE MAROC
LE KOWEÏT
BAHREÏN (m.)
L'ANCIEN SAHARA OCCIDENTAL (m.)
L'ALGÉRIE (f.)
LA LIBYE
L'ÉGYPTE (f.)
L'ARABIE SAOUDITE (f.)
LE QATAR
LA MAURITANIE
Nouakchott
LE BURKINA-FASO
LE NIGER
LE TCHAD
LE YÉMEN L'OMAN (m.)
LE SÉNÉGAL
Tombouctou
Niamey
LE SOUDAN
Djibouti
LA GAMBIE
Dakar
LE MALI
Bamako
N'Djamena
DJIBOUTI (m.)
LA GUINÉE-BISSAU
Conakry
Ouagadougou
LE NIGERIA
L'OUGANDA (m.)
L'ÉTHIOPIE (f.)
LES SEYCHELLES (f. pl.)
LA GUINÉE
Abidjan
Lomé
Porto-Novo
LE CAMEROUN
LA RÉPUBLIQUE CENTRAFRICAINE
LA SOMALIE
LA SIERRA LEONE
LA CÔTE-D'IVOIRE
LE BÉNIN
Yaoundé
Bangui
LE KENYA
LES COMORES (f. pl.)
LE LIBERIA
LE TOGO
LE GHANA
Libreville
LE GABON
LA RÉPUBLIQUE DÉMOCRATIQUE DU CONGO
Kigali
MAYOTTE (f.)
Brazzaville
LE RUANDA
Bujumbura
LA GUINÉE-ÉQUATORIALE
Kinshasa
LE BURUNDI
LA TANZANIE
L'ANGOLA (m.)
LA ZAMBIE
LE MALAWI
Antananarivo
LE ZIMBABWE
LE MOZAMBIQUE
MADAGASCAR (m.)
LA NAMIBIE
LE BOTSWANA
LA RÉUNION (LA FRANCE)
LE LESOTHO
LE SWAZILAND
L'ÎLE MAURICE (f.)
L'AFRIQUE DU SUD (f.)

Langues maternelles

☐ Le français langue maternelle majoritaire
▨ Le français langue maternelle d'une minorité importante
▨ Le français et un créole français langues maternelles
☐ Créole français langue maternelle majoritaire

Langues officielles

☐ Le français est la seule langue officielle
▨ Le français est une des langues officielles du pays ou de l'état
▨ Le français sert de langue administrative ou dans l'enseignement
☐ Le français est la langue de culture ou des affaires pour une partie importante de la population

0 200 400 600 800 MILLES

0 400 800 1,200 KILOMÈTRES

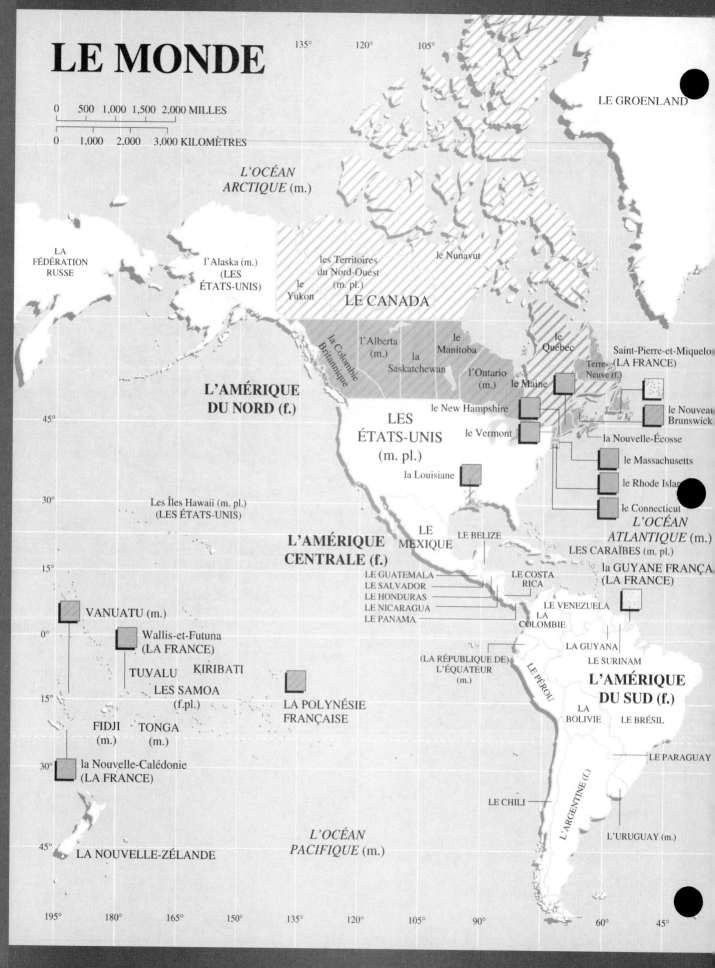

LE MONDE

0   500 1,000 1,500 2,000 MILLES

0   1,000 2,000 3,000 KILOMÈTRES

135°   120°   105°

LE GROENLAND

L'OCÉAN ARCTIQUE (m.)

LA FÉDÉRATION RUSSE

l'Alaska (m.) (LES ÉTATS-UNIS)

les Territoires du Nord-Ouest (m. pl.)

le Nunavut

le Yukon

LE CANADA

la Colombie Britannique

l'Alberta (m.)

la Saskatchewan

le Manitoba

l'Ontario (m.)

le Québec

Terre-Neuve (f.)

Saint-Pierre-et-Miquelon (LA FRANCE)

L'AMÉRIQUE DU NORD (f.)

LES ÉTATS-UNIS (m. pl.)

le Maine

le New Hampshire

le Vermont

le Nouveau Brunswick

la Nouvelle-Écosse

le Massachusetts

le Rhode Island

le Connecticut

la Louisiane

45°

30°

Les Îles Hawaii (m. pl.) (LES ÉTATS-UNIS)

L'AMÉRIQUE CENTRALE (f.)

LE MEXIQUE

LE BELIZE

LE GUATEMALA
LE SALVADOR
LE HONDURAS
LE NICARAGUA
LE PANAMA

LE COSTA RICA

L'OCÉAN ATLANTIQUE (m.)

LES CARAÏBES (m. pl.)

la GUYANE FRANÇAISE (LA FRANCE)

15°

LE VENEZUELA

LA COLOMBIE

LA GUYANA

LE SURINAM

VANUATU (m.)

0°

Wallis-et-Futuna (LA FRANCE)

TUVALU   KIRIBATI

LES SAMOA (f.pl.)

15°

LA POLYNÉSIE FRANÇAISE

(LA RÉPUBLIQUE DE) L'ÉQUATEUR (m.)

LE PÉROU

L'AMÉRIQUE DU SUD (f.)

FIDJI (m.)   TONGA (m.)

LA BOLIVIE

LE BRÉSIL

30°

la Nouvelle-Calédonie (LA FRANCE)

LE PARAGUAY

L'ARGENTINE (f.)

LE CHILI

L'URUGUAY (m.)

45°

L'OCÉAN PACIFIQUE (m.)

LA NOUVELLE-ZÉLANDE

195°   180°   165°   150°   135°   120°   105°   90°   60°   45°

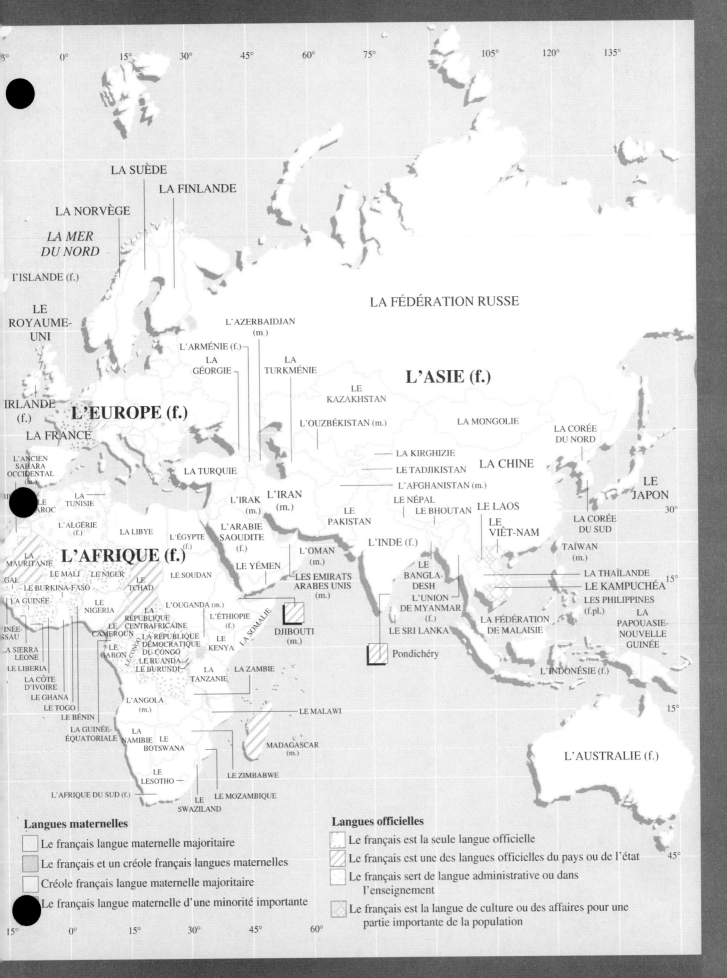

Langues maternelles

- Le français langue maternelle majoritaire
- Le français et un créole français langues maternelles
- Créole français langue maternelle majoritaire
- Le français langue maternelle d'une minorité importante

Langues officielles

- Le français est la seule langue officielle
- Le français est une des langues officielles du pays ou de l'état
- Le français sert de langue administrative ou dans l'enseignement
- Le français est la langue de culture ou des affaires pour une partie importante de la population

Chapitre préliminaire ○ ○ ○ ○ ○ ○ ○

Premiers contacts

PARTIE ÉCRITE

Bonjour, tout le monde!

Conversations. Using expressions you've learned on pages 2–3 of your text, fill in the blanks.

1.

Karine. _____ , je m'appelle _____ , je m'appelle toi ?

Je _____ Benoît .

2.

Bonjour, _____ . Comment _____ appelez - vous ?

_____ , Monsieur . _____ Sébastien Olivier .

3.

_____ , Madame . _____ allez - vous ?

Très _____ , _____ . Et vous ?

4.

Au _____ , Didier .

À tout _____ revoir, Xavier _____ .

Dans la salle de classe

Qu'est-ce que c'est? In the space provided, write a sentence identifying each of the numbered objects.

EXEMPLE *C'est un crayon.*

1. _____   7. _____

2. _____   8. _____

3. _____   9. _____

4. _____   10. _____

5. _____   11. _____

6. _____   12. _____

C'est quel jour?

Quel jour? One of your jobs at a ticket sales office is to tell customers on what days of the week certain dance performances and other events are held. Using the following schedule as a guide, give the information your customers request.

EXEMPLE   (La) Fondation Jean-Pierre Perreault?
C'est lundi et mardi.

Hydro-Québec
présente le

festival
International de Nouvelle
danse

Montréal

29 septembre-9 octobre

	Place des Arts Théâtre Maisonneuve	Salle Pierre-Mercure	Musée d'art contemporain Salle multimédia	Théâtre d'Aujourd'hui	Agora de la Danse Studio	Agora de la Danse Espace Tangente	Cinéma O.N.F.	Complexe Desjardins
	20 h 30	21 h	18 h 30	19 h	19 h	17 h 30	19 h	12 h
Oct S 2	Compagnie Marie Chouinard	Compagnie Michèle Anne De Mey	Shob... ingh C... any Complet	DV8 Physical Theatre	Dansers Studio / Beppie Blankert	Annamirl van der Pluijm	Film Strange Fish (DV8)**	
D 3	Compagnie Marie Chouinard		Shob... ngh D... 14 Complet	DV8 Physical Theatre	Dansers Studio / Beppie Blankert	Annamirl van der Pluijm	Film Strange Fish (DV8)	
L 4		Fondation Jean-Pierre Perreault*					Film Strange Fish (DV8) SUPPLÉMENTAIRE à 20 h 30	Danse Midi
M 5		Fondation Jean-Pierre Perreault		DV8 Physical Theatre	Jona... G... ws Complet	Annamirl van der Pluijm		Danse Midi
M 6	Ultima Vez		Héla... C... n Complet	DV8 Physical Theatre	Jonathan Burrows Group	Ann... P... r Complet		
J 7		Dancemakers	Hélène Blackburn Cas public	DV8 Physical Theatre		Annamirl van der Pluijm		
V 8	Bill T. Jones / Arnie Zane Dance Company			DV8 Physical Theatre	Àngels Margarit** Mudances	Annamirl van der Pluijm		
S 9	Bill T. Jones / Arnie Zane Dance Company	Le Ballet du Fargistan**			Àngels Margarit Mudances			

*Première mondiale
**Première nord-américaine

| | Communications Canada | Gouvernement du Québec Ministère de la Culture | CONSEIL DES ARTS | Ville de Montréal Commission d'initiative et de développement culturels (CIDEC) | Affaires extérieures et Commerce extérieur Canada | Hydro-Québec Le meilleur de nous-mêmes |

1. Ultima Vez? _____

2. Danse Midi? _____

3. Dancemakers? _____

4. Compagnie Marie Chouinard? _____

5. Angels Margarit Mudances? _____

6. Le Ballet du Fargistan? _____

Les nombres de 0 à 31

Températures. The following weather page from *Le Monde* gives high and low temperatures for international cities. In the space provided, write out the temperatures for the cities listed.

		maximum	**minimum**
EXEMPLE	Varsovie	*seize* degrés	*quatorze* degrés

TEMPÉRATURES			
du 25 juillet **maxima/minima**			

FRANCE		GRENOBLE	29/16	TOURS	27/13	CHICAGO	24/17	LISBONNE	24/18	PRETORIA	14/8
		LILLE	16/11	**ÉTRANGER**		COPENHAGUE	25/13	LONDRES	25/14	RABAT	26/21
		LIMOGES	28/18	ALGER	39/23	DAKAR	30/23	LOS ANGELES	26/19	RIO DE JAN.	31/22
		LYON	26/15	AMSTERDAM	17/11	DJAKARTA	32/23	LUXEMBOURG	18/11	ROME	30/20
		MARSEILLE	33/21	ATHÈNES	32/22	DUBAI	45/31	MADRID	34/17	SAN FRANC.	17/12
AJACCIO	29/18	NANCY	20/10	BANGKOK	29/25	DUBLIN	23/16	MARRAKECH	39/20	SANTIAGO	18/3
BIARRITZ	28/18	NANTES	27/16	BARCELONE	29/22	FRANCFORT	21/13	MEXICO	26/14	SÉVILLE	34/19
BORDEAUX	29/17	NICE	27/21	BELGRADE	22/11	GENÈVE	27/13	MILAN	29/15	ST-PÉTERS.	21/15
BOURGES	26/14	PARIS	24/14	BERLIN	19/14	HANOÏ	33/27	MONTRÉAL	28/18	STOCKHOLM	24/14
BREST	21/12	PAU	30/17	BOMBAY	31/26	HELSINKI	20/14	MOSCOU	22/12	SYDNEY	19/13
CAEN	22/11	PERPIGNAN	33/22	BRASILIA	26/11	HONGKONG	34/29	MUNICH	20/14	TENERIFE	27/23
CHERBOURG	22/11	POINTE-À-PIT.	31/25	BRUXELLES	16/14	ISTANBUL	26/20	NAIROBI	21/10	TOKYO	32/25
CLERMONT-F.	26/15	RENNES	27/12	BUCAREST	32/14	JÉRUSALEM	28/20	NEW DELHI	32/26	TUNIS	39/25
DIJON	26/13	ST-DENIS-RÉUNION	23/16	BUDAPEST	23/15	KIEV	26/15	NEW YORK	28/21	VARSOVIE	16/14
FORT-DE-FR.	28/24	ST-ÉTIENNE	25/12	BUENOS AIRES	12/1	KINSHASA	29/21	PALMA DE M.	40/23	VENISE	29/19
		STRASBOURG	22/11	CARACAS	–	LE CAIRE	32/22	PÉKIN	31/23	VIENNE	23/16
		TOULOUSE	32/20			LIMA	17/14	PRAGUE	16/13		

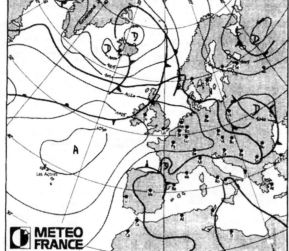

Situation le 26 juillet, à 0 heure, temps universel

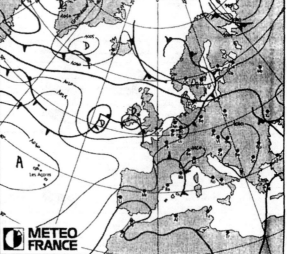

Prévisions pour le 28 juillet, à 0 heure, temps universel

	maximum	**minimum**
1. Sydney	_____ degrés	_____ degrés
2. Bombay	_____ degrés	_____ degrés
3. Buenos Aires	_____ degrés	_____ degrés
4. Chicago	_____ degrés	_____ degrés
5. Rome	_____ degrés	_____ degrés
6. Ajaccio	_____ degrés	_____ degrés
7. Nairobi	_____ degrés	_____ degrés
8. Lille	_____ degrés	_____ degrés

À vous de lire

Le Robert mini. **Dictionnaires Le Robert** publishes French dictionaries for a variety of purposes. This ad describes *Le Robert mini*, a condensed dictionary of the French language and proper nouns.

Before you read the ad for specific information, find at least ten cognates (e.g., **page**) and near cognates (e.g., **dictionnaire**) and list them in the space provided. Then read to find information from the three numbered sections.

cognates and near cognates

_____

_____

_____

_____

_____

_____

_____

_____

_____

1. What are some of the basic features of *Le Robert mini*?

■ Length of dictionary: _____

■ Number of words: _____

■ Number of proper nouns: _____

2. List three or more features of this dictionary.

_____

_____

3. List three or more categories of proper nouns that *Le Robert mini* provides.

_____

_____

PARTIE ORALE

Bonjour, tout le monde!

CD1, Track 2

0.1 Conversations. You will hear four short conversations. For each one, decide if what the second person says responds correctly to what the first person says and check the appropriate box. You will hear each item twice.

> **EXEMPLE**   You hear: —Bonjour, Anne. Comment allez-vous?
> —À demain.
> You check: *non*

	oui	non
1.	☐	☐
2.	☐	☐
3.	☐	☐
4.	☐	☐

Dans la salle de classe

CD1, Track 3

0.2 Qu'est-ce qu'il y a? Jean-Luc is telling a friend which objects are in his classroom. Looking at the drawing below, decide whether each statement is **vrai** *(true)* or **faux** *(false)*, and mark the appropriate column. You will hear each item twice.

> **EXEMPLE**   You hear: Il y a un tableau.
> You mark: *vrai*

	vrai	faux
1.		
2.		
3.		
4.		
5.		

Quelques expressions utiles

CD1, Track 4

0.3 En classe. You are going to hear five statements made by a teacher. In the space provided, jot down in English what you would say or do to respond to the teacher. You will hear each item twice.

> **EXEMPLE**   You hear: Répétez, s'il vous plaît.
> You write: *I would repeat what I just said.*

1. _____
2. _____
3. _____
4. _____
5. _____

Bien prononcer, c'est important!

CD1, Track 5

0.4 Abonnement. You work in the subscription department of *Réponse à tout!* magazine and are taking information over the phone. Complete the form with the information you hear. You will hear each item twice.

> **EXEMPLE**   You hear: Nom: Ballan b a deux l a n
> You write: **Ballan**

BULLETIN D'ABONNEMENT

RÉPONSE À TOUT!

OUI, JE M'ABONNE JE BÉNÉFICIE D'UN NUMÉRO GRATUIT

Ci-joint   **par :** ☐ chèque bancaire ☐ chèque postal
☐ Carte Bleue   *à l'ordre de « Réponse à tout ! »*
Nom et prénom du titulaire_____

N° de carte ☐☐☐☐ ☐☐☐☐ ☐☐☐☐ ☐☐☐☐

Expire le ☐☐☐ Date............. Signature

NOM .... BALLAN

PRÉNOM ....

ADRESSE ... 10 rue

....

VILLE ....

CODE POSTAL ....

Glissez ce bon d'abonnement et votre règlement dans une enveloppe. Renvoyez les à :

«Réponse à tout !» / Service abonnements
DIP 70, rue Compans 75019 Paris.

Offre valable en France métropolitaine. Pour vous abonner à l'étranger : règlement uniquement par mandat, merci de nous consulter au 01.44.84.85.19.

Conformément à la loi informatique et libertés du 6 Janvier 1978, vous disposez d'un droit d'accès et de rectification aux données vous concernant. Si vous ne souhaitez pas être prospecté(e), merci de nous le signaler par écrit à « Réponse à tout ! ».

EN 84

C'est quel jour?

CD1, Track 6

0.5 La musique française. Your friend Sabine wants to know when certain concerts will be performed. Using the calendar of events as a guide, write the day of the week in English when each concert Sabine mentions is held. You might find it helpful to read through the concert listings before hearing Sabine's questions. You will hear each item twice.

EXEMPLE   You hear: Trois géants: Franck, Saint-Saëns, Roussel
                You write: *Friday*

1. _____

2. _____

3. _____

4. _____

5. _____

MERCREDI   25   SEPTEMBRE
- Auditorium. 20 h 30.
  Berlioz: Béatrice et Bénédict.

JEUDI   26   SEPTEMBRE
- Eglise St François-de-Sales. 17 h 30.
  Le Berlioz du piano.
- Auditorium. 20 h 30.
  L'héritage de Lalo.

VENDREDI   27   SEPTEMBRE
- Salle Molière. 17 h 30.
  Le piano orchestral.
- Auditorium. 20 h 30.
  Trois géants: Franck, Saint-Saëns, Roussel.

SAMEDI   28   SEPTEMBRE
- Transbordeur. 11 h.
  Aspects du XXe siècle.
- Salle Molière. 17 h.
  Du baroque au classicisme.
- Auditorium. 20 h 30.
  Les triomphes de l'opérette.

DIMANCHE 29 SEPTEMBRE
- Salle Molière. 9 h 30.
  Concert lecture (entrée libre).
- Salle Molière. 11 h 30.
  Anciens et modernes.
- Salle Molière. 15 h.
  La musique chorale de Debussy à Messiaen.
- Salle Molière. 18 h.
  Chefs-d'œuvre de la virtuosité.

Les nombres de 0 à 31

CD1, Track 7

0.6 C'est dans quel quartier? *Pariscope,* a weekly guide covering cultural events, movies, and restaurants, divides Paris into numbered **quartiers** *(districts)* that readers can use to locate restaurants in the guide. For each **quartier** indicated, first write the number you hear in the space provided. Then, based on the information from *Pariscope,* decide whether that number is correct and check the appropriate box. You will hear each item twice.

EXEMPLE   You hear: Vaugirard-Grenelle—quartier numéro huit
You write: *8;* and you mark: ***non***

Paris par quartiers

Pariscope a divisé le grand Paris en 27 quartiers.
Pour situer votre restaurant, consultez cette carte et reportez-vous
dans le quartier choisi.

Les 27 quartiers

1. Trocadéro-Passy-Auteuil
2. Etoile-Champs-Elysées
3. Ternes-Villiers
4. Clichy-Montmartre-Pigalle
5. St-Lazare-Trinité
6. Gare de l'Est-Gare du Nord
7. République-Grands Boulevards
8. Concorde-Madeleine-Opéra
9. Halles-Louvre-Palais-Royal
10. Marais-Beaubourg
11. Bastille-Nation
12. Invalides-Champ-de-Mars
13. Montparnasse
14. St-Germain-des-Prés
15. Quartier Latin-St-Michel
16. Quais-Cité-Ile-St-Louis
17. Mouffetard-Gobelins
18. Vaugirard-Grenelle
19. Pte Champerret-Levallois
20. Pte Maillot-Neuilly
21. Pte St Cloud-Boulogne
22. Pte de Versailles-Sèvres
23. Denfert-Porte d'Orléans
24. Italie-Pte d'Ivry
25. Belleville-Pte de Bagnolet
26. Porte de la Villette-Pantin
27. Environs de Paris

	oui	non		oui	non
1. Montparnasse _____	☐	☐	**5.** Italie-Porte d'Ivry _____	☐	☐
2. St-Lazare-Trinité _____	☐	☐	**6.** Bastille-Nation _____	☐	☐
3. Environs de Paris _____	☐	☐	**7.** Ternes-Villiers _____	☐	☐
4. Mouffetard-Gobelins _____	☐	☐	**8.** Étoile-Champs-Élysées _____	☐	☐

Chapitre un ○ ○ ○ ○ ○ ○

La vie à l'université

(1)

PARTIE ÉCRITE

Point de départ

Ⓐ Conversation. Sabine and Saïd are talking about their courses. Choosing words from those provided, complete their statements.

SABINE: Moi, j'adore l'informatique. Et toi?

SAÏD: Oui, moi _____, j'aime _____ l'informatique.
                 aussi / après   regarder / étudier

Je trouve ça _____. J'aime aussi la littérature. Et toi?
                 désagréable / intéressant

SABINE: Oui, j'aime _____, mais j'aime _____ l'histoire. Et j'aime étudier.
                les sciences / la littérature   mieux / mais

SAÏD: Pas moi! Je _____ étudier! Je trouve ça _____.
               travaille / déteste   ennuyeux / facile

_____ mieux parler avec mes amis.
Je m'appelle / J'aime

Ⓑ Comparaisons. You and Marie-France are comparing your interests. Using the examples as a guide and words you know, write your responses to Marie-France's statements.

    EXEMPLE MARIE-FRANCE: J'aime marcher.
                   VOUS: *Moi aussi, j'aime marcher.* or
                         Pas moi, je n'aime pas marcher. Je trouve ça fatigant.

1. MARIE-FRANCE: J'aime étudier avec des amis.

    VOUS: _____

2. MARIE-FRANCE: Je déteste la littérature. Je trouve ça inutile.

    VOUS: _____

3. MARIE-FRANCE: Après les cours, j'aime bien nager.

VOUS: _____

4. MARIE-FRANCE: J'adore les vacances.

VOUS: _____

5. MARIE-FRANCE: J'aime les sciences. Je trouve ça facile.

VOUS: _____

6. MARIE-FRANCE: Je déteste regarder la télévision.

VOUS: _____

⊙ Préférences. Write sentences telling whether you like or dislike each of the following and what you think of each.

     EXEMPLE parler français
          J'aime parler français. Je trouve ça intéressant.

1. nager _____

2. regarder la télévision _____

3. écouter des CD _____

4. étudier les langues étrangères _____

5. naviguer sur Internet _____

Les noms et les articles

Êtes-vous prêts? Les noms et les articles

This section is designed to help you decide whether you are ready to do the exercises in this activities manual. Indicate on a scale of 1 (not comfortable) to 5 (very comfortable) how well you can handle each of the following tasks and place the number in the box provided. If you answer 1 to 3 for any of the tasks, you should go back and review the explanations and exercises in your book.

☐ Name the French definite and indefinite articles and tell what they mean.

☐ Know when to use the definite article and when to use the indefinite article.

☐ Identify people or things using the appropriate definite articles and nouns.

☐ Use the appropriate definite articles and nouns to tell what your interests are and what school subjects you like.

☐ Tell what you generally like to do on different days of the week.

Ⓐ Journaux et revues. The following clippings were taken from various Canadian and French magazines and newspapers. Fill in the blanks in the first six clippings with the appropriate forms of the definite article; in the last six clippings, use appropriate forms of the indefinite article.

■ **Utilisez l'article défini.**

1.
   OUVERT MERCREDI JUSQU'À 21h 00

2. ____ professeurs d'université sont bien perçus mais leur travail est mal compris

3. ____ **commerce international**

4. **Laissez-les regarder ____ télé !**

5. **À ____ radio : Duval et Pothier se joignent à Gilles Tremblay**

6. Métiers de ____ Informatique

■ **Utilisez l'article indéfini.**

7. ____ *Stylo plume multicolore* + 4 cartouches courtes encre bleue

8. ____ ordinateurs personnels ...de la physique et de l'astro...

9.
   19€ ____ CHAISE DACTYLO (voir page 4)

10. ____ *Tables* gourmandes

11. ____ **WEEK-END EN POCHE**

12. **LE ROBERT MINI** *l'essentiel d'____dictionnaire*

B Impressions. Solange and Laurent are exchanging their impressions of university life. Complete their conversation by filling in the blanks with the appropriate forms of the definite article.

LAURENT: Moi, j'aime bien _____ université, et toi?

SOLANGE: Moi, aussi. Je trouve _____ campus très agréable. J'étudie _____ physique et _____ biologie.

LAURENT: Je déteste _____ sciences. Moi, j'étudie _____ langues. J'adore _____ espagnol.

SOLANGE: Moi, j'aime mieux _____ anglais. J'étudie aussi _____ philosophie. Et toi?

LAURENT: Oui, j'aime bien Madame Mairet, _____ professeure de philosophie. Tu aimes étudier?

SOLANGE: J'aime mieux regarder _____ télévision ou écouter _____ radio.

C Préférences. Virginie is talking about the things she and her friends like and don't like to do on various days of the week. Using the example as a guide, write what she says.

EXEMPLE like to swim / on Tuesdays
Le mardi, nous aimons nager.

1. don't like to study / on Fridays

_____

2. like to listen to CDs / on Sundays

_____

3. like to study at the library / on Wednesdays

_____

4. like to eat with friends / on Mondays

_____

5. like to surf the Internet / on Saturdays

_____

Les verbes du premier groupe

Êtes-vous prêts? Les verbes du premier groupe

Indicate on a scale of 1 (not comfortable) to 5 (very comfortable) how well you can handle each of the following tasks and place the number in the box provided. If you answer 1 to 3 for any of the tasks, you should go back and review the explanations and exercises in your book.

- ☐ Tell what the subject pronouns are in French and give their English equivalents.
- ☐ Name at least eight **-er** verbs and give their meanings in English.
- ☐ Conjugate **-er** verbs (i.e., put the right endings on the verbs to correspond to their appropriate subject pronouns).
- ☐ Tell what activities you enjoy doing.
- ☐ Use adverbs to tell how often, how well, and when you do these activities.

Ⓐ La vie du campus. Janine is telling how she and her friend Samir feel about campus life. Complete her statements by filling in the blanks with appropriate verbs from the lists provided. Certain verbs can be used more than once.

1st paragraph: **aimer, détester, étudier, travailler, trouver**

À l'université, Samir _____ les maths et moi, j(e) _____ l'anglais. Nous

_____ le campus très agréable. Les étudiants _____ à la bibliothèque. Ils

_____ bien les cours, mais ils _____ les examens.

2nd paragraph: **aimer, manger, danser, écouter, marcher, nager, regarder**

Samir _____ souvent la radio; il aime aussi _____ la télévision. Le samedi, j'aime

_____ dans les discothèques. Nous détestons le restaurant universitaire, mais nous aimons bien

_____ avec des amis. Nous _____ le sport: nous _____ et nous

_____ .

Ⓑ Occupations. Describe what the people in each of the following illustrations are doing.

EXEMPLE

La famille Vincent *voyage.* or
La famille Vincent *aime voyager.*

1.

¡Buenas tardes!

¡Hola! ¿Cómo estaś?

Annette et Jacques _____ .

2. Jean et moi, _____.

3. Les étudiants _____.

4. Vous _____.

5. Stéphanie et Séverin _____.

C Activités et préférences. Using the adverbs and expressions you've learned and the verbs provided, create sentences that tell when or how often you or people you know do certain activities.

> EXEMPLES   écouter la radio
> *Jérôme et Anne écoutent souvent la radio.*
>
> travailler
> *Je travaille le lundi et le mercredi.*

1. étudier à la bibliothèque

_____

2. nager

_____

3. parler français

_____

4. regarder la télévision

_____

5. manger au restaurant universitaire

_____

6. travailler

_____

La forme interrogative et la forme négative

Êtes-vous prêts? La forme interrogative et la forme négative

Indicate on a scale of 1 (not comfortable) to 5 (very comfortable) how well you can handle each of the following tasks and place the number in the box provided. If you answer 1 to 3 for any of the tasks, you should go back and review the explanations and exercises in your textbook.

- [ ] Name two ways to change a statement into a question.
- [ ] Change an affirmative statement into a negative one using both **ne... pas** and **ne... jamais.**
- [ ] Ask someone questions about his or her interests and activities.
- [ ] Tell what activities you don't do or never do.
- [ ] Give several expressions that you can use to agree or disagree with someone.

A Mais pas du tout! Sophie is fairly happy with her life at the university. Her friends, however, do not feel the same way. Using the cues in parentheses, re-create their replies by making the following sentences negative.

> **EXEMPLE** J'aime nager. (ne... pas)
> *Mais non, tu n'aimes pas nager.*

1. Tu étudies à la bibliothèque. (ne... pas)

_____

2. Paul regarde souvent la télé. (ne... jamais)

_____

3. Nous téléphonons à des amis. (ne... pas)

_____

4. On mange bien à l'université. (ne... pas)

_____

5. Les étudiants trouvent les cours passionnants. (ne... pas)

_____

6. Philippe et Odile étudient ensemble. (ne... jamais)

_____

7. Les étudiants aiment manger au resto. (ne... pas)

_____

8. Nous aimons bien la vie à l'université. (ne... pas)

_____

ⓑ Questions. You have just met Georges, a student from Quebec, and you want to find out more about him. What questions would you ask to find out the following information? Be sure to use either **est-ce que** or **n'est-ce pas** and appropriate pronouns.

> **EXEMPLE** Find out if he likes the dorm.
> *Est-ce que vous aimez la résidence universitaire?* or
> *Vous aimez la résidence universitaire, n'est-ce pas?*

Find out:

1. if he is studying computer science

_____

2. if he works a lot

_____

3. if he speaks English well

_____

4. if he watches DVDs often

_____

5. if he likes to study at the library

_____

ⓒ Compatibilité. Your roommates this year are students from Quebec. In the space provided, write at least six questions you can ask to find out about their interests and studies. Vary the vocabulary and expressions you use as much as possible, but be sure to use words you know.

> **EXEMPLES** *Est-ce que vous aimez le campus?*
> *Vous regardez quelquefois la télé, n'est-ce pas?*

Intégration et perspectives

A Chez nous en France: Destination la région Poitou-Charentes. Amélie, a young French student, is about to start studying at the **Université de La Rochelle.** She is corresponding with Lauren, an American college student who has been studying French for a semester. She introduces herself. Check the map at the beginning of the workbook to see where **Poitou-Charentes** is located.

Chère Laurent,

Bonjour! Je m'appelle Amélie. J'habite à La Rochelle, dans l'ouest de la France. J'ai dix-huit ans.

En octobre, je commence mes études à l'université de La Rochelle. Au revoir la vie facile et les amis du lycée!... C'est vrai que je n'aime pas beaucoup étudier... J'aime mieux passer mon temps avec mes amis, et ne pas toujours parler des problèmes de la vie!... J'aime aussi chatter sur Internet, et j'adore les jeux vidéo! Papa et maman pensent que c'est stupide, mais moi, je trouve ça passionnant.

Après les cours, j'étudie le piano et la flûte avec un professeur privé. J'aime beaucoup ça, mais, entre (between) un passe-temps agréable et une profession, il y a une différence considérable!... En général, j'aime bien les activités artistiques.

Ma famille et moi, nous habitons dans une région assez agréable, au bord de l'océan Atlantique. La Rochelle est une ville très pittoresque et un port de mer autrefois (formerly) très important pour la défense du pays et pour l'industrie de la pêche (fishing). J'aime bien visiter la région en moto avec papa. Un jour, c'est l'île de Ré, à l'ouest; un autre, c'est le Parc Régional du Marais Poitevin, au nord, ou bien la région de Cognac, au sud. Maman préfère les promenades sur la plage (beach).

Moi, je n'aime pas marcher, mais j'aime bien aller (to go) à la plage et nager dans l'océan. J'aime aussi préparer des crêpes—ou une bonne pizza—et inviter les amis!

Au revoir et à plus tard.

Avez-vous compris?

1. What are some of Amélie's likes and dislikes?

_____

_____

2. How does she feel about school?

_____

3. Give several facts about **La Rochelle.**

_____

4. What areas of **Poitou-Charentes** does she visit with her father?

_____

_____

B À vous de lire: Choix de filières. Amélie is going to be a first-year student at the **Université de La Rochelle** and is thinking about what she will study once she is there. Following is a sampling of the majors (**filières**) and programs of study available at the university. Look over the majors and in the space provided, make a list of cognates and near cognates. Next choose five majors and give your opinion about each one (e.g., **le génie—je trouve ça facile / difficile, agréable / désagréable, intéressant / ennuyeux, utile / inutile**).

Nouvelles filières

◄ IUP Génie *(m)* des Équipements et des Procédés
◄ IUP Génie des Matériaux
◄ Licence *(f)* d'administration publique
◄ Licence Professionelle Système d'information géographique
◄ Licence Professionelle «Conduite de Projet en Agro-Alimentaire et Gestion de la Qualité»
◄ DESS Ingénierie *(f)* du bâtiment (3 options)
◄ DESS Multimédia *(m)* «Jeux vidéo et médias interactifs»
◄ DEA Environnement et paysage

Formations professionnalisantes

◄ LUP Danse *(f)* et Sciences (Dossier d'inscription)
◄ Licence Professionnelle Lettres Cultures et Nouveaux Médias
◄ IUP Commerce et Vente
◄ IUP de Biotechnologie et Alimentaire
◄ IUP Génie Civil et Infrastructure
◄ IUP de Génie Informatique
◄ IUP Management et Gestion des Entreprises option Asie-Pacifique
◄ IUP Génie des Équipements et des Procédés
◄ IUP Génie des Matériaux

◄ Licence Professionnelle «Création Multimédia»
◄ Licence Professionnelle «Systèmes d'Information Géographiques»
◄ Licence Professionelle «Conduite de Projet en Agro-Alimentaire et Gestion de la Qualité»
◄ DRT Technologie de l'Information appliquée aux Systèmes Industriels

Formations initiales

◄ UFR Sciences Fondamentales et Sciences pour l'Ingénieur (SCIENCES)
◄ UFR de Sciences Juridiques, Politiques, Économiques et de Gestion (DROIT)
◄ UFR Langues, Lettres, Arts et Sciences Humaines (FLASH)
◄ Centre *(m)* Inter-pôles d'Enseignement des Langues (CIEL)
◄ Institut *(m)* Universitaire de Technologie (IUT)

Formations transversales

◄ IUT Licence Professionnelle «Environnement et Construction»
◄ DESS Management *(m)* de Projet

---

cognates and near cognates

_____   _____
_____   _____
_____   _____
_____   _____
_____   _____

mes opinions

_____
_____
_____
_____
_____
_____
_____
_____

C **Petite conversation.** You are talking with Amélie, and she asks you the following questions. Write what you would say in the space provided.

AMÉLIE: Bonjour, Je m'appelle Amélie. Et toi?

VOUS: _____

AMÉLIE: Ça va?

VOUS: _____

AMÉLIE: Est-ce que tu aimes la vie à l'université?

VOUS: _____

AMÉLIE: Tu étudies le français, n'est-ce pas?

VOUS: _____

AMÉLIE: Est-ce que tu préfères étudier les mathématiques ou l'histoire?

VOUS: _____

AMÉLIE: Est-ce que les étudiants américains aiment bien les jeux vidéo?

VOUS: _____

AMÉLIE: Au revoir. À demain!

D **À vous d'écrire: Logement.** You are going to study at the **Université de La Rochelle.** As part of the application process for student housing, the **service des résidences** asks students to write a description of themselves so they can be matched with suitable residences and roommates. Follow these four steps to develop a description of yourself.

1. Préparation

Fill in the grid that follows with information in French about yourself.

Nom	Pays d'origine	Langues parlées	Études	Activités	Préférences

2. Brouillon

Use these ideas to describe yourself (at least eight sentences), telling about the courses you're taking, what you like and dislike, and what you like and do not like to do. Write this first draft on a separate sheet of paper. Vary the verbs you use, and be sure to use definite and indefinite articles correctly. Don't forget to include adverbs to indicate how often you do something (**rarement, souvent**) how well you do it (**bien, assez bien**), or when you do it (**lundi, mardi,** etc.).

3. Révision

Now that you have finished writing your first draft, read through what you have written and check the following.

- Did you use definite and indefinite articles correctly?
- Did you use verbs that refer to both likes and dislikes?
- Did you use adverbs to describe how often or how well you do certain activities?
- Using vocabulary you know, what other things could you say about yourself?

4. Rédaction

Write the final draft of your description in the space provided here. Make the corrections and insert the additions you noted in step #3. Then reread your description to be sure you are satisfied with it.

PARTIE ORALE

Point de départ

CD1, Track 8

1.1 Préférences. Jeanne is telling what she thinks about the university. For each of the statements you hear, first jot down in English what she says. Then decide whether Jeanne likes a particular aspect of university life and check the appropriate box. You will hear each item twice.

> **EXEMPLE** You hear: Moi, j'aime bien la philosophie. Je trouve ça facile.
> You write: *likes philosophy; finds it easy;* and you check: ***oui***

	oui	non
1. _____	☐	☐
2. _____	☐	☐
3. _____	☐	☐
4. _____	☐	☐
5. _____	☐	☐

Les noms et les articles

CD1, Track 9

*1.2 Situation: Visite du campus. (p. 18) Laure is showing a friend around her campus and is telling her what some of the buildings are. You will hear the conversation twice. Listen the first time as you hear it read, paying attention to intonation, tone, and pronunciation. During the second reading, repeat each line of the conversation after it is read to you.

CD1, Track 10

*1.3 Petits boulots. (p. 18 A) Several of your friends have part-time jobs. Using the cues you hear, ask where they are working. Then say how another student will respond.

> **EXEMPLE** You hear: Laurent / centre sportif
> You say: ***Où est-ce que Laurent travaille?***
> ***Dans un centre sportif.***

CD1, Track 11

*1.4 Les études universitaires. (p. 19 C) Several French students are preparing for their end-of-year exams. Using the cues you hear, first ask what courses a student is taking; then give the other student's response.

> **EXEMPLE** You hear: Sophie: biologie, chimie
> You say: ***Qu'est-ce que Sophie étudie?***
> ***La biologie et la chimie.***

CD1, Track 12

1.5 Préférences. Some students are discussing different aspects of campus life. Listen for the definite and indefinite articles each person uses and write them in the space provided. You will hear each item twice.

> **EXEMPLE** You hear: Isabelle aime le campus et surtout la bibliothèque.
> You write: *le, la*

1. _____

2. _____

3. _____

4. _____

5. _____

6. _____

Les verbes du premier groupe

CD1, Track 13

*1.6 Situation: On mange ensemble? (p. 22) Guillaume calls Sophie and Denis to see if they can go out for dinner. You will hear the conversation twice. Listen the first time as you hear it read, paying attention to intonation, tone, and pronunciation. During the second reading, repeat each line of the conversation after it is read to you.

CD1, Track 14

*1.7 Après les cours. (p. 23 B) Several friends are asking about what they and others are doing tonight. Tell what they do. Repeat the correct response after it is given.

> **EXEMPLE** You hear: Paul et Omar / regarder la télé
> You say: *Ils regardent la télé.*

CD1, Track 15

1.8 Descriptions. You will hear five statements describing these drawings. Write the number of each statement below the drawing it describes. You will hear each item twice.

a. _____

b. _____

c. _____

d. _____

e. _____

La forme interrogative et la forme négative

CD1, Track 16

*1.9 Situation: Anglais ou français? (p. 28) Antoine has just found out that Nathalie has an American room-mate and is asking questions about her. You will hear the conversation twice. Listen the first time as you hear it read, paying attention to intonation, tone, and pronunciation. During the second reading, repeat each line of the conversation after it is read to you.

CD1, Track 17

*1.10 Absolument pas. (p. 28 B) Fabienne and Thibaut are talking about their interests. Fabienne is positive about things; Thibaut is somewhat negative and contradicts everything that Fabienne says. What does Thibaut say?

> **EXEMPLE**   You hear: Moi, j'aime bien le prof d'anglais.
> You say: *Moi, je n'aime pas le prof d'anglais.*

CD1, Track 18

1.11 C'est une question? You overhear some people talking. Decide whether you hear a question each time and mark the appropriate box. You will hear each item twice.

> **EXEMPLE**   You hear: Est-ce que Robert aime étudier à la bibliothèque?
> You mark: *oui*

	oui	non			oui	non
1.	☐	☐		4.	☐	☐
2.	☐	☐		5.	☐	☐
3.	☐	☐		6.	☐	☐

Intégration et perspectives

CD1, Track 19

1.12 Salut! A young French-Canadian woman is talking about her life. After you listen to what she says, decide whether each statement is **vrai** *(true)* or **faux** *(false)* and mark the appropriate column. You will hear the passage twice.

vrai	faux	
		1. The woman speaking is named Catherine.
		2. She attends a university in Montreal.
		3. She lives alone in an apartment.
		4. She doesn't speak English well.
		5. When she isn't studying, she likes to have friends over to her apartment.

CD1, Track 20

1.13 À l'université. Several students are talking about their studies. Complete their conversation in the space provided. Each line will be read twice, then the entire conversation will be read once again so that you can check your work.

MICHELINE: Pauline, _____ l'université?

PAULINE: Oui, beaucoup. _____ campus _____. Mais je

_____ universitaire!

ROBERT: Moi, _____ les cours. J'étudie _____. Je trouve ça

_____!

CD1, Track 21

*1.14 Bien prononcer. (p. 38) **Liaison** refers to a consonant sound that is added to link one word to another. In French, a **liaison** may occur when a word that normally ends in a silent consonant (**s, t, x,** or **n**) is followed by a word that begins with a vowel sound. For a **liaison** to occur, the first word must in some way modify or qualify the second. Note also that in a **liaison,** "s" and "x" are pronounced "z." Repeat the following words.

CD1, Track 22

*1.15 Petite conversation. Practice repeating the following conversation.

B Présentations. Using vocabulary you know and the information provided, introduce the following people to your French friends. Begin your introductions with **Je vous présente…**

    Sabine Delisle: Canadian / from Trois-Rivières but lives in Montreal / single / computer programmer
    Martin Blanchard: Swiss / lives in Zurich / married / accountant
    Romeo Tiburon: Italian / from Rome but lives in New York / single / doctor
    Alexandra Castillo: Spanish / lives in Madrid / psychologist

_____

_____

_____

_____

_____

_____

_____

_____

Le verbe *être* et quelques adjectifs

Êtes-vous prêts? Le verbe *être* et quelques adjectifs

Indicate on a scale of 1 (not comfortable) to 5 (very comfortable) how well you can handle each of the following tasks and place the number in the box provided. If you answer 1 to 3 for any of the tasks, you should go back and review the explanations and exercises in your book.

☐ Tell what **être** means in English and conjugate the verb.

☐ Give the meaning of **c'est** and tell which group of pronouns follows it.

☐ List 10 or more adjectives and tell what they mean in English.

☐ Use adjectives appropriately to describe your personality and that of people you know.

A Origines. All of the following people live in Martinique. Indicate the town each is from by filling in the blanks in the following sentences with appropriate forms of the verb **être.**

1. Alain _____ de Sainte-Anne.

2. Isabelle et moi, nous _____ de Fort-de-France.

3. Les parents de Claudine _____ de Belle Fontaine.

4. Vous _____ de Basse-Pointe, n'est-ce pas?

5. Hélène _____ du Prêcheur, dans la région de la montagne Pelée.

6. Moi, je _____ de Vert-Pré.

B Et vous? Complete each of the following sentences so that they express your opinions of university life. Use the appropriate form of **être** and adjectives and adverbs in each sentence.

> **EXEMPLE** Nous, les étudiants, nous *sommes très optimistes.*

1. L'université _____.

2. Je _____.

3. Nous, les étudiants, nous _____.

4. Les examens _____.

5. La classe de français _____.

Les adjectifs qualificatifs

Êtes-vous prêts? Les adjectifs qualificatifs

Indicate on a scale of 1 (not comfortable) to 5 (very comfortable) how well you can handle each of the following tasks and place the number in the box provided. If you answer 1 to 3 for any of the tasks, you should go back and review the explanations and exercises in your book.

☐ List several adjectives like **content**, tell what they mean in English, and then give their feminine and plural forms.

☐ Do the same for adjectives like **sportif, heureux,** and **italien.**

☐ Use adjectives appropriately to describe yourself and people you know.

A Contre-attaque. Jean Chauvin is bragging about all the qualities he believes that men have. Stéphanie insists that women have these same qualities. Re-create Stéphanie's statements by rewriting the following paragraph in the space provided. Be sure to change each of the underlined adjectives to the feminine and make the other necessary substitutions of feminine nouns and pronouns.

En général, je trouve les hommes très <u>sympathiques</u>. Ils sont très <u>sportifs</u>. Ils ne sont jamais <u>paresseux</u>. Ils sont <u>indépendants</u>, <u>sérieux</u> et <u>intelligents</u>. Les hommes sont <u>doués</u> pour les maths et les sciences. Ils sont <u>ambitieux</u>, c'est vrai, mais ils sont aussi <u>honnêtes</u>. Et ils sont très <u>patients</u> avec les femmes. Ils ne sont pas <u>impulsifs</u> et <u>naïfs</u> comme les femmes. Les hommes sont <u>formidables</u>, n'est-ce pas?

En général, je trouve les femmes _____

_____

_____

_____

_____

_____

_____

B Descriptions. Complete each of the following sentences by adding one or more adjectives to make a complete and meaningful statement. Be sure the adjectives agree with the nouns they modify.

> **EXEMPLE**   Le film n'est pas très intéressant.
> *Il est ennuyeux.*

1. Julie aime beaucoup travailler.

   Elle n'est pas _____.

2. Marc est triste.

   Il n'est pas _____.

3. Maryse et Annick sont de Paris.

   Elles sont _____.

4. Madeleine aime nager et marcher.

   Elle est _____.

5. Les examens dans la classe de français ne sont pas difficiles.

   D'habitude, ils sont assez _____.

6. Katarina est de Berlin.

   Elle est _____.

C Opinions. The following questions are addressed to you personally. Write appropriate responses, using one or more adjectives in each answer.

> **EXEMPLE**   Quelle sorte de femmes / d'hommes aimez-vous?
> *J'aime les femmes indépendantes (les hommes indépendants).*

1. Quelle sorte de professeurs est-ce que les étudiants aiment?

   _____

2. Et vous, quelle sorte de professeurs est-ce que vous aimez?

   _____

3. Quelle sorte d'étudiants est-ce que les professeurs aiment?

   _____

4. Quelle sorte de films est-ce que vous aimez en général?

   _____

5. Quelle sorte de femmes / d'hommes est-ce que vous aimez?

   _____

6. Quelle sorte de gens détestez-vous?

   _____

Compter jusqu'à 100

Êtes-vous prêts? Compter jusqu'à 100

Indicate on a scale of 1 (not comfortable) to 5 (very comfortable) how well you can handle each of the following tasks and place the number in the box provided. If you answer 1 to 3 for any of the tasks, you should go back and review the explanations and exercises in your book.

☐ Say and write out the numbers through 100.

☐ Ask and tell how much something costs.

☐ Give and understand addresses and phone numbers.

Numéros de téléphone. The telephone numbers listed here would be helpful to an American tourist visiting Paris. Write out each number.

EXEMPLE Télégrammes: 01 42 33 44 11
C'est le zéro un, quarante-deux, trente-trois, quarante-quatre, onze.

1. American Express: 01 47 14 50 00

_____

2. Ambassade américaine: 01 43 12 22 22

_____

3. Hôpital Lariboisière, Service des urgences: 01 49 95 64 43

_____

4. Objets trouvés *(Lost and found):* 01 45 31 14 80

_____

5. Musée du Louvre: 01 40 20 53 17

_____

6. Tour Eiffel: 01 44 11 23 33

_____

Intégration et perspectives

A Chez nous en France: Destination le Pays basque. Pablo and Micaëla describe **le Pays basque,** located in the southwest corner of France. They imitate the approach taken by Claude Gauthier in his poem about Quebec to tell us about their region, its language **(le basque),** and the difficulties of the Basque people whose region lies partly in Spain and partly in France. Check the map at the beginning of the book to see where **le Pays basque** is located.

> Nous sommes d'océan, de montagnes,
> de lacs et de rivières.
> Nous sommes de petits villages,
> de vallées et de collines *(hills)*.
> Nous sommes d'une langue
> différente des autres langues d'Europe,
> une langue différente dans son vocabulaire,
> et dans sa grammaire,
> une langue qui a ses origines dans le sanscrit.
> Nous sommes d'un sport que vous appelez «jai alai».
> Et que nous appelons «la pelote basque».
> Nous sommes d'océan Atlantique
> et de Pyrénées.
> Nous sommes de France et d'Espagne.
> Nous sommes d'une région divisée
> entre ces deux pays *(countries)*.
> Nous sommes d'une région
> qu'on appelle un pays
> mais qui n'est pas un pays.

Avez-vous compris? What do Pablo and Micaëla say about the following topics? Jot down at least two pieces of information in English for each item.

location and geography of **le Pays basque:**

_____

_____

_____

the Basque language:

_____

la pelote basque:

_____

B À vous de lire: Identité basque. The geography of **le Pays basque, la langue basque,** and **la pelote basque** are all important aspects of the identity of the region and its inhabitants. Read the following information taken from several Web sites on **le Pays basque** and answer the questions in the **Avez-vous compris?** that follows.

Villes & Villages

- Le Pays basque (*Euskal Herria*) est à cheval sur la France (Pays basque nord) et l'Espagne (Pays basque sud).
- Le pays en lui-même comprend 7 provinces (*Zazpiak Bat*: «les 7 font 1»).
- Le Pays basque sud (*Euzkadi*) se compose de 4 provinces: **la Navarre, l'Alava, la Biscaye, le Guipuzcoa.**
- Le Pays basque nord (*Ipharalde*) se compose de 3 provinces: **la Basse-Navarre, le Labourd, la Soule.**

La culture

La langue basque

La langue basque—l'euskara—est le ciment de l'identité basque. *Euskal herria* (le Pays basque) signifie «le pays où l'on parle basque». *Euskalduna* (habitant du Pays basque) signifie littéralement «la personne qui parle basque».

Des origines mystérieuses

S'il y a aujourd'hui de fortes probabilités pour que la langue basque remonte à la préhistoire, ses origines réelles sont, et resteront semble-t-il, un mystère.

La Pelote basque

Le jeu de pelote basque se décline en plusieurs variantes en fonction du terrain et de la pelote utilisés. Ce sport occupe une grande place dans la vie des Basques et nécessite force et dextérité. Chaque village possède son fronton...

Avez-vous compris?

Villes et villages

1. What is the Basque name for **le Pays basque**?

_____

2. How many provinces are there in **le Pays basque**?

_____

3. What are the provinces in the north? in the south?

_____

La langue basque

1. What is the Basque term for the Basque language?

_____

2. What does **Euskalduna** mean?

_____

3. What are the origins of the Basque language?

_____

La pelote basque

1. There are many variations of **la pelote basque** (called *jai alai* in the U.S.). What are these variations a function of?

_____

2. What athletic characteristics does **la pelote basque** require?

_____

3. In **la pelote basque,** the ball is hit against a wall. What is the French word for this wall?

_____

C À l'auberge de jeunesse. While you're staying at a youth hostel in Biarritz, a beautiful city on the Basque coast known for its magnificent beaches, you strike up a conversation with Mila, a local student. Write what you would say in French to introduce yourself and to find out about her.

1. Ask Mila if she is from Biarritz. Find out if she speaks Basque.

_____

2. Ask her what she is studying.

_____

3. Find out what kind (**Quelle sorte de…**) of restaurants she likes, and tell her what kind you like (e.g., Spanish, Italian).

_____

_____

4. Tell Mila what you're studying and whether you work.

_____

_____

5. Find out if she is athletic, and if she likes **la pelote basque.**

_____

D À vous d'écrire: Autoportrait. You are writing a letter to the French family you are going to visit in Saint-Jean-de-Luz, a beautiful seaside resort and active fishing port near the Spanish border, and you want to tell them about yourself and about what you like and dislike. Follow these four steps to develop a description of yourself.

1. Préparation

In the space provided, make a list of the adjectives that describe you (**très impatient[e], assez optimiste,** etc.), and then list things you like and activities that you enjoy (**Je ne voyage pas souvent, j'aime beaucoup nager**). Don't forget to use adverbs to make your writing more precise.

_____

_____

_____

_____

2. Brouillon

Use your notes to write a short letter (eight or more sentences) to your French family. Write this first draft on a separate piece of paper. Start your letter with **Chers amis** and end it with **À bientôt** and your name.

3. Révision

Now that you have finished your first draft, read through what you have written and check the following.

- How many adjectives did you use? What other adjectives could you add to make your paragraph more interesting? Did you include adverbs to modify your statements?
- Did your adjectives agree with the nouns modified?
- Did you write about several things that you like and that you dislike? What others do you need to add?
- What else can you add to make your description complete?

4. Rédaction

Write the final draft of your letter in the space provided here. Make the corrections and insert the additions you noted in step #3. Then reread your letter to be sure you are satisfied with it.

PARTIE ORALE

Point de départ

CD1, Track 23

2.1 À la douane. You overhear a customs officer's conversation with a traveler going through customs at Charles de Gaulle Airport. Write down how the traveler answers each of the officer's questions.

FICHE D'ÉTRANGER

CH. N° _____

NOM : _____
Name in capital letters   (écrire en majuscules)
Name in Druckschrift

Nom de jeune fille : _____
Maiden name
Mädchenname

Prénoms : _____
Christian names
Vornamen

Date de naissance : _____
Date of birth
Geburtsdatum

Lieu de naissance : _____
Place of birth
Geburtsort

Domicile habituel : _____
Permanent address
Gewöhnlicher Wohnort

Profession : _____
Occupation
Beruf

NATIONALITÉ
Nationality
Nationalität

Passeport N° : _____
Pass - Ausweis ·

Date d'arrivée en France : _____
Date of arrival in France
Einreisedatum in Frankreich

Date probable de sortie : _____
Probable date of your way out
Voraussichtliches Ausreisedatum

_____ , le _____
Signature :
Unterschrift :

Nombre d'enfants de moins de 15 ans
accompagnant le voyageur
Accompaning children under 15
Zahl der begleitenden Kinder unter 15 Jahren   **109258 ORLANDI**

Le verbe *être* et quelques adjectifs

CD1, Track 24

*2.2 Situation: À la gare. (p. 49) Catherine and Gérard are at the train station in Nantes with their friends Claude and Suzanne waiting for the arrival of Daniel Johnson, an American student who is going to spend a semester at the **École supérieure de commerce de Nantes.** You will hear the conversation twice. Listen the first time as you hear it read, paying attention to intonation, tone, and pronunciation. During the second reading, repeat each line of the conversation after it is read to you.

CD1, Track 25

*2.3 De quelle ville est-ce que tu es? (p. 50 A) Students at Laval University in Quebec are telling where they are from. Based on the cues you hear, tell what they say.

> **EXEMPLE**   You hear: De quelle ville est Geneviève? (Trois-Rivières)
> You say: *Elle est de Trois-Rivières.*

CD1, Track 26

2.4 C'est un compliment? Some professors at Laval University in Quebec are discussing their classes and the university. Decide whether a comment you hear is favorable and check the appropriate box. You will hear each item twice.

> **EXEMPLE**   You hear: Les étudiants sont trop timides.
> You check: *non*

	oui	non			oui	non
1.	☐	☐		4.	☐	☐
2.	☐	☐		5.	☐	☐
3.	☐	☐		6.	☐	☐

Les adjectifs qualificatifs

CD1, Track 27

*2.5 Situation: Possibilité de promotion. (p. 53) Several employees are up for a promotion. Madame Mermet, the personnel director, asks her assistant, Gilbert Lacoste, his opinion of the candidates. You will hear the conversation twice. Listen the first time as you hear it read, paying attention to intonation, tone, and pronunciation. During the second reading, repeat each line of the conversation after it is read to you.

CD1, Track 28

*2.6 Et les femmes alors? (p. 54 A) You overhear a conversation between Hubert, who thinks that men are superior to women, and Suzanne, who doesn't agree at all. What do they say?

> **EXEMPLE**   You hear: ambitieux
> You say: *Les hommes sont ambitieux.*
> *Les femmes aussi sont ambitieuses.*

CD1, Track 29

*2.7 Qualités et défauts. (p. 54 C) Madame Besnard and her associate are evaluating different part-time employees at Quick Snack. What do they say about each one?

> **EXEMPLE**   You hear: Candice? assez gentil / pas assez sérieux
> You say: *Candice est assez gentille, mais elle n'est pas assez sérieuse.*

CD1, Track 30

2.8 Compétence. A group of attorneys are discussing the clerks who work for their firm. Listen to the comments made about each person and jot down in English what you hear. You will hear each item twice.

EXEMPLE   You hear: Je suis content de Joëlle. Elle est très compétente.
         You jot down: Joëlle: *happy with her; very competent*

1. Georges: _____

2. Sabine: _____

3. Benoît: _____

4. Jean-François et Martin: _____

5. Marie-Anne: _____

6. Arnaud: _____

Compter jusqu'à 100

CD1, Track 31

*2.9 Situation: Demande d'emploi. (p. 57) Mireille Rivière is applying for a job. The interviewer is asking her questions to fill out the personnel form. You will hear the conversation twice. Listen the first time as you hear it read, paying attention to intonation, tone, and pronunciation. During the second reading, repeat each line of the conversation after it is read to you.

CD1, Track 32

*2.10 Services publics et sociaux. (p. 58 B) You are an employee of the **Syndicat d'Initiative** in **Châtillon sur Chalaronne** and are giving out emergency phone numbers for special services. Using the text provided as a guide, give the phone numbers the callers request. You will hear each item twice.

EXEMPLE   You hear: La mairie. Les services administratifs, s'il vous plaît?
         You say: *C'est le zéro quatre, soixante-quatorze, cinquante-cinq, zéro quatre, trente-trois.*

CANTON DE CHATILLON SUR CHALARONNE

CHATILLON SUR CHALARONNE
SERVICES PUBLICS ET SOCIAUX

MAIRIE -	
Services Administratifs - Place de la Mairie	Tél : 04 74 55 04 33
Services Techniques - Place de l'Hôtel de Ville	Tél : 04 74 55 01 90
Services Techniques de Voirie - 65 rue Bergerat	Tél : 04 74 55 23 13
LA POSTE : Avenue de la Poste	
Renseignements	Tél : 04 74 55 02 56
Receveur	Tél : 04 74 55 02 32
POMPIERS	Tél : 18
GENDARMERIE	Tél : 17
URGENCES MEDICALES	Tél : 15
SAMU Bourg	Tél : 04 74 23 15 15
G.D.F. Dépannage Sécurité	Tél : 04 74 04 92 23
E.D.F. Dépannage Sécurité	Tél : 04 74 04 04 50
ECLAIRAGE PUBLIC	N° Vert (appel gratuit) : 0800 28 77 93
ASSISTANTE SOCIALE	Tél : 04 74 55 01 15

CD I, Track 33

2.11 Universités. You want to know more information about some universities that offer a degree in music. For each university listed, write the telephone number you can call for more information. You will hear each item twice.

> **EXEMPLE**   You hear: Université Lumière—Lyon II: c'est le zéro quatre, soixante-dix-huit, soixante-neuf, soixante-dix, zéro quatre
>
> You write: **04 78 69 70 04**

1. Université de Provence—Aix-Marseille I: _____

2. Université de Rennes II—Haute Bretagne: _____

3. Université de Paris VIII: _____

4. Université de Bordeaux III: _____

5. Université de Bourgogne—Dijon: _____

Intégration et perspectives

CD I, Track 34

2.12 Description. Listen as Nicole talks about herself and her friend Clémentine. Then decide if the following statements are **vrai** (*true*) or **faux** (*false*) and mark the appropriate column. You will hear the passage twice.

vrai	faux	
		1. Nicole est une femme timide et modeste.
		2. Nicole et Clémentine travaillent à Paris.
		3. Clémentine est médecin, et elle travaille avec les enfants.
		4. Nicole est informaticienne.
		5. Elle pense que c'est une profession passionnante.

CD I, Track 35

2.13 Opinions. Patrice has asked three friends for their opinions about Monsieur Renaud, their history professor. Complete what each person says in the space provided. Each line will be read twice, then the entire conversation will be read once again so that you can check your work.

ANNE: _____ Monsieur Renaud, _____.

_____ et patient.

PAUL: Oui, je trouve _____.

DAVID: _____ Monsieur Renaud. _____, mais les

examens _____.

CD I, Track 36

*2.14 Bien prononcer. (p. 68) Masculine and feminine forms of many adjectives differ in sound as well as in spelling. The spoken form of the feminine adjective ends in a pronounced consonant; the consonant sound is dropped in the masculine. Compare and repeat the following pairs of words.

CD I, Track 37

*2.15 Petite conversation. Practice repeating the following conversation.

Chapitre trois ○ ○ ○ ○ ○ ○

La famille et le logement ③

PARTIE ÉCRITE

Point de départ

Ⓐ Possessions. The following drawing shows items in Jean-Claude's apartment. Using vocabulary you know, list as many items as you can.

> **EXEMPLE** *Dans l'appartement de Jean-Claude, il y a des livres…*

Dans l'appartement de Jean-Claude, _____

_____

_____

_____

_____

B **Échange de maisons.** As part of your summer internship in Quebec, you are working for a company that specializes in exchanges of homes. A prospective client has called about the furnished house below and has asked you to describe the rooms in the house as well as the furniture and appliances. In the space provided, list each of the rooms and indicate what is found there.

EXEMPLE *Dans la cuisine, il y a un frigo et une cuisinière.*

Rez-de-chaussée: 141,30 m² (1570 pi²)

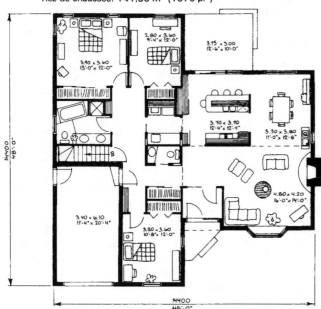

Le verbe *avoir* et les membres de la famille

Êtes-vous prêts? Le verbe *avoir* et les membres de la famille

Indicate on a scale of 1 (not comfortable) to 5 (very comfortable) how well you can handle each of the following tasks and place the number in the box provided. If you answer 1 to 3 for any of the tasks, you should go back and review the explanations and exercises in your textbook.

- [ ] Conjugate **avoir** and give its meaning.
- [ ] List the French names for family members and give their English equivalents.
- [ ] Tell how to say "there is/are" in French, what you need, or what you feel like doing.
- [ ] Tell some of the things you or other people have.
- [ ] Talk about members of your family.

Ⓐ Arbre généalogique. Hélène Dupont's family tree is shown here. Refer to it as you complete the following items, which describe family relationships between various people shown in the family tree.

EXEMPLE   Véronique Dupont et Michèle Thibaut *sont les sœurs* d'Hélène Dupont.

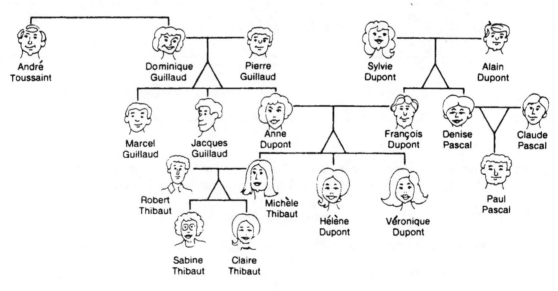

1. Marcel et Jacques Guillaud _____ d'Anne Dupont.

2. Robert Thibaut _____ de Michèle Thibaut.

3. Sylvie Dupont et Dominique Guillaud _____ d'Hélène Dupont.

4. Hélène Dupont _____ de Sabine et Claire Thibaut.

5. Pierre Guillaud _____ de Jacques Guillaud.

6. Alain Dupont _____ de Paul Pascal.

7. Sabine et Claire Thibaut _____ de Michèle Thibaut.

8. François Dupont _____ de Sylvie et Alain Dupont.

B **La vie n'est pas parfaite.** Régine is talking about the various things she and her friends have and don't have. Using the words and phrases provided, re-create Régine's statements. Then, in the space provided, tell some of the things you have or don't have.

> **EXEMPLE** je / chaîne stéréo (oui) / magnétoscope (non)
> ***J'ai une chaîne stéréo mais je n'ai pas de magnétoscope.***

1. Marie / sœurs (oui) / frère (non)

_____

2. vous / téléviseur (oui) / radio (non)

_____

3. tu / four à micro-ondes (non) / ordinateur (oui)

_____

4. je / crayons (oui) / stylo (non)

_____

5. nous / chaises (oui) / canapé (non)

_____

6. Jacques et Robert / lecteur CD (non) / chaîne stéréo (oui)

_____

Et vous? _____

_____

C **Camarades de chambre.** Samira Abibi is talking about herself and her roommate, Clémentine Reynaud. Fill in the blanks in her statements with appropriate forms of the verbs **avoir** and **être**.

1. Clémentine et moi, nous _____ camarades de chambre. Nous _____ étudiantes

en sciences politiques à l'université de Grenoble. Clémentine _____ de Paris. Elle

_____ trois frères. Moi, j(e) _____ de Strasbourg, et je n(e) _____

pas de frères.

2. Nous habitons dans une résidence universitaire. La chambre _____ agréable: il y

_____ un ordinateur, et j(e) _____ un téléviseur. En général, les étudiants ici

_____ un lecteur CD et des CD, mais un jour, je voudrais _____ un lecteur DVD.

3. La vie à l'université _____ intéressante, et nous _____ des amis très sympa. Moi,

j(e) _____ des classes difficiles, mais les profs _____ toujours excellents.

D Dans une librairie. You are talking to a clerk at the **Fnac** in Lyon. Write what you would say in French to convey the following information.

1. Tell the clerk that he has some very interesting books.

_____

2. Tell him what kind of books you like.

_____

3. Find out if there are any American books.

_____

4. Say that you would like to have some French books.

_____

5. Say that you need a French–English dictionary.

_____

La préposition *de* et les adjectifs possessifs

Êtes-vous prêts? La préposition *de* et les adjectifs possessifs

Indicate on a scale of 1 (not comfortable) to 5 (very comfortable) how well you can handle each of the following tasks and place the number in the box provided. If you answer 1 to 3 for any of the tasks, you should go back and review the explanations and exercises in your textbook.

☐ Give the possessive adjectives and their English equivalents.

☐ Tell when **mon, ton,** and **son** are used with feminine adjectives. Give three ways to express possession.

☐ Say "her house," "his house," "their house," "his cars," "their cars."

☐ Use possessive adjectives and other adjectives you know to talk about your family, friends, classes, and possessions.

A Équipement de bureau. Monsieur Fontaine is telling the staff in his office supply store the names of the customers who have purchased different pieces of office equipment. What does he say?

EXEMPLE   le professeur Rollet
C'est le magnétophone du professeur Rollet.

1.   Annette Joubin

_____

2. le docteur Ravel

_____

3. le fils de Xavier Morin

_____

4. le professeur Sauviat

_____

5. la secrétaire de Catherine Métayer

_____

6. les enfants de Madame Beauvalet

_____

B La famille et les amis. Several people are talking to Richard about their families and friends. Re-create their statements by filling in the blanks with the appropriate forms of the possessive adjective.

CLAIRE: Dans notre région, les gens sont contents de _____ vie. Chaque *(Each)* famille possède

_____ maison ou _____ appartement. Nous habitons dans une rue

agréable et _____ maison est très confortable.

ANDRÉ: _____ parents ont un magasin d'articles de sport. Il y a quatre personnes qui travaillent

dans _____ magasin. _____ employés aiment _____ travail.

RENÉE: _____ amie Lise habite rue Laugier. _____ parents sont professeurs. Et toi,

Richard, comment est la ville où tu habites? Comment sont _____ amis? Est-ce que tu

es content de _____ vie et de _____ travail?

ⓒ La vie à l'université. Sandrine is asking you about your experiences at your university. Write an appropriate response to each of her questions using complete sentences.

1. SANDRINE: Est-ce que vous êtes content(e) de votre vie à l'université?

   VOUS: _____

2. SANDRINE: Est-ce que vous trouvez vos cours intéressants?

   VOUS: _____

3. SANDRINE: En général, est-ce que les étudiants sont contents de leurs cours?

   VOUS: _____

4. SANDRINE: Est-ce que vous avez des professeurs intéressants?

   VOUS: _____

5. SANDRINE: Quelle est votre classe favorite?

   VOUS: _____

6. SANDRINE: Est-ce que votre appartement ou votre chambre est agréable?

   VOUS: _____

Les adjectifs prénominaux

A Critiques. The teenage children in the Prévost family don't entirely agree with their parents' ideas. Using the examples as a guide, re-create their statements. Pay attention to both the agreement and the placement of the adjectives in parentheses. Depending on the adjectives used, you will have to make some of your sentences negative.

EXEMPLES   Notre maison est assez belle. (grand)
Oui, mais ce n'est pas une grande maison.

Notre magnétoscope marche bien. (vieux)
Oui, mais c'est un vieux magnétoscope.

1. Ta sœur a une belle voiture. (nouveau)

_____

2. Notre téléviseur marche bien. (vieux)

_____

3. Nous habitons dans une ville pittoresque. (intéressant)

_____

4. Vos grands-parents ont un grand appartement. (beau)

_____

5. Tu regardes un film amusant à la télé. (bon)

_____

6. Tu as une belle affiche. (vieux)

_____

7. Tes professeurs sont sympathiques. (ennuyeux)

_____

8. Notre ordinateur est en assez bonne condition. (nouveau)

_____

B Ça m'intéresse! Your job is taking you to Paris. You have received some listings for apartments in Paris from Just France, a U.S.-based company that offers properties for sale and rent in France, and you wish to discuss the listings with a Parisian friend. Using vocabulary you know, write in French the general descriptions that you would e-mail your friend for two of these apartments that follow (e.g., furnished apartment, large or small kitchen, number of bedrooms and baths).

RUE D'ALGER – 4th Floor. Near Place Vendôme and the Tuilerie Gardens, a large, comfortably appointed three-bedroom apartment with new kitchen and bathrooms, furnished in a modern style, perfect for a family with children who want to be near the Louvre, Seine River and other sites of interest. Small dining room. 3 bedrooms, 2 baths. Access to garage. Category: Comfortable.

RUE DE VARENNE. Available mid-April through September: A quiet, sunny, spacious and superbly decorated apartment with two beautiful bedrooms and two baths, high ceilings, living room, dining room, and a large and well-equipped kitchen (microwave, refrigerator, range), on an elegant street in the heart of the 7th arrondissement. 2 bedrooms, 2 baths. Category: Luxury.

RUE DE BAUNE. On the upper floor of a building without elevator, a pleasant and simply furnished small one-bedroom apartment with modern bath and kitchen, and a delightful terrace for dining or relaxing with a rooftop view of Paris. Recently renovated living room. Gas/electricity included. 1 bedroom, 1 bath. Category: Affordable.

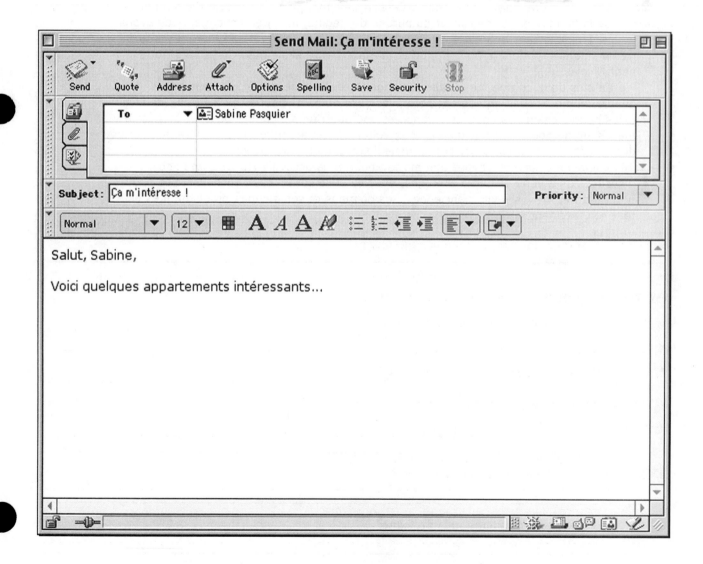

Intégration et perspectives

A **Chez nous en France: Destination la Bretagne.** Patrick Magnien is sending an e-mail (**un courriel**) to his Canadian relatives announcing the family's move from their apartment in Rennes to a new house in Cesson Sévigné, near Rennes. Before you read, look over the questions in **Avez-vous compris?** and locate **la Bretagne** on the map in the front of the book.

A : [   ]

Copie : [   ]

Objet : [   ]

Cher oncle et chère tante,

C'est demain le grand jour!… Eh oui, demain, nous quittons le petit appartement où nous habitons depuis *(since)* notre mariage. Un appartement, c'est suffisant pour des jeunes mariés, mais avec deux enfants, c'est beaucoup trop petit.

Notre nouvelle maison est située à Cesson-Sévigné, près de Rennes. C'est un peu loin de la banque où je travaille et du bureau de Régine, mais, en échange, nous avons la joie d'habiter dans un endroit vraiment agréable. Et en plus *(in addition)*, il y a une très bonne école primaire pour Marion et une excellente école maternelle pour notre petit Nicolas…

En plus de la cuisine, de la salle à manger et de la salle de séjour, nous avons quatre chambres: une grande chambre avec salle de bains pour Régine et moi, deux jolies petites chambres pour les enfants, et une quatrième chambre pour les invités! Il y a aussi un garage assez grand pour deux voitures, le matériel de jardin et les bicyclettes des enfants. La cour est assez petite, mais il y a une grande terrasse.

Maintenant que nous avons une maison pour vous accueillir *(to welcome you)*, n'hésitez pas à venir visiter la Bretagne, avec sa belle côte *(coast)* rocheuse, ses petits ports pittoresques, ses villes anciennes, ses dolmens et ses menhirs préhistoriques et tout son fascinant folklore.

Avez-vous compris?

1. Who are the different members of Patrick's family?

_____

2. Why are they glad to be moving to a new house?

_____

3. Where is the new house?

_____

4. Why is the house better than their apartment?

_____

5. What are some points of interest in **la Bretagne**?

_____

B À vous de lire: Gîtes ruraux. The two **gîtes ruraux** (*country vacation homes*) whose descriptions follow are located in the westernmost part of **la Bretagne** called **le Finistère** (*Land's end*). Brittany's Celtic heritage is evident in place names such as Plouhinec and Tregunc, where the **gîtes** are located; in people's names, such as Le Bihan, Le Goff, and Kerbol; in the regional language, **le breton,** now taught at the **Université de Bretagne;** in folk musical instruments, such as **le biniou** (*a kind of bagpipe);* and in many folk festivals and traditions.

- Scan the descriptions and find the French equivalents for five of the expressions listed in the **Vocabulaire** section.
- Reread the texts and for each property, list in English at least three features, amenities, or other pieces of information.

Gîtes de France en Finistère

Gîte N° 13971 ▮☰ |8 x🧍 | 🐕 | 🦟 Chèque-Vacances
Situé sur la commune de **Plouhinec**, dans **Le Finistère**.
Nombre de chambres : **4**   Superficie : **127 m²**

Description
Maison indépendante. Rdc : hall, cuisine/salle à manger, salon. 1er étage : 2ch 1lit 2p, s.eau, wc. 2ème étage : 2ch 2lits 1p, salle d'eau avec wc. Chauffage central au fuel, l-linge, s-linge, l-vais., m-ondes, TV, téléphone, magnétoscope. Chaise bébé. Garage. Jardin clos avec salon, barbecue, terrasse.$ Vue mer, face à l'océan et à l'entrée du port d'Audierne, cette maison traditionnelle présente l'avantage d'avoir une plage en contrebas à 20m et d'être au départ du sentier côtier. Le soin tout particulier apporté à sa décoration contribuera à rendre votre séjour confortable et accueillant.
🏴󠁧󠁢󠁥󠁮󠁧󠁿 ▮▮▮

Gîte N° 13181 ▮☰ |7 x🧍 | 🐕 | 🦟 Chèque-Vacances
Situé sur la commune de **Tregunc**, dans **Le Finistère**.
Nombre de chambres : **3**   Superficie : **90 m²**

Description
Maison contiguë à un autre logement et dans un village de gîtes. Rdc : séjour avec coin-cuisine, 1ch 1lit 2p avec salle d'eau, wc. Etage : 1ch 1lit 2p, 1ch 3lits 1p, s.de bains, wc. Chauf.élect, l.linge, l.vaisselle. Terrasse, jardin avec salon, barbecue. Animaux acceptés (chats et chiens de petite taille). Loc. draps.$Confort et calme dans ce petit coin de Bretagne où la nature est protégée. La rénovation soignée s'intègre bien dans le jardin où les enfants apprécieront l'aire de jeux. A Trégunc et Névez, une particularité dans la construction des maisons : les pierres debout. Juin/sept : prix 2personnes 274€.
🏴󠁧󠁢󠁥󠁮󠁧󠁿 ▮▮▮

Vocabulaire

high chair   _____   animals accepted   _____

central heat   _____   nature is protected   _____

shower room   _____   across from the ocean _____

comfort and calm   _____

Gîte n° 13181, Tregunc: _____

_____

Gîte N° 13971, Plouhinec: _____

_____

C **On loue un appartement.** You are going to spend a year at the **Université de Rennes II–Haute Bretagne** and will share a one-bedroom apartment (see floor plan that follows) with a French friend. In the space provided, describe the apartment, including number and type of rooms (**C'est un petit appartement**, etc.), and then tell what furniture and appliances you have and what you and your friend will need to get (e.g., **J'ai un… mais je n'ai pas de…; nous avons besoin de…**).

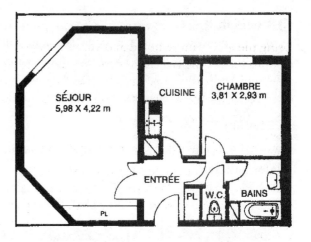

SÉJOUR
5,98 X 4,22 m

CUISINE

CHAMBRE
3,81 X 2,93 m

ENTRÉE

PL   W.C.   BAINS

PL

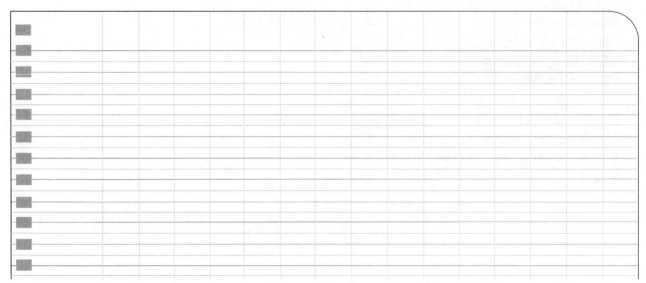

D **À vous d'écrire: La vie universitaire américaine.** A French friend from the **Institut d'Études Politiques de Rennes** is coming to study political science at your college. He has asked you to describe life on your campus. Follow these four steps to develop your description.

1. Préparation

Jot down in French the information you wish to include in your description.

logement— où et avec qui	activités typiques	nombre et type de cours	chambre typique	possessions

2. Brouillon

Using the ideas you've noted and vocabulary you know, write a paragraph (at least eight sentences) describing campus life for the typical student. Write this rough draft on a separate piece of paper. Vary the verbs, adjectives, and adverbs you use, and be sure to incorporate prenominal adjectives. Start your paragraph with an introductory sentence to catch your friend's interest, and then end with a concluding sentence.

3. Révision

Now that you've written the rough draft of your description, read through the draft and check the following.

- Did you write about all the topics listed in the grid? What else could you write about?
- Did you vary the adjectives you used, and were they in the proper form?
- Did you use adverbs to tell how often the typical student does certain activities?
- Did you write an introductory sentence? Does it capture the interest of the reader?
- Did you provide a conclusion?

4. Rédaction

Write the final draft of your description in the space provided here. Make the corrections and insert the additions you noted in step #3. Then reread your description to be sure you are satisfied with it.

PARTIE ORALE

Point de départ

CD1, Track 38

3.1 La chambre de Juliette. Juliette is talking about her possessions and her room, shown here. Decide whether the items Juliette mentions are in her room and mark the appropriate box. You will hear each item twice.

EXEMPLE   You hear: J'ai une voiture.
You mark: ***non***

	oui	non
1.	☐	☐
2.	☐	☐
3.	☐	☐
4.	☐	☐
5.	☐	☐
6.	☐	☐

Le verbe *avoir* et les membres de la famille

CD1, Track 39

*3.2 Situation: Étudiante au pair. (p. 78) Diane, a young American, is an au pair student in a French family. She is speaking with Claire. You will hear the conversation twice. Listen the first time as you hear it read, paying attention to intonation, tone, and pronunciation. During the second reading, repeat each line of the conversation after it is read to you.

CD1, Track 40

*3.3 Dans quelle ville? (p. 79 B) Some friends are telling where members of their families live. What do they say?

EXAMPLE You hear: Philippe / une tante / à Lille
You say: *Philippe a une tante à Lille.*

CD1, Track 41

3.4 La vie à l'université. André is talking about his life on campus. Decide whether you hear a form of the verb **avoir** in each of his statements and mark the appropriate box. You will hear each item twice.

EXAMPLE You hear: Il y a trente-cinq étudiants dans la classe de maths.
You mark: *oui*

	oui	non
1.	☐	☐
2.	☐	☐
3.	☐	☐
4.	☐	☐
5.	☐	☐
6.	☐	☐

La préposition *de* et les adjectifs possessifs

CD1, Track 42

*3.5 Situation: Qui est-ce? (p. 81) Jacques is showing his mother some photos of his new friend, Catherine Dupré, and her family. You will hear the conversation twice. Listen the first time as you hear it read, paying attention to intonation, tone, and pronunciation. During the second reading, repeat each line of the conversation after it is read to you.

CD1, Track 43

*3.6 Trousseau de clés. (p. 81 A) You have a set of seven keys (**les clés**), each of which is numbered. Your friend, who is going to house-sit for you, asks what each key is for. What do you say?

EXEMPLE   You hear: Le numéro un, c'est quelle clé? (voiture)
                    You say: ***C'est la clé de la voiture.***

CD1, Track 44

3.7 Qui est-ce? Anne is showing you a photo of a baptism in her family. In the space provided, jot down in English what Anne says about the people in the photo. You will hear each item twice.

EXEMPLE   You hear: La jeune femme sur la photo, c'est ma sœur, Catherine. C'est la maman du bébé.
           You jot down: *the young woman is her sister, Catherine; the baby's mother*

LE JEUNE HOMME
(AVEC LE BÉBÉ): _____

_____

LE BÉBÉ: _____

_____

L'AUTRE FEMME: _____

_____

L'AUTRE HOMME: _____

_____

Les adjectifs prénominaux

CD1, Track 45

*3.8 Situation: Tiens, Nicolas! (p. 83) Laurent and Nicolas have just run into one another and are catching up on each other's news. You will hear the conversation twice. Listen the first time as you hear it read, paying attention to intonation, tone, and pronunciation. During the second reading, repeat each line of the conversation after it is read to you.

CD1, Track 46

*3.9 Je suis d'accord. (p. 84 A) You and a friend are looking at a house. Your friend comments on the different rooms in the house, and you agree. What do you say?

> **EXEMPLE**   You hear: La cuisine n'est pas très grande.
> You say: ***Oui, c'est vrai; ce n'est pas une très grande cuisine.***

CD1, Track 47

*3.10 Conversation. (p. 84 C) You meet an old friend, Pierre, and you talk about how things are going. Answer Pierre's questions based on the cues you hear.

> **EXEMPLE**   You hear: Est-ce que tu as un appartement? (petit)
> You say: ***Oui, j'ai un petit appartement.***

CD1, Track 48

3.11 Mon nouvel appartement. Pascal has found an apartment in Paris, and he is describing it to his co-workers. Decide whether Pascal's statements accurately describe the floor plan shown here and check the appropriate box. You will hear each item twice.

> **EXEMPLE**   You hear: Il y a deux jolies chambres dans mon appartement.
> You check: ***faux***

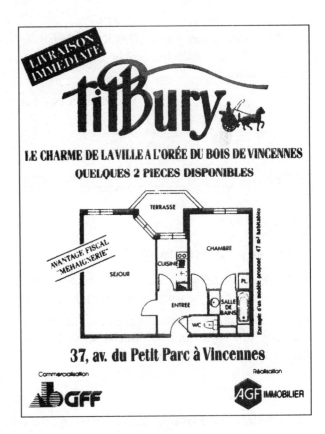

	vrai	faux			vrai	faux
1.	☐	☐		5.	☐	☐
2.	☐	☐		6.	☐	☐
3.	☐	☐		7.	☐	☐
4.	☐	☐		8	☐	☐

Intégration et perspectives

CD1, Track 49

3.12 Description. Listen as Christian Romo talks about his life. Then answer the following questions. You will hear the passage twice.

1. What nationality is Christian's wife?

_____

2. How many children do they have, and how old are they?

_____

3. Where do Christian and his wife work?

_____

4. Who else lives with them?

_____

5. What do they do together as a family? What do the children think of this?

_____

CD1, Track 50

3.13 C'est mon tour! Patrick Deschamps is talking about his family's life. During the pauses provided, complete what he says. Each line will be read twice, then the entire dictation will be read once again so that you can check your work.

1. _____ de la chance parce que nous habitons _____.

2. _____, mais elle _____.

3. _____ et moi, nous _____, mais nous sommes contents.

4. C'est vrai, _____ est différente de la vie _____.

CD1, Track 51

*3.14 Bien prononcer. (p. 94)

A. There are three basic nasal vowel sounds in French: /ɔ̃/ as in **mon**; /ɛ̃/ as in **magasin**; and /ɑ̃/ as in **étudiant**. Practice repeating the words containing the sound /ɔ̃/.

B. Note the difference between the pronunciation of **bon** with a nasal sound and **bonne.** Note also that **bon** becomes /bɔn/ (the same pronunciation as the feminine form **bonne**) when it is followed by a vowel sound. Repeat the following words.

CD1, Track 52

*3.15 Petite conversation. Practice repeating the following conversation.

Chapitre quatre ○ ○ ○ ○ ○ ○

Bon voyage!

④

PARTIE ÉCRITE

Point de départ

Ⓐ À l'agence de voyages. Fill out the following travel survey so that your favorite travel agency can have your preferences on hand. Mark each of the preferences in the categories listed (5 indicates the strongest interest, 1 the least interest), and then write a summary statement about your thoughts. For instance, if you marked 5 for airplane travel and 1 for bus travel, you might write the following statement.

> **EXEMPLE** *Je préfère voyager en avion et je n'aime pas voyager en autocar.*
> *Je trouve ça fatigant.*

Les moyens de transport:					
en avion	5	4	3	2	1
en train	5	4	3	2	1
en autocar	5	4	3	2	1
en voiture	5	4	3	2	1

Commentaires:

_____

_____

La saison:					
au printemps	5	4	3	2	1
en été	5	4	3	2	1
en automne	5	4	3	2	1
en hiver	5	4	3	2	1

Commentaires:

_____

_____

L'endroit:					
à la montagne	5	4	3	2	1
à la campagne	5	4	3	2	1
au bord de la mer	5	4	3	2	1
en ville	5	4	3	2	1
dans mon pays	5	4	3	2	1
à l'étranger	5	4	3	2	1

Commentaires:

_____

_____

Les activités:					
faire des excursions	5	4	3	2	1
acheter des souvenirs	5	4	3	2	1
aller à la plage	5	4	3	2	1
visiter des musées et des monuments	5	4	3	2	1
aller au concert, au cinéma ou au théâtre	5	4	3	2	1

Commentaires:

_____

_____

Le logement:					
dans un hôtel de luxe	5	4	3	2	1
dans un hôtel modeste	5	4	3	2	1
dans un camping	5	4	3	2	1
dans une auberge de jeunesse	5	4	3	2	1

Commentaires:

_____

_____

B **Voyage de luxe ou voyage à prix mini?** In the space provided, list the modes of transportation, activities, and so on that characterize a lavish trip versus a budget-oriented trip.

	voyage de luxe	voyage à prix mini
moyens de transport		
destinations		
logement		
activités		
endroits à visiter		

Le verbe *aller*

Êtes-vous prêts? Le verbe *aller*

Indicate on a scale of 1 (not comfortable) to 5 (very comfortable) how well you can handle each of the following tasks and place the number in the box provided. If you answer 1 to 3 for any of the tasks, you should go back and review the explanations and exercises in your textbook.

☐ Tell what **aller** means and give its different forms.

☐ Tell what **à** means and how it combines with the definite article.

☐ List the months of the year and use them to tell the dates of events.

☐ Use **aller** to tell where you and others are going and what you are going to do (e.g., on the weekend, on vacation, next year).

☐ Ask others what their plans are.

A La semaine prochaine. Fill in the following **agenda** page with at least six activities you and your friends are going to do next week. Then write out your activities in complete sentences in the space provided.

EXEMPLE lundi—*bibliothèque avec Paul*
Lundi matin, Paul et moi, nous allons étudier à la bibliothèque.

lundi 7 novembre

_____

_____

_____

mardi 8 novembre

_____

_____

mercredi 9 novembre

_____

_____

jeudi 10 novembre

_____

_____

_____

vendredi 11 novembre

_____

_____

_____

samedi 12 / dimanche 13 novembre

_____

_____

_____

B Nos vacances. Some students are discussing their summer vacation plans. Using the words and phrases provided and following the example, tell what each person is going to do.

> **EXEMPLE** Marc / travailler dans un magasin.
> *Marc va travailler dans un magasin.*

1. tu / rester à l'université pour étudier

_____

2. moi, je / passer dix jours à la plage

_____

3. Henri / voyager à l'étranger

_____

4. mes frères et moi, nous / aller à la montagne

_____

5. vous / acheter une petite voiture pour aller à la campagne

_____

6. Pascal et Julie / voyager à l'étranger

_____

C Pendant le week-end. Use the suggestions provided to create sentences telling where you and people you know go or do not go on the weekend. Be sure to use a different subject in each sentence.

> **EXEMPLE** *Mon ami Brett ne va pas souvent au théâtre; il préfère aller au cinéma.*

> **les personnes:** Moi; Mon ami(e) ___(nom)___; Mes amis et moi, nous; Mon frère / Ma sœur; Mon / Ma camarade de chambre; Mes amis
>
> **les endroits:** concert, restaurant, cinéma, campagne, bibliothèque, théâtre, université, plage

Les prépositions et les noms de lieux

Êtes-vous prêts? Les prépositions et les noms de lieux

Indicate on a scale of 1 (not comfortable) to 5 (very comfortable) how well you can handle each of the following tasks and place the number in the box provided. If you answer 1 to 3 for any of the tasks, you should go back and review the explanations and exercises in your textbook.

- [ ] Give the French names for countries.
- [ ] Tell which prepositions are used with different place names.
- [ ] Tell in which country you and others live or which countries you want to visit.
- [ ] Tell where different cities in the world are located.

A Projets de voyage. Tell where the following people plan to travel this summer. Using the words and phrases provided, re-create their statements. Be sure to use appropriate prepositions or definite articles.

EXEMPLE Suzanne / désirer / aller / Suisse / Italie
Suzanne désire aller en Suisse et en Italie.

1. nous / visiter / Espagne / Portugal

_____

2. les Renaud / aller / États-Unis / Canada

_____

3. mon frère / aller / voyager / Algérie / Maroc

_____

4. je / aller / visiter / Hollande / Belgique

_____

5. mon oncle et ma tante / avoir envie de / visiter / Nice / Monaco

_____

6. tu / aller / Japon / Chine

_____

B **Où est-ce qu'il faut aller?** Choose eight of the following sites (or others you can think of) and tell to what city or country one must go to visit each one.

EXEMPLE   la tour Eiffel
Il faut aller en France (à Paris) pour visiter la tour Eiffel.

suggestions:

les pyramides	le Kremlin	les chutes du Niagara
le Louvre	le Vatican	les ruines aztèques
les Alpes	le Parthénon	le Palais de Buckingham
la Casbah	le Prado	le Château Frontenac

Les nombres supérieurs à 100 et les nombres ordinaux

Êtes-vous prêts? Les nombres supérieurs à 100 et les nombres ordinaux

Indicate on a scale of 1 (not comfortable) to 5 (very comfortable) how well you can handle each of the following tasks and place the number in the box provided. If you answer 1 to 3 for any of the tasks, you should go back and review the explanations and exercises in your textbook.

☐ Give the French equivalents for numbers such as: three hundred, three hundred fifty, one thousand, five thousand, one million, ten million.

☐ Give the current year in French, say the year you were born, and give the dates of several historical events.

☐ Use numbers to give phone numbers, prices, and populations.

☐ Say and write ordinal numbers such as: first, fifth, ninth, twelfth, twenty-first, fiftieth, one hundredth.

A Distances. Julien and Dominique Vincent are planning a trip to Quebec and are checking the distances between various cities. Referring to the chart that follows, complete their statements.

EXEMPLE   Montréal est à *cinq cent trente-neuf* kilomètres de Rimouski.

Distances entre les principales villes du Québec

(En kilomètres)

Baie-Comeau	Chicoutimi	Gaspé	Hull	La Malbaie	Montréal	Québec	Rimouski	Rouyn-Noranda	Sept-Îles	Sherbrooke	Saint-Georges	Trois-Rivières	Joliette	Sorel	Sainte-Agathe-des-Monts
316															
337	649														
869	662	1 124													
273	186	572	596												
676	484	930	207	405											
422	211	700	451	149	253										
93	264	431	736	142	539	312									
1 304	831	1 559	536	1 032	638	882	1 167								
232	542	567	1 096	503	904	652	325	1 532							
662	451	915	347	388	147	240	527	782	886						
524	313	818	525	251	334	102	387	961	754	158					
545	367	831	331	304	142	135	442	747	779	158	233				
635	422	904	216	363	75	214	520	650	864	218	313	86			
631	419	924	281	357	101	208	494	718	860	143	266	82	34		
755	557	1 019	201	484	103	338	632	537	984	248	437	210	109	201	

1. Sorel est à _____ kilomètres de Sainte-Agathe-des-Monts.

2. Baie-Comeau est à _____ kilomètres de Sherbrooke.

3. Hull est à _____ kilomètres de Sorel.

4. Montréal est à _____ kilomètres de Sept-Îles.

5. La Malbaie est à _____ kilomètres de Joliette.

6. Chicoutimi est à _____ kilomètres de Sherbrooke.

B C'est combien? According to recent information on the Internet, the following are average prices for apartments and homes in the Val-de-Marne area near Paris. Write out each price in full.

EXEMPLE   69 868 € pour un studio: *soixante-neuf mille huit cent soixante-huit euros*

QUELQUES INDICATEURS POUR LE VAL-DE-MARNE

Les prix moyens par taille

Pour un appartement

112 576 € pour un 2 pièces: _____

173 118 € pour un 3 pièces: _____

245 973 € pour un 4 pièces: _____

397 504 € pour un 5 pièces: _____

Pour une maison

216 245 € pour 3 pièces: _____

269 466 € pour 4 pièces et moins: _____

352 999 € pour 5 pièces et moins: _____

502 498 € pour 6 pièces et plus: _____

Ⓒ Le Tour de France. The following chart lists the **étapes** *(stages)* across France of a typical **Tour de France** bicycle race. Using the example as a guide, tell the position in the race of each **étape** indicated.

　　EXEMPLE　Lamballe–Quimper? C'est la *huitième* étape.

1. Liège–Charleroi
2. Charleroi–Namur
3. Waterloo–Wasquehal
4. Cambrai–Arras
5. Amiens–Chartres
6. Bonneval–Angers
7. Châteaubriant–Saint-Brieuc
8. Lamballe–Quimper
9. Saint-Léonard-de-Noblat–Guéret
10. Limoges–Saint-Flour
11. Saint-Flour–Figeac
12. Castelsarrasin–La Mongie
13. Lannemezan–Plateau de Beille
14. Carcassonne–Nîmes
15. Valréas–Villard-de-Lans
16. Bourg d'Oisans–L'Alpe d'Huez
17. Bourg d'Oisans–Le Grand Bornand
18. Annemasse–Lons-le-Saunier
19. Besançon–Besançon
20. Montereau-Fault-Yonne–Paris Champs-Élysées

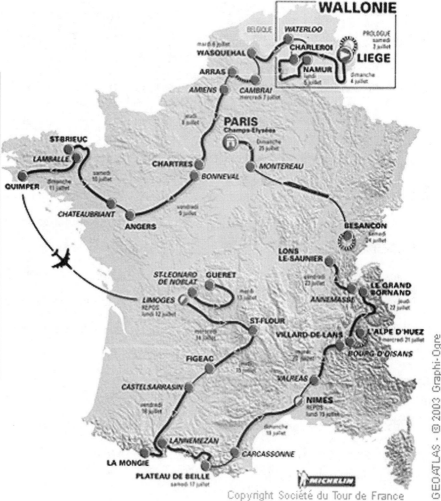

1. Montereau-Fault-Yonne–Paris Champs-Élysées? C'est la _____ étape.

2. Limoges–Saint-Flour? C'est la _____ étape.

3. Bourg d'Oisans–L'Alpe d'Huez? C'est la _____ étape.

4. Liège–Charleroi? C'est la _____ étape.

5. Cambrai–Arras? C'est la _____ étape.

6. Bonneval–Angers? C'est la _____ étape.

7. Annemasse–Lons-le-Saunier? C'est la _____ étape.

8. Castelsarrasin–La Mongie? C'est la _____ étape.

Ⓓ Quelques dates célèbres. Write out in words the years for the following events.

> **EXEMPLE** la mort *(death)* de Jeanne d'Arc à Rouen (1431)
> ***mille quatre cent trente et un***

1. la bataille d'Hastings (1066)

_____

2. la fondation de la Sorbonne (1275)

_____

3. la défaite de l'Armada (1588)

_____

4. la défaite de Napoléon à Waterloo (1815)

_____

5. la prise de la Bastille (1789)

_____

6. l'indépendance de l'Algérie (1962)

_____

7. le centenaire de la statue de la Liberté (1986)

_____

8. les jeux Olympiques de Vancouver (2010)

_____

Intégration et perspectives

Ⓐ Chez nous en France: Destination le Périgord. Madame Claire Dassier has written to the **Syndicat d'Initiative** in **le Périgord** for travel information on the region. An employee has answered her letter and has enclosed a brochure describing a 4-day excursion (see **À vous de lire**). Before you read the letter, look over the items in **Avez-vous compris?** and consult the map at the front of the workbook to see where **le Périgord** is located.

Madame,

Dans votre lettre du 27 juin, vous annoncez votre intention de visiter le Périgord en septembre ou en octobre prochain, et vous nous demandez des détails sur notre région. Vous nous demandez aussi si l'automne est une bonne saison pour visiter le Périgord.

Oui, l'automne est le moment parfait pour visiter notre région. En septembre et en octobre, le temps est magnifique et les touristes sont moins *(less)* nombreux. Vous allez trouver partout des chambres libres dans les hôtels et des restaurants heureux de vous aider à découvrir les excellentes spécialités de notre région: foie gras, truffes, champignons *(mushrooms)*, noix *(nuts)*, etc.

Vous savez probablement que la célèbre grotte de Lascaux est maintenant fermée au public pour la protection des peintures *(paintings)* préhistoriques contre la pollution, mais il existe une copie exacte de la grotte qui est ouverte au public. Il y a aussi de nombreuses autres grottes avec de très belles peintures datant d'il y a plus de 10 000 ans qu'il est encore possible de visiter.

Pour plus de détails sur notre région, consultez l'itinéraire ci-joint *(enclosed)*. Si vous avez accès à Internet, visitez notre site à http://www.perigord.tm.fr.

Avec nos meilleures salutations et nos remerciements pour l'intérêt que vous portez à notre région *(a customary formal closing formula)*.

Avez-vous compris? Based on what she read in the letter from the **Syndicat d'Initiative,** which of the following statements are accurate representations of what Mme Dassier might tell her husband about their upcoming visit to the **Périgord**?

1. **oui / non**   L'automne est une excellente saison pour visiter le Périgord parce qu'il n'y a pas beaucoup de touristes.

2. **oui / non**   C'est dommage, mais il va être difficile de trouver des chambres d'hôtel.

3. **oui / non**   Nous allons sûrement aimer les spécialités de la région, comme les truffes et le foie gras.

4. **oui / non**   Malheureusement, il est impossible de visiter la grotte de Lascaux.

5. **oui / non**   Mais il y a de nombreuses autres grottes à visiter dans la région.

B À vous de lire: Quatre jours dans le Périgord. You are planning to spend some time in the **Périgord** and have received the same information that the **Syndicat d'Initiative** sent to Mme Dassier.

Read over the itinerary, and jot down in English (1) what might be of interest to you on each of the four days and why, and (2) what doesn't interest you and why not. You should mention three or more places for each day.

Day 1: _____

_____

Day 2: _____

_____

Day 3: _____

_____

Day 4: _____

_____

Itinéraire

1. Le Périgord Vert
- Visite de la grotte préhistorique de Villars et du château de Puyguilhem: un des plus remarquables châteaux de la première Renaissance.
- Déjeuner libre (à Brantôme ou ses environs).
- Promenade dans Brantôme, la «Venise du Périgord»: son ensemble d'édifices médiévaux et ceux datant de la Renaissance, le charme de ses jardins au bord de la Dronne.
- Visite du Château de Bourdeilles (forteresse du XIIIe et XVe siècles et Palais de la Renaissance dominant la Vallée de la Dronne).
- Visite de l'Écomusée de la Truffe à Sorges.
- Installation dans un hôtel*** (Logis de France).
- Dîner et hébergement.

2. Du Périgord Blanc au Périgord Noir
- Départ de l'hôtel. Visite de Périgueux, ville d'art et d'histoire: circuit médiéval, Renaissance et gallo-romain.
- Déjeuner libre (dans la région des Eyzies).
- Visite du Musée National de Préhistoire.
- Abri Pataud, Grotte du Grand Roc, grottes préhistoriques.
- Parcours le long de la vallée de la Vézère.

- Visite d'un village troglodytique (La Madeleine à Tursac, la Roque Saint-Christophe ou Moustier).
- Installation dans un hôtel*** (Logis de France).
- Dîner et hébergement.

3. Vallées de la Vézère et de la Dordogne
- Départ de l'hôtel.
- Visite du fac-similé de la grotte de Lascaux, Lascaux II et du centre d'art préhistorique du Thot. «Espace Cro-magnon» à Thonac.
- Déjeuner libre (à Thonac ou ses environs).
- Visite de Sarlat, ville d'art et d'histoire.
- Cingle de Montfort, promenade dans la Bastide de Domme (panorama sur la vallée de la Dordogne).
- Installation dans un hôtel*** (Logis de France).
- Dîner et hébergement.

4. Le Bergeracois «Pays de Vignobles et de Bastides»
- Départ de l'hôtel.
- Musée du vin.
- Visite de la Vieille Ville.
- Musée du Vélocipède à Cadouin.
- Déjeuner libre à Monpazier ou ses environs.
- Visite du Château de Biron. Fin du circuit.

⊙ À vous d'écrire: Cartes postales. While on your trip in the **Périgord,** you write two postcards to French friends telling them about what you are doing or are going to do. Describe a different day on each postcard. Follow these four steps to develop your descriptions.

1. Préparation

In the preceding activity, you wrote what did and did not interest you on the different days of your four-day trip in the **Périgord.** Reread those answers (or do the activity if you have not already done so) and then choose those activities that you want to talk about on your postcards and list them in the following grid (**contenu**). Indicate also the recipient (**destinataire**) of each card. Remember that a postcard has only a limited amount of space, so you will have to be selective in what you write.

	destinataire	contenu
carte postale #1		
carte postale #2		

2. Brouillon

Using the ideas you've noted and vocabulary you know, write a draft of your two postcards on a separate piece of paper. Use a variety of sentence structures, and use the verb **aller** to tell what you are going to do (**Demain, nous allons visiter la ville de Sarlat, une ville célèbre pour son art et son histoire.**). Choose an opening and a closing from the list that follows.

Opening: **Chers amis, / Un petit bonjour de… / Salut les amis!**
Closing: **Bises** *(Hugs and kisses),* **/ Au revoir, / À bientôt, / Affectueusement,**

3. Révision

Now that you've written the rough drafts of your descriptions, read through the drafts and check the following.

• Did you write about things that might be of interest to the person to whom you are sending the postcard?
• Did you use **aller** correctly?
• Did you vary your sentence structure? For example, **Demain, nous allons visiter le musée du vin** or **Demain, c'est la visite du musée du vin.**
• Did you use a proper opening and closing for each message?

4. Rédaction

Write the final draft of your postcards in the space provided. Make the corrections and insert the additions you noted in step #3. Then reread your postcards to be sure you are satisfied with them.

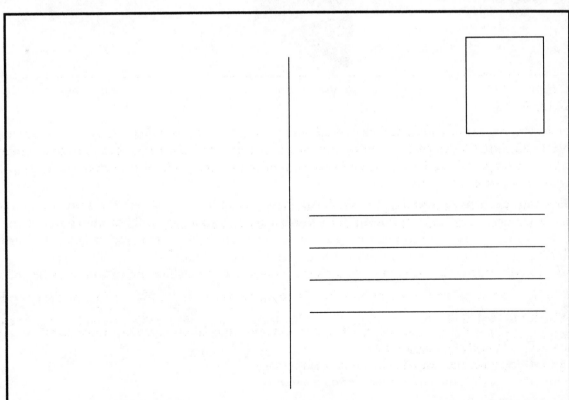

PARTIE ORALE

Point de départ

CD2, Track 2

4.1 On est en vacances. Listen as some people talk about their vacations. Decide whether their statements describe the following drawings and underline **oui** or **non.** You will hear each item twice.

EXEMPLE   You hear: Mon ami Jacques aime bien prendre des photos.
You underline: *non*

1.

oui   non

2.

oui   non

3.

oui   non

4.

oui   non

5.

oui   non

6.

oui   non

Le verbe *aller*

CD2, Track 3

*4.2 Situation: Fermeture annuelle. (p. 104) It is the last week of July, and a customer is wondering when Madame Dubourg's pharmacy will close for the family's annual vacation. You will hear the conversation twice. Listen the first time as you hear it read, paying attention to intonation, tone, and pronunciation. During the second reading, repeat each line of the conversation after it is read to you.

CD2, Track 4

*4.3 Pendant le week-end. (p. 104 A) Danielle and her friends have plans for this weekend. Using the cues you hear, tell where they are going.

EXEMPLE   You hear: Catherine / concert
You say: *Catherine va au concert.*

CD2 Track 5

*4.4 Le 1ᵉʳ mai. (p. 104 B) Several students are talking about their plans for the **fête du travail** (similar to Labor Day in the U.S.). What do they say?

   EXEMPLE   You hear: Jean-Claude / prendre des photos
            You say: *__Jean-Claude va prendre des photos.__*

CD2, Track 6

4.5 Projets. André has found out what different people in his dormitory are going to do this weekend. Jot down in English what each person is going to do. You will hear each item twice.

   EXEMPLE   You hear: Michelle va étudier à la bibliothèque avec ses amis.
       You jot down: *going to study at library with friends*

1. Marie et Jacques: _____

2. Henri: _____

3. Moi: _____

4. Vous, Anne et Gisèle: _____

5. Nous: _____

6. Mon camarade de chambre: _____

Les prépositions et les noms de lieux

CD2, Track 7

*4.6 Situation: Les grands départs. (p. 108) Paris, July 31. A reporter is interviewing vacationers who are caught in a traffic jam on their way out of the city. You will hear the conversation twice. Listen the first time as you hear it read, paying attention to intonation, tone, and pronunciation. During the second reading, repeat each line of the conversation after it is read to you.

CD2, Track 8

*4.7 Projets de voyage. (p. 108 B) Where are the following people going this summer? Use the cues you hear to tell what they say.

   EXEMPLE   You hear: Henri / Espagne et Portugal
        You say: *__Henri va en Espagne et au Portugal.__*

CD2, Track 9

4.8 À l'agence de voyages. You're working at a travel agency, and you need to keep track of places people ask about. For each statement you hear, write the English name of the country mentioned. You will hear each item twice.

   EXEMPLE   You hear: Et au Brésil, comment est le climat?
       You write: *__Brazil__*

1. _____ **4.** _____

2. _____ **5.** _____

3. _____ **6.** _____

Les nombres supérieurs à 100 et les nombres ordinaux

CD2, Track 10

*4.9 Situation: Réservation d'une chambre d'hôtel. (p. 111) Laurence Rivière is calling to reserve a room at the **Hôtel du Mont Blanc** for a business trip to Geneva. You will hear the conversation twice. Listen the first time as you hear it read, paying attention to intonation, tone, and pronunciation. During the second reading, repeat each line of the conversation after it is read to you.

CD2, Track 11

*4.10 Agence de voyages. (p. 112 C) You are working at **Nouvelles Frontières** and are answering customers' questions about the prices of different trips. Using the information shown, how would you respond to your customers' questions?

> **EXEMPLE** Tunisie (1 023 €)
>
> You hear: Combien coûte le voyage en Tunisie?
> You say: *Mille vingt-trois euros.*

1. Le Viêt Nam (1 715 €)

2. Découverte de la Chine (2 090 €)

3. L'ouest Canadien (1 840 €)

4. L'Afrique du Sud (1 610 €)

5. La Turquie (797 €)

6. L'Espagne (803 €)

CD2, Track 12

4.11 Appartements. The following advertisement shows some luxury apartments available in the **sixième arrondissement** in Paris. Write the price you hear for each one. You will hear each item twice.

> **EXEMPLE** You hear: cent trente-sept mille cinq cent neuf euros
> You write: *137 509 €*

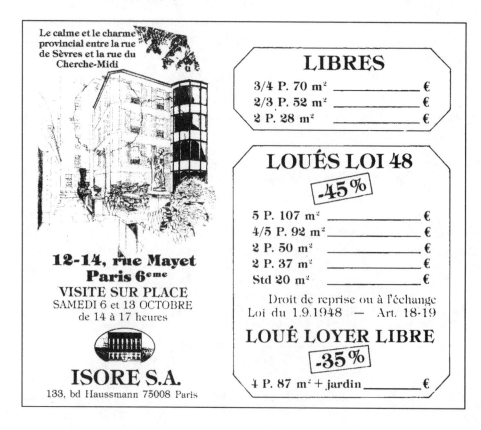

Le calme et le charme provincial entre la rue de Sèvres et la rue du Cherche-Midi

12-14, rue Mayet Paris 6ᵉᵐᵉ
VISITE SUR PLACE
SAMEDI 6 et 13 OCTOBRE
de 14 à 17 heures

ISORE S.A.
133, bd Haussmann 75008 Paris

LIBRES

3/4 P. 70 m²	_____ €
2/3 P. 52 m²	_____ €
2 P. 28 m²	_____ €

LOUÉS LOI 48
-45%

5 P. 107 m²	_____ €
4/5 P. 92 m²	_____ €
2 P. 50 m²	_____ €
2 P. 37 m²	_____ €
Std 20 m²	_____ €

Droit de reprise ou à l'échange
Loi du 1.9.1948 — Art. 18-19

LOUÉ LOYER LIBRE
-35%

4 P. 87 m² + jardin _____ €

Intégration et perspectives

CD2, Track 13

4.12 Une histoire d'amour entre ciel et mer. Listen to the following description of Martinique, an island in the French West Indies situated above the South American coast. Then decide if the following statements are **vrai** or **faux** and mark the appropriate column. You will hear the passage twice.

vrai | **faux**

1. The people of Martinique speak Creole, French, and English.

2. Carnaval is celebrated in December.

3. Tourists like to visit the villages around Mount Pelée.

4. Tourists are also attracted to the exotic restaurants of the capital.

5. Tourists prefer the hotels located in the small villages.

CD2, Track 14

4.13 En vacances. Véra and Xavier Dufreigne are discussing their upcoming vacation. During the pauses provided, complete what they say. Each line will be read twice, then the entire conversation will be read once again so that you can check your work.

VÉRA: _____.

Qu'est-ce que nous allons faire cette année?

XAVIER: Moi, je voudrais bien _____.

VÉRA: Bon. Alors, _____?

XAVIER: _____.

CD2, Track 15

*4.14 Bien prononcer (p. 122)

A. Practice repeating the nasal sound /ɛ̃/ as in **province** and note the different letter combinations associated with this sound.

B. Note the difference in the pronunciation of the masculine and feminine forms of nouns and adjectives whose masculine form ends in /ɛ̃/. This change occurs whenever **in, ain,** or **ien** is followed by a vowel or by another **n** or **m.**

CD2, Track 16

*4.15 Petite conversation. Practice repeating the following conversation.

Chapitre cinq ○ ○ ○ ○ ○ ○

Bon appétit!

⑤

PARTIE ÉCRITE

Point de départ

🅐 **Qu'est-ce que vous aimez?** You are visiting the Lair family in Tours, and Madame Lair has asked you to help her in meal planning by writing down the types of foods you like. Write your preferences in the space provided.

J'aime…

les fruits

_____les pommes_____

_____

_____

_____

les viandes

_____

_____

_____

_____

les légumes

_____

_____

_____

_____

les boissons

_____

_____

_____

_____

les desserts

_____

_____

_____

_____

autres

_____

_____

_____

_____

🅑 **Préférences.** Name three or more foods that the following people like or dislike.

1. Les étudiants aiment _____

_____

2. Mes amis végétariens n'aiment pas _____

_____

3. Moi, je déteste _____

_____

mais j'aime _____

_____

4. En général, les Américains n'aiment pas beaucoup _____

_____

5. Les enfants adorent _____

_____

mais ils détestent _____

_____

6. Les Français aiment _____

_____

Les adjectifs démonstratifs

Êtes-vous prêts? Les adjectifs démonstratifs

Indicate on a scale of 1 (not comfortable) to 5 (very comfortable) how well you can handle each of the following tasks and place the number in the box provided. If you answer 1 to 3 for any of the tasks, you should go back and review the explanations and exercises in your textbook.

- [ ] List the demonstrative adjectives and give their English equivalents.
- [ ] Tell which adjective is used with masculine nouns beginning with a vowel sound.
- [ ] Know when to use the definite article, indefinite article, or demonstrative adjective.
- [ ] Use the demonstrative adjective to point out people, specific things you like, things you want to buy, etc.

Ⓐ Au marché. Marie is looking at some produce at an outdoor market. Fill in the blanks in the conversation with the appropriate demonstrative articles.

LE MARCHAND: Qu'est-ce que vous désirez, madame?

MARIE: Je voudrais acheter _____ haricots verts, _____ carottes, _____ melon et

_____ oignons. Est-ce que vos tomates sont bonnes?

LE MARCHAND: Oui, _____ tomates sont très bonnes.

MARIE: Et vos fruits?

LE MARCHAND: _____ poires et _____ cerises sont excellentes.

MARIE: Et vos oranges, elles sont comment?

LE MARCHAND: Regardez _____ orange: est-ce qu'elle n'a pas l'air bonne?

ⓑ Critiques. G. Bongoût rarely finds anything to his liking. Using the cues provided and following the example, re-create his statements.

EXEMPLE affiche (pas beau / trop petit)
Cette affiche-ci n'est pas belle et cette affiche-là est trop petite.

1. quartier (trop vieux / pas très tranquille)

_____

2. femme (trop impulsif / pas assez indépendant)

_____

3. hommes (pas assez honnête / trop impatient)

_____

4. hôtel (pas confortable / trop petit)

_____

5. maisons (trop vieux / trop moderne)

_____

6. appartement (pas assez moderne / trop grand)

_____

Le partitif

Êtes-vous prêts? Le partitif

Indicate on a scale of 1 (not comfortable) to 5 (very comfortable) how well you can handle each of the following tasks and place the number in the box provided. If you answer 1 to 3 for any of the tasks, you should go back and review the explanations and exercises in your textbook.

☐ List the partitive articles and tell what they mean.

☐ Know when to use the definite article, the indefinite article, and the partitive article—tell the meanings of **le pain, un pain, du pain.**

☐ Talk about quantities, weights, and measures using the appropriate expression.

☐ Tell what ingredients you would use to make different meals and dishes.

A Houra. Sabine and Thibaut Girard are doing their grocery shopping online at houra.fr. Based on the products they've placed in their **panier** *(shopping basket),* tell what they are going to buy. (You do not need to give the brand names of these items.)

Sabine et Thibaut vont acheter _____

_____

_____

_____

B La cuisine française. What do you know about French cuisine? Reconstruct the following sentences to tell what ingredients are and are not in various French dishes.

> EXEMPLE   Dans le bœuf bourguignon: vin (oui), oignons (oui), pommes de terre (non)
> ***Dans le bœuf bourguignon, il y a du vin et des oignons, mais il n'y a pas de pommes de terre.***

1. Dans la quiche lorraine: jambon (oui), œufs (oui), vin (non), sucre (non)

_____

_____

2. Dans la salade niçoise: tomates (oui), haricots verts (oui), fruits (non)

_____

_____

3. Dans la fondue suisse: fromage (oui), vin (oui), viande (non)

_____

_____

4. Dans le pain: eau (oui), lait (non), œufs (non)

_____

_____

C Au Bistrot d'à côté. Jacques is sitting at the restaurant **Le Bistrot d'à côté** *(The Bistro next door)* looking at the menu; the waiter is trying to take his order. Fill in the blanks in their conversation with the correct definite, indefinite, or partitive articles.

LE GARÇON: Au menu, il y a _____ poulet avec _____ haricots verts.

JACQUES: Oh, je déteste _____ haricots verts. Est-ce que vous avez _____ petits pois et _____ pommes de terre?

LE GARÇON: Nous avons _____ pommes de terre mais nous n'avons pas _____ petits pois.

JACQUES: Alors, je vais prendre _____ poisson et _____ salade et je vais boire _____ eau minérale et _____ vin.

LE GARÇON: Et comme fruit, vous aimez _____ pêches?

JACQUES: Non, je préfère _____ pommes et _____ cerises.

D Qu'est-ce qu'on va acheter? In the space provided, prepare shopping lists for each of the following situations.

1. vos provisions habituelles pour la semaine

_____

_____

_____

2. un repas typiquement américain pour des amis étrangers

_____

_____

_____

3. un pique-nique à la campagne

_____

_____

_____

Le verbe *prendre* et le verbe *boire*

Êtes-vous prêts? Le verbe *prendre* et le verbe *boire*

Indicate on a scale of 1 (not comfortable) to 5 (very comfortable) how well you can handle each of the following tasks and place the number in the box provided. If you answer 1 to 3 for any of the tasks, you should go back and review the explanations and exercises in your textbook.

☐ Conjugate the verbs **prendre** and **boire** and give their English equivalents. Give a second meaning of **prendre.**

☐ List two other verbs conjugated like **prendre** and give their English equivalents.

☐ Say "I'm hungry" and "I'm thirsty" in French.

☐ List beverages and give their English equivalents.

☐ Order something to eat and drink in a café or restaurant.

Ⓐ Apprentis-cuisiniers. Marc and his wife, Élise, are apprentice cooks in a Parisian restaurant. Marc is describing their work. Complete his statements with the appropriate forms of the following verbs: **apprendre, comprendre, prendre.**

Ma femme et moi, nous sommes apprentis-cuisiniers. Nous _____ des leçons dans un

grand restaurant parisien. C'est passionnant, mais ce n'est pas facile. Nous travaillons beaucoup pour

_____ notre métier (*profession*). Notre patron (*boss*) est un homme qui adore faire la cuisine,

mais il ne _____ pas toujours les gens qui ont beaucoup à _____. Cette

semaine, j(e) _____ à faire des hors-d'œuvre. Élise _____ à faire des sauces.

Nous _____ tous des choses différentes. Certains _____ à préparer les

viandes: d'autres _____ à préparer les spécialités de la maison. Nous avons des clients de

pays différents et ça aide (*helps*) quand on _____ une langue étrangère. Élise et moi, nous

_____ l'anglais. Un des employés _____ des leçons d'espagnol et deux de

nos amis _____ l'allemand.

Ⓑ Habitudes. Roxanne is telling an American friend what French people like to drink at different times of the day. Complete her statements with the correct forms of the verb **boire.**

Tu aimerais savoir si les Français _____ souvent du vin. C'est vrai que les Français aiment

bien _____ du vin blanc avec le poisson et du vin rouge avec les viandes rouges. Aux États-

Unis, on _____ souvent des cocktails, n'est-ce pas? En France, on _____

rarement des cocktails, mais il y a des gens qui _____ un apéritif avant (*before*) le dîner ou

un digestif après—pour aider la digestion, bien sûr! Il y a d'autres boissons qui sont importantes dans la vie de

tous les jours. Par exemple, les enfants _____ souvent du lait ou du jus de fruits le matin.

Moi, je _____ surtout de l'eau minérale ou du jus de fruits. Quand il rentre (*returns*) de son travail, mon père _____ quelquefois un petit verre de vin dans un café avec ses amis. Le

dimanche, nous _____ quelquefois un petit digestif après le dîner. Et toi, qu'est-ce que tu

_____?

C Au Chat qui fume. You have been invited by some French friends to eat in one of their favorite restaurants. Look at the following menu. How would you answer your friends' questions?

Soupes
Soupe à l'oignon gratinée
Soupe aux petits pois
Consommé de boeuf

Viandes
Rôti de porc jardinière
Filet de sole sauce au beurre
Boeuf bourguignon
Poulet aux olives et aux tomates

Légumes
Tomates provençales
Pommes de terre dauphinoises
Artichaut sauce vinaigrette
Frites

Salades
Salade de laitue

Desserts
Gâteau au chocolat
Tarte aux poires
Pêche Melba
Glaces assorties
Fromages assortis

Boissons
Eau minérale
Vin (rouge, blanc)
Bière (allemande, hollandaise, française)
Café

1. Est-ce que vous allez prendre de la soupe?

_____

2. Qu'est-ce que vous prenez comme viande? Leur rôti de porc est toujours excellent.

_____

3. Et comme légumes, qu'est-ce que vous prenez?

_____

4. Est-ce que vous allez prendre de la salade?

_____

5. Qu'est-ce que vous prenez comme dessert? Je recommande leurs glaces et leur tarte aux poires.

_____

6. Est-ce que vous allez boire du vin avec votre repas?

_____

7. Est-ce que vous désirez un café après le repas?

_____

Intégration et perspectives

Ⓐ Chez nous en France: Destination la Bourgogne du Sud. André Dumercy, the chef at the **Auberge du Cheval Blanc,** is always happy to hear that his customers enjoy the food he prepares. He responds to a favorable review in the regional newspaper. Before you read his letter, look over the **Avez-vous compris?** that follows, and check the map at the front of the workbook to see where **la Bourgogne** is located.

Vous êtes contents de votre visite dans notre établissement? Eh bien, je suis ravi de l'apprendre, et je vous assure que nous allons continuer à faire tout notre possible pour donner entière satisfaction à notre aimable clientèle.

Notre restaurant n'est pas un établissement de grand luxe, mais nous essayons de préparer une cuisine agréable, faite avec les excellents produits de notre région. Le bon bœuf charolais, les excellents poulets fermiers *(free-range)* et même les poulets de Bresse avec appellation contrôlée *(label guaranteeing the origin of the chickens)*, les superbes fromages fabriqués dans les fermes de la région, les légumes frais de nos jardins et, bien sûr, les bons vins du Mâconnais et du Beaujolais: voilà les produits qu'on trouve à notre table! Et comme spécialités régionales, nous servons aussi les traditionnels escargots *(snails)* de Bourgogne et les cuisses de grenouilles *(frog legs)*!

Le service reste simple et modeste parce que nous avons seulement un minimum de personnel. Moi, je suis occupé à la cuisine. Ma femme est à la caisse *(is the cashier)* et surveille le service dans la salle à manger. Alors, si vous aimez cette ambiance familiale, nous sommes prêts à vous accueillir!

Avez-vous compris? Based on the information in the **Chez nous** reading, give the information you would include about **le Cheval Blanc** on a regional Web site.

Nom du restaurant _____

Nom du chef _____

Cuisine _____

Spécialités _____

Vins _____

Ambiance _____

ⓑ À vous de lire: La cuisine bourguignonne. Burgundy is well known for its excellent cuisine, and one of the favorite regional **specialités** is **le bœuf bourguignon.** Read the following information about a recipe for this dish and complete the activities in **Avez-vous compris?**

petit lexique de termes culinaires

le gîte *round (cut of beef)*, **la macreuse** *shoulder (cut of beef)*, **les lardons** *(m) cubed bacon*, **le bouquet** *(m)* **garni** *bunch of mixed fresh herbs*, **l'ail** *(m) garlic*, **une cuillerée** *a spoonful*, **ajoutez** *add*, **émincez** *slice thinly*, **faites revenir** *brown, fry*, **doré** *golden*, **la cocotte** *casserole (dish)*, **mijoter** *to simmer*, **retirez** *remove*

Le bœuf bourguignon
Pour 4 personnes

1 kg de gîte ou de macreuse en morceaux	1 carotte
1 bouteille de bourgogne rouge	1 bouquet garni
200 g de champignons de Paris	1 gousse d'ail
150 g de lardons	1 cuillerée à soupe de concentré de tomate
2 gros oignons	

1. Pelez et émincez les oignons. Épluchez la carotte et coupez-la en rondelles. Faites chauffer 20 g de beurre et une cuillerée à soupe d'huile dans une cocotte. Faites revenir les oignons et les lardons. Quand ils sont dorés, retirez-les.
2. Remplacez les oignons et les lardons par la viande et faites-la également dorer, puis remettez les lardons et les oignons. Poivrez et versez le vin. Ajoutez le bouquet garni, la carotte et l'ail haché. Couvrez et laissez mijoter 2 heures.
3. Nettoyez les champignons et émincez-les. Faites-les revenir au beurre. Ajoutez-les 15 minutes avant la fin de la cuisson, avec le concentré de tomate. Mélangez bien.
4. Servez dans la cocotte, en ayant pris soin de retirer le bouquet garni.

Conseil: Le bœuf bourguignon est traditionnellement accompagné de pommes de terre vapeur persillées mais vous pouvez aussi vous régaler avec une purée de pommes de terre ou des pâtes fraîches.

Astuce: Si vous voulez corser le goût, vous pouvez faire mariner la viande pendant quelques heures dans du vin rouge avec des aromates.

Boisson conseillée: Bourgogne rouge, évidemment!

Avez-vous compris?

1. On fait des courses. Based on the information in the recipe for **le bœuf bourguignon,** mark those ingredients that should be on your shopping list.

	oui	non		oui	non
white wine	☐	☐	tomatoes	☐	☐
tomato paste	☐	☐	garlic	☐	☐
mushrooms	☐	☐	champagne	☐	☐
eggs	☐	☐	red wine	☐	☐
onions and carrots	☐	☐	cream	☐	☐

2. Dans quel ordre? The following recipe for **le bœuf bourguignon** wasn't copied in the right order. Number the steps for completing the recipe in the right order, starting with 1.

_____ Servez le plat bien chaud.

_____ Laissez tout (sauf les champignons) mijoter pendant deux heures.

_____ Ajoutez le vin rouge.

_____ Pelez les oignons et faites-les cuire dans du beurre.

_____ Faites dorer la viande.

_____ Ajoutez les champignons et le concentré de tomate.

3. Et en plus? The recipe gives additional information about the dish. What are the answers to these questions?

What is **le bœuf bourguignon** typically served with? What are other possibilities?

_____

What can you do to enhance the flavor of the dish?

_____

What wine is recommended as an accompaniment?

_____

Ⓒ À vous d'écrire: Un bon restaurant. Some French friends from Dijon are visiting your town and have asked you to recommend a restaurant. Follow these four steps to develop a description of the restaurant.

1. Préparation

Choose a restaurant you like and jot down information about it in the categories given here.

prix	
type de cuisine	
qualité de la cuisine	
spécialités	
boissons	
un repas typique	
autre	

2. Brouillon

Use these ideas and vocabulary you know to write your description (at least 8 sentences) of the restaurant on another piece of paper. Include a quote or two from satisfied customers. Vary your sentences and the vocabulary you use as much as possible. Be sure to use the partitive and the verbs **prendre** and **boire** correctly.

3. Révision

Now that you have written the rough draft of your description, look over the draft and check for the following.

- Have you included enough information to give your friends an idea of what the restaurant is like?
- Did you use partitive articles and the verbs **prendre** and **boire** correctly?
- Did you use varied sentence structures and a variety of food-related vocabulary?
- What else can you add to make your friends want to eat at this restaurant?

4. Rédaction

Write the final draft of your description in the space provided here. Make the corrections and insert the additions you noted in step #3. Then reread your description to be sure you are satisfied with it.

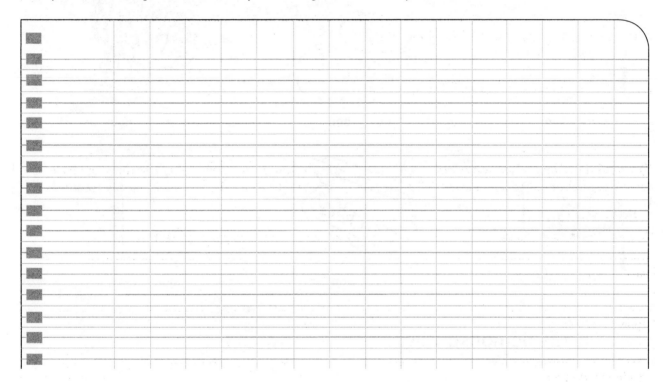

PARTIE ORALE

Point de départ

CD2, Track 17

5.1 Au supermarché. Paul Reynaud is doing his shopping at Carrefour, a French supermarket. For each of the following drawings, decide whether he mentions the foods shown and underline **oui** or **non.** You will hear each item twice.

EXEMPLE You hear: Je vais acheter des fraises.
You underline: *non*

1.

oui   non

2.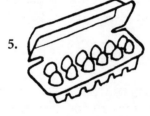

oui   non

3.

oui   non

4.

oui   non

5.

oui   non

6.

oui   non

Les adjectifs démonstratifs

CD2, Track 18

*5.2 Situation: Au marché. (p. 132) Madame Vallois is shopping at an open-air market and stops at her favorite fruit and vegetable stand. You will hear the conversation twice. Listen the first time as you hear it read, paying attention to intonation, tone, and pronunciation. During the second reading, repeat each line of the conversation after it is read to you.

CD2, Track 19

*5.3 Ça coûte combien, s'il vous plaît? (p. 133 A) You are shopping at an outdoor market and ask the price of different items. What do you ask?

> **EXEMPLE**   You hear: les petits pois
> You say: *Combien coûtent ces petits pois?*

CD2, Track 20

5.4 L'heure du déjeuner. Anne Collet and Françoise Lannes are having lunch together at the restaurant **La Coupole.** Decide whether you hear a demonstrative adjective in each of their statements and check the appropriate box. You will hear each item twice.

EXEMPLE   You hear: Ce café est excellent, n'est-ce pas?
                You check: *oui*

	oui	non			oui	non
1.	☐	☐		5.	☐	☐
2.	☐	☐		6.	☐	☐
3.	☐	☐		7.	☐	☐
4.	☐	☐		8	☐	☐

Le partitif

CD2, Track 21

*5.5 Situation: Le goûter. (p. 136) Henri has just come home from school and wants his after-school snack. You will hear the conversation twice. Listen the first time as you hear it read, paying attention to intonation, tone, and pronunciation. During the second reading, repeat each line of the conversation after it is read to you.

CD2, Track 22

*5.6 Au restaurant universitaire. (p. 136 A) You are asking French friends how often the following foods are served in the **restaurant universitaire.** Based on the cues you hear, first ask your question and then tell what your friends say.

EXEMPLE   You hear: soupe (quelquefois)
                You say: *Est-ce qu'il y a souvent de la soupe au menu?*
                          Oui, on mange quelquefois de la soupe.

CD2, Track 23

5.7 Réponses. Patrick is asking a friend about his food preferences. Listen to the questions he asks, and fill in the blanks with the articles needed to answer each question correctly. You will need to decide whether to use definite, indefinite, or partitive articles. You will hear each item twice.

EXEMPLE   You hear: Qu'est-ce que tu détestes?
                You write: *le* jambon

1. _____ poisson

2. _____ tarte

3. _____ bœuf

4. _____ pomme

5. _____ lait

6. _____ eau minérale

7. _____ pêches

8. _____ carottes

Le verbe *prendre* et le verbe *boire*

CD2, Track 24

*5.8 Situation: Au restaurant. (p. 141) Julie and Mathieu are ready to order lunch. You will hear the conversation twice. Listen the first time as you hear it read, paying attention to intonation, tone, and pronunciation. During the second reading, repeat each line of the conversation after it is read to you.

CD2, Track 25

*5.9 Préférences. (p. 141 A) Several friends are telling you what they generally drink with their dinner. What do they say?

> **EXEMPLE**   You hear: Michel / vin
> You say: ***Michel boit du vin.***

CD2, Track 26

*5.10 Préférences. (p. 142 C) Dorothée's friend, her friend's husband, and their children are coming to spend the weekend, and Dorothée wants to find out what their food preferences are. What does she ask?

> **EXEMPLE**   You hear: Marc / pour le petit déjeuner
> You say: ***D'habitude, qu'est-ce que Marc prend pour le petit déjeuner?***

CD2, Track 27

5.11 Habitudes et préférences. Some people are discussing their food preferences. Jot down what each person says in English. You will hear each item twice.

> **EXEMPLE**   You hear: Paul et Hélène prennent chaque jour un bon petit déjeuner.
> You jot down: Paul et Hélène: *have a good breakfast every day*

1. les enfants: _____

2. Alain: _____

3. toi: _____

4. ma femme et moi: _____

5. Sophie: _____

6. moi: _____

Intégration et perspectives

CD2, Track 28

5.12 Au restaurant. You work in a restaurant, and you are the only person there who can take the dinner order of a French couple. Jot down their order briefly but completely in English. The order will be given twice.

	Femme	**Homme**
1. appetizer		
2. meat		
3. vegetables		
4. salad / bread		
5. beverage		
6. dessert		

CD2, Track 29

5.13 On fait le marché. Jean and Danièle Damon are doing the shopping together for tonight's dinner. Write what they say during the pauses provided. Each line will be read twice, then the entire conversation will be read once again so that you can check your work.

JEAN: _____

DANIÈLE: _____

JEAN: _____

DANIÈLE: _____

JEAN: _____

DANIÈLE: _____

CD2, Track 30

*5.14 Bien prononcer. (p. 152)

A. The French /r/ is very different from the *r* sound in English. It is pronounced at the back of the mouth—almost in the throat—and resembles the sound one makes when gargling. It is also similar to the sound produced when saying the name of the German composer **Bach,** pronounced with a guttural **ch.** To learn the pronunciation of the French /r/, (1) start with a familiar sound, as in **Bach,** or (2) start with words where the sound that precedes or follows the **r** is also pronounced toward the back of the mouth: /a/ as in **garage** or /k/ as in **parc.**

Now practice repeating the following words that end with an /r/ sound.

B. Practice repeating the following pairs of words, starting with words where the **r** is in final position, then moving to words where **r** is in the middle.

C. Practice repeating the words where the **r** is preceded by another consonant sound.

CD2, Track 31

*5.15 Petite conversation. Practice repeating the following conversation.

Chapitre six ○ ○ ○ ○ ○ ○ ○

Le cadre de vie

(6)

PARTIE ÉCRITE

Point de départ

Ⓐ Qu'est-ce que c'est? Many maps have **légendes,** which give icons that represent different things that one might find in a city. What do the following symbols represent? Check your answers by comparing them to the **légende** for Lyon on p. 157 of your textbook.

EXEMPLE *C'est une synagogue.*

1. _____

2. _____

3. _____

4. _____

5. _____

6. _____

7. _____

8. _____

B Où est-ce qu'on va? Some people are talking about their town and about the places they go. Using words and expressions from pages 156–158 of your text, fill in the blanks in their statements.

   EXEMPLE   AUDE: Nous allons _à la bibliothèque_ municipale pour étudier et pour chercher
                  des livres intéressants.

   CORINNE: Les touristes vont _____ pour demander des renseignements sur

   la région.

PIERRE-FRANÇOIS: J'adore nager, mais il n'y a pas de _____ dans cette ville.

   VINCENT: Ghislaine et moi, nous préférons aller _____ Joseph Gibert Presse

   pour acheter des livres et des cartes postales.

   THIERRY: J'ai envie de voir un bon film. Qu'est-ce qu'il y a _____ Odéon?

   SANDRINE: Je vais _____ parce que ma grand-mère va arriver au train de

   10 heures. Après ça, je vais _____ pour faire du sport.

   FRÉDÉRIC: _____ où je prépare mon permis de conduire a une réputation

   excellente.

   OMAR: Nous, nous n'avons pas besoin de voiture parce que les _____

   publics sont excellents.

   AMÉLIE: Mes parents n'aiment pas le centre-ville; ils préfèrent habiter

   _____.

Les prépositions

Êtes-vous prêts? Les prépositions

Indicate on a scale of 1 (not comfortable) to 5 (very comfortable) how well you can handle each of the following tasks and place the number in the box provided. If you answer 1 to 3 for any of the tasks, you should go back and review the explanations and exercises in your textbook.

☐ List expressions used in asking for and giving directions and give their English equivalents.

☐ List expressions used in talking about locations and give their English equivalents.

☐ Give and understand directions on how to get to different locations.

☐ Tell where buildings and other sites are located (e.g., the parking lot is next to the stadium).

A Le campus. Marie-Claire wants to know where different buildings in the university area are located. Write what you would say in French to convey the following information.

Tell Marie-Claire:

1. The student restaurant is near the library.

_____

2. The stadium is far from the bookstore.

_____

3. There is a restaurant across from the subway stop.

_____

4. The bus stop is in front of the bank.

_____

5. There isn't a parking lot behind the library.

_____

6. There is a bakery between the department store and the pharmacy.

_____

7. There is a movie theater next to the church.

_____

8. The post office isn't far from the hospital.

_____

B Où est... ? While you are sitting on a bench in the **place Gambetta** in Bordeaux, several people ask you for directions. Use the map provided to tell them how to get to these places.

> **EXEMPLE** Où est le Musée des Douanes, s'il vous plaît?
> *Prenez la rue St-Rémi, jusqu'à la place de la Bourse. Tournez à droite. Le Musée des Douanes est au coin de la place sur le Quai Louis XVIII.*

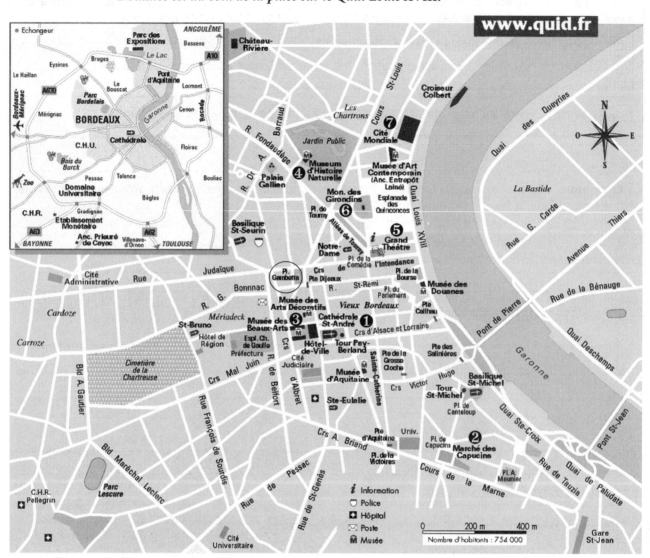

1. Excusez-moi, je cherche la Cathédrale Saint-André, s'il vous plaît.

_____

_____

_____

2. Pardon, je désire aller au Marché des Capucins, situé place des Capucins.

_____

_____

_____

3. Je cherche le Musée des Beaux-Arts. Est-ce que c'est loin d'ici?

_____

_____

_____

4. Bonjour, pour aller au Museum d'Histoire Naturelle, au Jardin Public, qu'est-ce que je fais?

_____

_____

_____

5. Comment est-ce qu'on va au Grand Théâtre, situé Cours de l'Intendance?

_____

_____

_____

6. Le Monument des Girondins, s'il vous plaît?

_____

_____

_____

7. Où est la Cité Mondiale, s'il vous plaît?

_____

_____

_____

Le verbe *faire*

Êtes-vous prêts? Le verbe *faire*

Indicate on a scale of 1 (not comfortable) to 5 (very comfortable) how well you can handle each of the following tasks and place the number in the box provided. If you answer 1 to 3 for any of the tasks, you should go back and review the explanations and exercises in your textbook.

- [ ] Conjugate the verb **faire** and tell what it means.
- [ ] List expressions that contain **faire** and give their English equivalents.
- [ ] Give other expressions you've learned for talking about household chores.
- [ ] Talk about your activities (and those of other people), including daily and weekly chores.

Ⓐ Occupations. Monsieur Lambert is telling a friend about the activities of members of his family. Complete his statements by filling in the blanks with the appropriate forms of the verb **faire.**

1. Ma femme et moi, nous _____ une promenade chaque matin.

2. Les enfants _____ leurs devoirs, mais ils n'aiment pas _____ leur chambre!

3. Nous _____ du sport en famille.

4. Je ne _____ pas souvent la cuisine. D'habitude, c'est ma femme qui

_____ la cuisine, et ce sont les enfants qui _____ la vaisselle.

5. Le mois prochain, je vais _____ du camping avec mes enfants.

6. Et vous, qu'est-ce que vous _____ pendant les week-ends?

B Questions. Using the expressions with **faire** that you've learned and vocabulary you know, write at least six questions you might ask a French person about family interests and activities.

    EXEMPLE *Dans votre famille, est-ce que c'est votre père ou votre mère qui fait le ménage?*

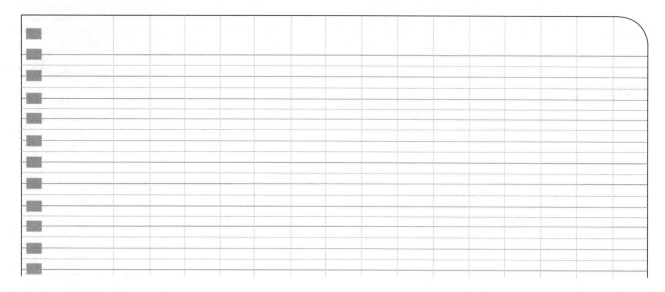

C Qu'est-ce qu'on fait? Using vocabulary you know, write at least six sentences telling who does what chores in your family (or in your apartment or dorm) and when these things are done. You may want to use the **Situation** on page 165 of your text as a guide.

    EXEMPLE *Mes camarades de chambre et moi, nous faisons le marché ensemble le samedi matin.*

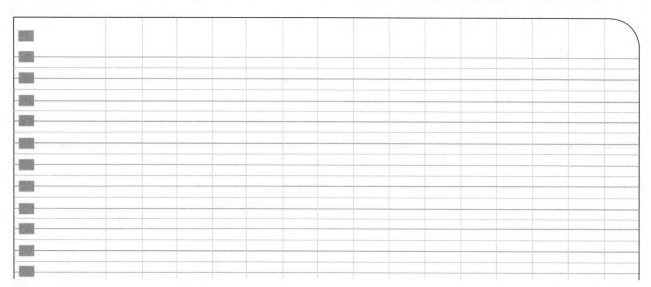

Les mots interrogatifs et l'inversion

Êtes-vous prêts? Les mots interrogatifs et l'inversion

Indicate on a scale of 1 (not comfortable) to 5 (very comfortable) how well you can handle each of the following tasks and place the number in the box provided. If you answer 1 to 3 for any of the tasks, you should go back and review the explanations and exercises in your textbook.

☐ List interrogative words and give their English equivalents.

☐ Use inversion to make questions from these statements: **Il habite à Paris. Les enfants sont dans leur chambre.**

☐ List all the ways you've learned for making questions.

☐ Ask questions on topics that you've studied so far.

☐ Ask questions about someone's interests and activities using the different interrogative words you've learned.

Ⓐ Le week-end. André is asking questions about what various people are doing this weekend. Use inversion and the cues provided to form André's questions.

> **EXEMPLE** Où / vous / aller ce week-end?
> *Où allez-vous ce week-end?*

1. Mathis / rester à la maison?

_____

2. Éric et Robert / faire du sport avec leurs amis?

_____

3. Pourquoi / vous / être / fatigué?

_____

4. Quand / Paul / prendre le train pour Lyon?

_____

5. Quand / les enfants / aller faire leur chambre?

_____

6. Comment / tu / trouver ta nouvelle voiture?

_____

7. Que / tu / faire samedi soir?

_____

8. Marianne / aller au concert avec Henri?

_____

B Dialogue. While traveling in Bordeaux, Baptiste Leroux asked a policeman some questions. Based on the policeman's answers, write questions that Baptiste might have asked. Use inversion in each question.

EXEMPLE   BAPTISTE: *La banque est-elle près d'ici?*
              L'AGENT: Oui, la banque est près d'ici.

1. BAPTISTE: _____?

L'AGENT: Oui, c'est un restaurant français.

2. BAPTISTE: _____?

L'AGENT: Oui, les touristes étrangers trouvent notre région très agréable.

3. BAPTISTE: _____?

L'AGENT: Il y a trois restaurants italiens dans ce quartier.

4. BAPTISTE: _____?

L'AGENT: Non, on ne parle pas anglais dans les magasins.

5. BAPTISTE: _____?

L'AGENT: Oui, il y a un arrêt d'autobus près de la Bibliothèque centrale.

6. BAPTISTE: _____?

L'AGENT: Oui, bien sûr, les touristes aiment visiter notre région!

7. BAPTISTE: _____?

L'AGENT: Non, je ne comprends pas toujours les questions des touristes.

8. BAPTISTE: _____?

L'AGENT: Non, le musée Goupil n'est pas loin d'ici.

Intégration et perspectives

A Chez-nous en France: Destination la région Nord–Pas-de-Calais. In an open letter to his constituents, Monsieur Grappelli, the new "deputy mayor" of a town in the north of France, explains how he views his job and the future of his town. Before you read, consult the map at the front of the book to locate **Nord–Pas-de-Calais.**

Depuis les dernières élections, je suis votre nouveau Premier Adjoint au maire, et je suis chargé du développement économique de notre ville. C'est une responsabilité que je prends très au sérieux, et je suis heureux de pouvoir participer au développement de notre région.

Située dans la riche plaine de Flandre, à 50 kilomètres de l'entrée du Tunnel sous la Manche, à quelques kilomètres de la frontière belge d'un côté, et du port de Dunkerque de l'autre, notre ville occupe une position privilégiée pour les transports, le commerce et les échanges de tous genres. Le problème est de concilier le développement économique avec la préservation de notre héritage culturel, de nos monuments anciens, de nos traditions et de notre environnement. Nous avons, bien sûr, des projets pour maintenir l'intégrité structurelle des remparts (city walls) qui entourent le centre de la ville, et nous allons aussi faire tout notre possible pour assurer la continuation du grand marché du lundi. Mais nous avons aussi besoin de créer de nouveaux quartiers pour accueillir (welcome) les jeunes familles. Et avec les nouveaux quartiers, il va être nécessaire d'envisager (to consider) la construction d'une nouvelle école et d'une «Maison de la Jeunesse».

Notre ville a un riche passé historique mais, c'est aussi une ville dynamique, tournée vers l'avenir (future). Il y a donc toujours des projets à envisager, des contrats à négocier et des travaux à inspecter. Être un «élu» (elected official), c'est aussi rester en contact avec les habitants, savoir écouter et échanger des idées. Alors, n'oubliez pas que mon bureau est ouvert au public le jeudi matin de 9 h à midi.

Avez-vous compris? The deputy mayor indicated that he needs to deal with issues concerning historical preservation and with those that relate to modernizing his town. Make a list in English of issues relating to each of these areas in the space provided.

La préservation historique

_____

_____

_____

_____

_____

La modernisation

_____

_____

_____

_____

_____

B À vous de lire: On consulte une encyclopédie Internet. You have downloaded some information from Wikipédia, an online encyclopedia, to find out more about the région **Nord–Pas-de-Calais.** Read the following texts, and jot down in English three or more pieces of information about each in the space provided.

Nord-Pas-de-Calais

Un article de Wikipédia, l'encyclopédie libre.

Le **Nord-Pas-de-Calais** est une région administrative française, autrefois appelée Nord, comprenant deux départements:

- Nord (59)
- Pas-de-Calais (62)

On trouve deux langues régionales parlées dans la région Nord-Pas-de-Calais:

- le flamand occidental, dans une partie de la Flandre française, c'est-à-dire dans la partie du département du Nord correspondant à l'arrondissement de Dunkerque, dans la région de Cassel et jusqu'à Lille.
- le picard, dans tout le reste de la région. Il y est le plus souvent dénommé *chtimi* ou *chti*, ou *rouchi* (dans le Valenciennois), ou tout simplement *patois*.

_____

_____

_____

Tunnel sous la Manche

Un article de Wikipédia, l'encyclopédie libre.

Le **tunnel sous la Manche** est un tunnel ferroviaire reliant la Grande-Bretagne et la France. Il est long de 50 km, dont 39 km sous la Manche. Il fut inauguré le 6 mai 1994.

On l'appelle aussi **Eurotunnel** (du nom de la société franco-britannique qui l'exploite), ou parfois **Chunnel** (par contraction de *Channel Tunnel* en anglais).

Le tunnel sous la Manche est selon l'American Society of Civil Engineers (*l'association américaine des ingénieurs en génie civil*) l'une des *sept merveilles du monde moderne*.

_____

_____

Dunkerque

Un article de Wikipédia, l'encyclopédie libre.

Dunkerque est une ville du nord de la France, chef-lieu d'un arrondissement du département du Nord (59), sur la mer du Nord. Son nom provient du flamand *Duyn Kerke*, qui signifie «église dans les dunes».

La commune s'est considérablement agrandie en absorbant les communes voisines de Malo-les-Bains en 1970, Petite-Synthe et Rosendaël en 1972, et Mardyck en 1980 (cette dernière bénéficiant du statut de commune associée). Une grande partie de Petite-Synthe a ultérieurement été détachée de Dunkerque et rattachée à Grande-Synthe.

La Communauté Urbaine de *Dunkerque Grand Littoral* regroupe 18 communes.

Économie

L'économie de Dunkerque profite de sa position de plaque tournante européenne. Elle est en effet située à moins de 300 kilomètres de 5 capitales: Londres, Paris, Bruxelles, Amsterdam et Luxembourg.

- Port de transit de marchandises (3ème port français après Marseille et Le Havre)
- Pétrochimie
- Agroalimentaire

_____

_____

_____

C À vous d'écrire: Où habitez-vous? A French friend would like to spend the year in your area and has asked you to describe the town where you live. Follow these four steps to develop your description.

1. Préparation

First of all, make notes in French about the town where you live (e.g., geographical location, shops, services, historical monuments, tourist attractions, and activities). Then jot down the advantages and disadvantages of living in your town.

description de la ville

_____

_____

_____

avantages

_____

_____

inconvénients

_____

_____

_____

2. Brouillon

Using the ideas you collected and vocabulary you know, write a description (at least 12 sentences) describing where you live. Be sure to use vocabulary related to cities and towns and the advantages and disadvantages of living there. You will also want to use prepositions of location (**en face de, près de, loin de**) to describe where things are located. You should write three paragraphs. The first paragraph describes your town; start your paragraph with an introductory sentence such as **Dans la ville où j'habite** or **J'habite dans une assez grande ville de l'Indiana.** The second paragraph focuses on the advantages of your town (**Voici les principaux avantages de la ville où j'habite.** or **Notre ville présente certains avantages, par exemple,…**). The third paragraph discusses the disadvantages of your town. You might start out with **Par contre** (*On the other hand*) or **Malheureusement, il y a aussi des inconvénients.** Write this first draft on another sheet of paper.

3. Révision

Now that you have finished your first draft, read through what you have written and check the following.

- Did you discuss a variety of shops, services, points of interest, and so on?
- Did you include prepositions of location in your discussion of what your town offers?
- Did you include advantages and disadvantages? Are there other advantages and disadvantages that you could include?
- When your friend has finished reading about your town, will he or she have a good idea of what it is like? If not, what else can you add to make your description complete?

4. Rédaction

Write the final draft of your description in the space provided here. Make the corrections and insert the additions you noted in step #3. Then reread your description to be sure you are satisfied with it.

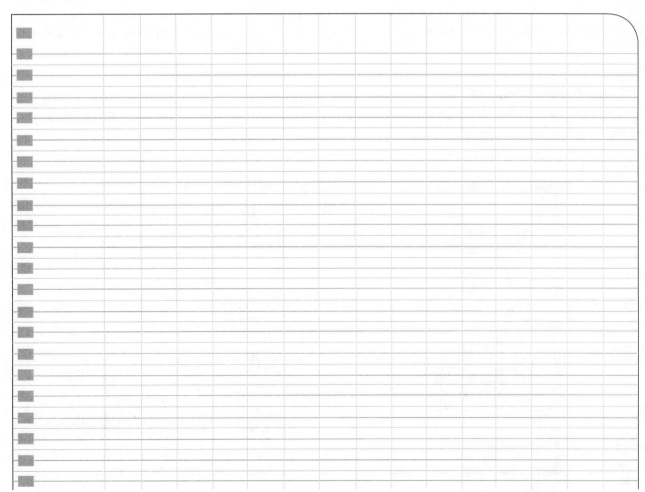

PARTIE ORALE

Point de départ

CD2, Track 32

6.1 Où? People are talking about where they are going or where they can be found. Decide whether they give appropriate reasons for going to these places and check the appropriate box. You will hear each item twice.

> **EXEMPLE** You hear: Nous sommes à l'auto-école pour acheter une nouvelle voiture.
> You check: *non*

	oui	non			oui	non			oui	non
1.	☐	☐		3.	☐	☐		5.	☐	☐
2.	☐	☐		4.	☐	☐		6.	☐	☐

Les prépositions

CD2, Track 33

*6.2 Situation: Excusez-moi, monsieur l'agent. (p. 162) Alain Rollet is asking a police officer for directions. You will hear the conversation twice. Listen the first time as you hear it read, paying attention to intonation, tone, and pronunciation. During the second reading, repeat each line of the conversation after it is read to you.

CD2, Track 34

*6.3 Où est-ce qu'ils habitent? (p. 163 A) Manu is explaining where his friends live. Tell whether his statements are true. The numbers on the map indicate the approximate location of his friends' apartments.

> **EXEMPLE** You hear: François, numéro 7, habite près de la piscine.
> You say: *Non, il n'habite pas près de la piscine.*

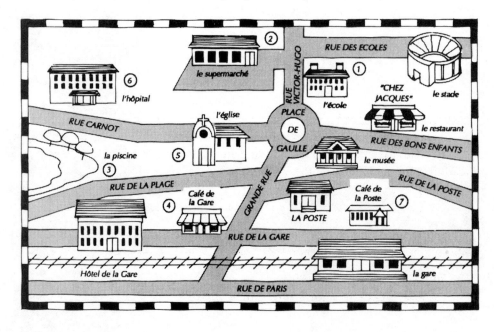

CD2, Track 35

6.4 Où? Using the map that follows as a guide, decide whether the statements you hear are **vrai** or **faux** and check the appropriate column. You will hear each item twice.

EXEMPLE   You hear: Le bureau de poste est en face de la gare.
You check: *faux*

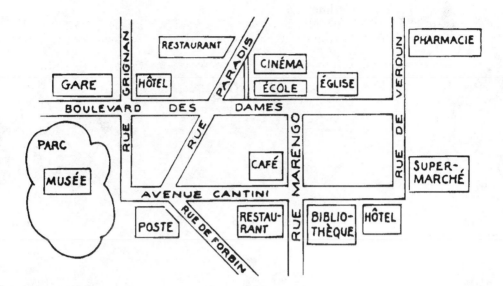

	vrai	faux
1.		
2.		
3.		
4.		
5.		
6.		

Le verbe *faire*

CD2, Track 36

*6.5 Situation: Qui fait quoi à la maison? (p. 165) Madeleine and Nathalie are talking during their lunch hour. Madeleine is asking Nathalie how she manages to get everything done at home. You will hear the conversation twice. Listen the first time as you hear it read, paying attention to intonation, tone, and pronunciation. During the second reading, repeat each line of the conversation after it is read to you.

CD2, Track 37

*6.6 Qu'est-ce que tu fais? (p. 166 A) Thibaut and a friend are making plans for the weekend and need to figure out what everyone is doing. What questions do they ask?

EXEMPLE   You hear: Fabien / samedi
You say: *Qu'est-ce que Fabien fait samedi?*

CD2, Track 38

6.7 Descriptions. Decide whether the statements you hear describe the following drawings, and underline **oui** or **non**. You will hear each item twice.

EXEMPLE   You hear: Paul fait ses courses pendant le week-end.
You underline: **non**

1.   oui   non

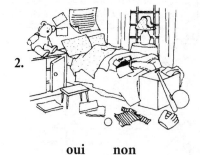

2.   oui   non

3.   oui   non

4.   oui   non

5.   oui   non

6.   oui   non

Les mots interrogatifs et l'inversion

CD2, Track 39

*6.8 Situation: Travail et résidence. (p. 169) A journalist is doing research on working conditions in Paris. He is speaking with Madame Simon. You will hear the conversation twice. Listen the first time as you hear it read, paying attention to intonation, tone, and pronunciation. During the second reading, repeat each line of the conversation after it is read to you.

CD2, Track 40

*6.9 À l'agence immobilière. (p. 169 A) Bernard is looking for a new apartment. Listen to the real estate agent's answers and, using the appropriate interrogative words, give the questions that Bernard asks about the apartment.

EXEMPLE   You hear: Un vieux monsieur habite maintenant dans l'appartement.
You say: *Qui habite maintenant dans l'appartement?*

CD2, Track 41

6.10 À l'agence de voyages. While waiting at a travel agency, you overhear people talking. Decide whether you hear a question each time, and check the appropriate box. You will hear each item twice.

EXEMPLE   You hear: Et Nice? Est-ce une ville agréable?
You check: *oui*

	oui	non		oui	non
1.	☐	☐	4.	☐	☐
2.	☐	☐	5.	☐	☐
3.	☐	☐	6.	☐	☐

Intégration et perspectives

CD2, Track 42

6.11 La ville de Pons. Marie-Claire is talking about her hometown, Pons, in southern France. Listen to what she says, and then decide whether each of the following statements is **vrai** or **faux** and mark the appropriate column. You will hear the passage twice.

vrai	faux	
		1. Pons is a city of fewer than 7,000 residents.
		2. The churches there date back many centuries.
		3. The pace of life in Pons is slow.
		4. People must leave Pons to do their shopping.
		5. Young people enjoy the beaches and going to the movies in Pons.

CD2, Track 43

6.12 Où est la bibliothèque? You have asked a police officer for directions to get to the library. Write down in French what he tells you. Each line will be said twice, then the entire set of directions will be given once again so that you can check your work.

1. _____

2. _____

3. _____

4. _____

5. _____

CD2, Track 44

*6.13 Bien prononcer (p. 180)

A. Some vowels, like /i/ in **ici,** are pronounced with the lips spread; others, like /y/ in **tu,** are produced with the lips tightly rounded. Both these sounds are pronounced in the front of the mouth. Thus /i/ and /y/ differ only by the shape of the lips. In fact, if you have difficulty pronouncing the French /y/, try saying /i/ with your lips rounded. Compare and repeat.

B. Practice repeating words and phrases containing the sound /y/. Remember to have your lips tightly pursed and reaching forward as if you were going to whistle or give a kiss.

C. Note the difference between the sound /y/ as in **tu** and the sound /u/ as in **tout,** which is also pronounced with the lips rounded, but with the tongue more toward the back of the mouth. Compare and repeat.

D. The following summarizes the differences in the way /i/, /y/, and /u/ are pronounced. Practice contrasting these sounds.

CD2, Track 45

*6.14 Petite conversation. Practice repeating the following conversation.

Chapitre sept ○ ○ ○ ○ ○ ○

Le temps passe

⑦

PARTIE ÉCRITE

Point de départ

🅐 **Vos émissions favorites.** Make a list of 10 television programs that Americans like to watch; include a variety of program types. Then briefly describe each program: tell what type it is, when it's on, etc.

> **EXEMPLE** *J'aime beaucoup regarder «General Hospital». C'est un feuilleton que les étudiants aiment beaucoup. C'est à la télé tous les jours.*

1. _____

_____

_____

2. _____

_____

_____

3. _____

_____

_____

4. _____

_____

_____

5. _____

_____

_____

6. _____

_____

_____

7. _____
_____
_____

8. _____
_____
_____

9. _____
_____
_____

10. _____
_____
_____

Ⓑ Comparaisons. You and some French friends are talking about movies. Write what you would say in French to convey the following information.

1. Find out what films your friends like.

_____
_____

2. Tell what types of movies you prefer and why.

_____
_____

3. Ask your friends if they go to the movies often.

_____

4. Ask them who their favorite actor or actress is and in what film(s) he / she appears.

_____
_____

5. Ask your friends what they prefer in a film—the actors, the story, or the characters.

_____
_____

L'heure

A Heures de travail. The employees of a Quick fast-food restaurant want to know their work schedules. Using the information provided on the schedule, tell when each employee works. Convert times to the 12-hour system.

EXEMPLE *Mathieu travaille de huit heures du matin à une heure de l'après-midi.*

Employé(e)	Période de travail
Mathieu	8:00–13:00
Benoît	11:15–13:30
Laurent	12:30–14:30
Annabelle	15:00–19:45
Pascal	20:30–2:30
Céline	1:00–5:30

1. Laurent

_____

2. Céline

_____

3. Benoît

_____

4. Pascal

_____

5. Annabelle

_____

B Difficultés de circulation *(Traffic problems).* The following chart lists the times of anticipated weekend traffic jams around France. For each of the areas indicated, write out in full the times given in the chart. Convert 24-hour times to the 12-hour system.

EXEMPLE   départs: Nantes, Pornic (18)
entre dix heures du matin et une heure de l'après-midi

départs

1. Val-de-Saône (2) _____

2. Tain, Livron (6) _____

3. Orange, Nîmes (11) _____

retours

4. Val-de-Saône (15) _____

5. Jonction (17) _____

6. Souillac Uzerche (3) _____

☉ Le Thalys de Paris à Bruxelles. **Le Thalys** is a TGV line that connects Paris to Belgium, the Netherlands, Germany, and Switzerland. You are planning to take **le Thalys** from Paris to Brussels and are looking at possible departure times. Using the schedule provided, answer the following questions. Write out the times in full, and convert 24-hour time to the 12-hour system.

EXEMPLE   À quelle heure est-ce que le dernier train arrive à Bruxelles?
À minuit moins quatre.

VIVEZ L'EUROPE ••• THALYS

FR EN NL DE

HORAIRES : Paris Nord > Bruxelles-Midi DU 14 DÉCEMBRE 2003 AU 12 JUIN 2004 - RETOUR -

THALYS		9307	9409	9311	9313	9315	9417	9319	9321	9323	9325	9327	9429	9331	9333	9339
Paris-Nord	D	06:25	06:55	07:25	07:55	08:25	08:55	09:25	09:55	10:25	10:55	11:25	11:55	12:25	12:55	14:25
Bruxelles-Midi	A	07:50	08:20	08:50	09:20	09:50	10:20	10:50	11:20	11:50	12:20	12:50	13:20	13:50	14:20	15:50
lundi à jeudi		+	+	+	+	+	+	+	+	+	+	+	+	+	+	+
vendredi		+	+	+	+	+	+	+	+	+	+	+	+	+	+	+
samedi		-	+	-	+	-	+	-	+	-	+	-	+	-	+	-
dimanche		-	+	-	+	-	+	-	+	-	+	-	+	-	+	+

THALYS		9441	9343	9345	9347	9349	9351	9453	9355	9357	9361	9365	9369	9371
Paris-Nord	D	14:55	15:25	15:55	16:25	16:55	17:25	17:55	18:25	18:55	19:55	20:55	21:55	22:31
Bruxelles-Midi	A	16:20	16:50	17:20	17:50	18:20	18:50	19:20	19:50	20:20	21:20	22:20	23:20	23:56
lundi à jeudi		+	+	+	+	+	+	+	+	+	+	+	+	-
vendredi		+	+	+	+	+	+	+	+	+	+	+	+	-
samedi		+	-	+	-	+	-	+	-	+	+	-	+	-
dimanche		+	-	+	-	+	+	+	+	+	+	+	+	+

+ circule   **- ne circule pas**

Vocabulaire: D = départ *(m) departure*; A = arrivée *(f) arrival*; circule *runs*

1. À quelle heure est le premier départ pour Bruxelles?

_____

2. À quelle heure arrive ce train à Bruxelles?

_____

3. Et le dernier départ le matin, c'est à quelle heure?

_____

4. Quels sont les trains qui partent de Paris vers deux heures de l'après-midi?

_____

_____

5. Pour arriver à Bruxelles entre six et sept heures du soir, quel(s) train(s) est-ce qu'il faut prendre?

_____

_____

6. À quelles heures sont les trains qui quittent Paris entre midi et une heure?

_____

_____

7. Si on quitte Paris à neuf heures moins cinq du soir, est-il possible d'arriver à Bruxelles avant minuit?

_____

_____

8. J'ai un rendez-vous important à Bruxelles à six heures et demie du soir. Il est maintenant quatre heures. Est-ce qu'il est possible d'arriver à Bruxelles avant six heures?

_____

_____

Ⓓ Projets. Using vocabulary you know, tell what you are going to do today at a *specific* time around each of the *general* times given. If you don't know the words for a certain activity, find another way to say what you're going to do.

> **EXEMPLE** vers 12h
> *À midi et quart, je vais retrouver des amis au resto U.*

vers 10h _____

vers 11h _____

vers 12h _____

vers 1h _____

vers 2h _____

vers 3h _____

vers 4h _____

vers 5h _____

vers 6h _____

vers 7h _____

Le passé composé

Êtes-vous prêts? Le passé composé

Indicate on a scale of 1 (not comfortable) to 5 (very comfortable) how well you can handle each of the following tasks and place the number in the box provided. If you answer 1 to 3 for any of the tasks, you should go back and review the explanations and exercises in your textbook.

☐ Explain what the **passé composé** means and how it is formed for **-er** verbs.

☐ List the verbs you've learned that have irregular past participles and give these past participles.

☐ List words commonly used when talking about the past and tell what they mean in English (e.g., "yesterday").

☐ Tell what you and others did yesterday (last week, last summer, etc.); for example, what you watched on TV, what your friends did last weekend.

ⓐ Pendant le week-end. Using the words and phrases provided, tell what various people did over the weekend.

> **EXEMPLE** tu / étudier pour un examen de sciences politiques
> ***Tu as étudié pour un examen de sciences politiques.***

1. nous / regarder un documentaire à la télévision

_____

2. Jeanne et Michelle / faire une promenade à vélo

_____

3. je / décider d'aller au cinéma avec des amis

_____

4. vous / acheter un lecteur DVD

_____

5. tu / téléphoner à tes parents

_____

6. Roger / avoir des difficultés avec sa voiture

_____

ⓑ Qu'est-ce qui a changé? Mathis wants to know why his friends suddenly changed their daily habits. Write the questions he asks by changing the verbs in each of the following sentences to the **passé composé.**

> **EXEMPLE** En général, le soir, tu regardes les informations.
> ***Alors, pourquoi est-ce que tu n'as pas regardé les informations aujourd'hui?***

1. Souvent Marine et vous, vous buvez de l'eau minérale avec vos repas.

_____

2. Après le dîner, Paul et moi, nous faisons la vaisselle ensemble.

_____

3. D'habitude, Madeleine travaille de 9 heures à 5 heures.

_____

4. D'habitude, tu as le temps de faire une promenade après le dîner.

_____

5. Souvent, vous faites votre marché à Carrefour.

_____

6. En général, les enfants sont très gentils.

_____

⊙ La semaine dernière. In the space provided, tell whether you did the following activities last week.

1. étudier à la bibliothèque _____

2. faire le marché _____

3. avoir des difficultés avec votre voiture _____

_____

4. regarder des émissions intéressantes à la télé _____

_____

5. être à l'heure pour votre premier cours _____

_____

6. aller faire du sport _____

_____

Choisir et les verbes du deuxième groupe

Êtes-vous prêts? Les verbes du deuxième groupe

Indicate on a scale of 1 (not comfortable) to 5 (very comfortable) how well you can handle each of the following tasks and place the number in the box provided. If you answer 1 to 3 for any of the tasks, you should go back and review the explanations and exercises in your textbook.

☐ List verbs ending in **-ir** and tell what they mean in English.

☐ Explain how to conjugate these verbs in the present tense and in the **passé composé.**

☐ Use verbs like **choisir** to say things such as where you grew up, when you and your friends finish for the day, and so forth.

A **Retravailler.** Among other activities, the organization **Retravailler** helps women as well as men reenter the workforce after raising a family. The following statements were made at a recent meeting. Fill in the blanks in the statements with the appropriate form and tense of the following verbs: **choisir, finir, grandir, réussir.**

1. Les enfants _____ si vite *(quickly)* de nos jours.

2. Les femmes ne _____ pas toujours à trouver le temps de tout faire.

3. _____ une bonne gardienne d'enfants n'est pas une chose facile.

4. Les femmes qui désirent retravailler _____ souvent un travail qui laisse du temps libre pour la famille.

5. Je suis sûre que vous allez _____ à trouver du travail.

6. Je _____ mon travail au bureau à cinq heures du soir, mais en réalité, ma journée de

   travail ne _____ pas avant dix heures.

B **Choix d'une université.** How would you answer your French friend's questions about why you have selected the university where you are studying and how happy you are with your choice?

1. Pourquoi avez-vous choisi cette université?

   _____

   _____

2. Est-elle située dans la région où vous avez grandi?

   _____

   _____

3. Quand avez-vous commencé vos études ici?

   _____

   _____

4. Êtes-vous content(e) du programme d'études que vous avez choisi? Pourquoi ou pourquoi pas?

   _____

   _____

5. En général, réussissez-vous bien dans vos études? Pourquoi ou pourquoi pas?

   _____

   _____

6. Quand allez-vous finir vos études, et qu'est-ce que vous allez faire après?

   _____

   _____

7. Qu'est-ce que vous espérez accomplir au cours de votre vie?

   _____

   _____

8. À votre avis, est-ce que vos études sont une bonne préparation pour la vie ou pour la carrière que vous avez choisie?

_____

_____

Intégration et perspectives

🅐 **Chez nous en France: Destination la région Midi-Pyrénées.** Karim, a student at the **université de Toulouse,** describes his city and his favorite musical group, Zebda, also from Toulouse. Before reading what Karim says, look for Toulouse on the map at the front of the workbook.

Située sur la Garonne, à une courte distance des Pyrénées, Toulouse est la principale ville de la région Midi-Pyrénées. C'est la quatrième ville de France (741 000 habitants avec ses banlieues), avec une grande université et de très importantes écoles d'aéronautique. C'est aussi un centre commercial et industriel très important, surtout dans les domaines de la chimie et de l'aérospatiale. C'est ici, à Toulouse, que pendant de nombreuses années, on a construit le célèbre avion supersonique Concorde. Le projet Concorde est maintenant terminé, mais Toulouse continue à être le premier centre européen de production d'avions civils (comme Airbus, par exemple). C'est aussi le second centre spatial dans le monde après Los Angeles, et le leader européen dans le domaine des satellites.

Et, chose très importante pour nous les jeunes, c'est dans notre ville que le groupe musical Zebda est né! Ils ont commencé ici, pendant les années 80, dans une association de quartier, et ils ont enregistré leur premier album en 1991. En 1995, ils ont fait une entrée très remarquée sur la scène nationale avec leur album «Le bruit et l'odeur», et leur évident engagement (commitment) politique. En 2000, ils ont été nommés «meilleur (best) groupe musical de l'année», et maintenant ils ont une réputation internationale. Leurs chansons sont même à l'origine du récent film d'Éric Pittard, intitulé «Le bruit, l'odeur et quelques étoiles».

J'aime beaucoup ce groupe parce que ce sont des artistes «engagés» qui n'ont pas peur de dire ce qu'ils pensent et d'aborder (broach) des sujets difficiles. Leur musique métissée (drawing from a variety of cultures) exprime dans un langage artistique les problèmes et les choix de notre société moderne, spécialement en ce qui concerne l'immigration, la xénophobie et les problèmes de justice sociale. Ils n'ont pas peur, non plus, de participer à la vie politique, et quand il y a des catastrophes (comme les récentes inondations qui ont dévasté plusieurs quartiers de Toulouse), ils sont les premiers à organiser des concerts pour aider les victimes. À mon avis, ce sont des types qui ont beaucoup de talent, qui ont vraiment quelque chose à dire et pour qui il n'y a pas seulement l'argent et le succès qui comptent.

Avez-vous compris? You work for an online encyclopedia, and your assignment is to write two brief entries in French of 50 words each: the first on Toulouse, and the second on the group Zebda. You have only enough words to give the highlights for each of these topics, so plan carefully. In the space provided, write the two entries—be concise, but include as much information as you can.

Toulouse _____

_____

_____

_____

Zebda _____

_____

_____

_____

B À vous de lire: Une fiche artiste. The following **fiche** *(information sheet)* about the group Zebda appeared on mcm.net, a French music Web site; what you learned in **Chez nous** will help you understand this text. As you read, look for information that describes the group (e.g., origins, types of music played, recent albums), and jot it down in the space provided.

Zebda

Zebda est un groupe de musique citoyenne, entendez par là que ces Toulousains, depuis leurs débuts dans les années 80, ont exprimé de manière artistique un état des lieux d'urgence avec une musique métissée et plutôt burlesque sans l'être vraiment dans le fond. Zebda, c'est sept petits gars qui en 85, faisaient tous partie d'une asso de quartier. Zebda enregistre son premier album en 91 mais commence à se faire connaître sur la scène nationale avec le second *Le Bruit et l'Odeur*, en 95, réponse à un commentaire de Jacques Chirac sur l'immigration. Zebda sans squatter les ondes radios et télés, se forge une notoriété de bouche à oreilles lors de ses concerts; Zebda, artistes engagés avant tout, sont devenus les emblèmes d'une France pluri-ethnique combattant la xénophobie et une certaine idée de l'intégration. En 98, Zebda sort *Essence Ordinaire*, l'album de la consécration. *Tomber la Chemise, Je Crois Que Ça Va Pas Être Possible, Y'a Pas d'Arrangement* ou *Oualalaradime* sont autant de tubes prouvant leur investissement politique. Après de nombreux projets parallèles, *Les Motivés* ou *100% collègues,* Zebda continue son combat social dans les banlieues toulousaines qu'ils n'ont pas oublié. Consécration aux Victoires de la Musique 2000, Zebda est meilleur groupe de l'année et *Tomber la Chemise* meilleure chanson de l'année. Deux ans plus tard, les Toulousains reviennent avec *Utopie d'Occase*. En 2003, Zebda fait un break et sort le live *La Tawa*.

Avez-vous compris? In the space provided, jot down in English five or more pieces of information about Zebda.

Zebda _____

_____

_____

_____

_____

C À vous d'écrire: Les étudiants et les médias. You are giving a French friend a brief overview of the preferences of American students in the following categories: music, television, places to go on the weekend, and movies. Follow these four steps to develop your description.

1. Préparation

Jot down ideas about student preferences in *two* of the following categories. You will find it helpful to review the vocabulary in the **Point de départ.**

• La musique qu'ils préfèrent _____

_____

• Le type d'émissions qu'ils aiment regarder à la télé _____

_____

• Leurs sorties pendant le week-end _____

_____

• Le cinéma et leurs acteurs / actrices favori(te)s _____

_____

2. Brouillon

Using the ideas you collected about the topics you chose and vocabulary you know, write the first draft of your essay (12 or more sentences) on another sheet of paper. Because you are presenting an overview of preferences from your own perspective, you might find phrases such as the following useful: **à mon avis** *(in my opinion)*; **je pense que; j'ai l'impression que; je suis sûr(e) que; en général, la plupart des étudiants; la plupart du temps; en ce qui concerne** *(as far as . . . is concerned)*.

3. Révision

Now that you have finished your first draft, read through what you have written and check the following.

• Did you include information on both of your chosen topics in your composition?
• Did you use as much vocabulary as possible from the **Point de départ**?
• Does your description present an overview of the preferences of university-level students in this regard? If not, what needs to be changed?
• Did you use expressions indicating that you were giving your personal opinion, such as those suggested in step #2?

4. Rédaction

Write the final draft of your description in the space provided here. Make the corrections and insert the additions you noted in step #3. Then reread your description to be sure you are satisfied with it.

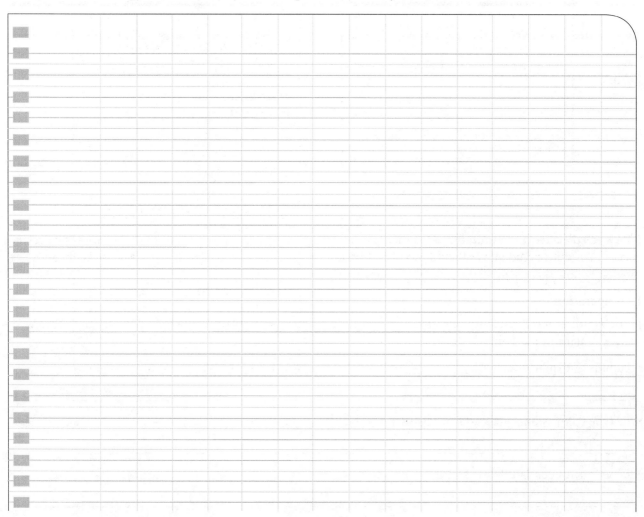

PARTIE ORALE

Point de départ

CD3, Track 2

7.1 Sur France 2. Sophie is looking at the schedule of programs that are on France 2 today. Decide if her statements correctly describe the schedule reproduced here and check the appropriate boxes. You will hear each item twice.

EXEMPLE   You hear: Je vais regarder «La montagne perdue», un documentaire qui passe à 15h35.
You check: *oui*

6.15 Petits matins.cool Dessins animés.
Iznogoud • Casper.   8747881
7.00 Thé ou café
Magazine. Par Catherine Ceylac. Invitées :
Jeanne Moreau et Ludmila Mikaël.   38336
8.00 Rencontre à XV Magazine .   45107
8.20 Expression directe «L'UDF».   1556152
8.30 Emissions religieuses
Voix bouddhistes • 8.45 Islam • 9.15 Source
de vie • 10.00 Présence protestante • 10.30
Jour du Seigneur • 11.00 Messe célébrée en
l'église Notre-Dame-du-Val à Bussy-Saint-
Georges (Seine-et-Marne). L'homélie sera
prononcée par le père Luc Crepy • 11.50
Midi moins 7.   65733249
12.05 DMA (Dimanche midi Amar) 6998775
Magazine présenté par Paul Amar. *Pour
connaître le nom de l'invité, appelez notre
«Téléphone plus» ou consultez le Minitel.*
13.00 Journal Présenté par Béatrice Schönberg.
13.25 Météo, rapports du Loto
13.35 Vivement dimanche ! Divertissement.
Présenté par Michel Drucker. Invité princi-
pal : le cuisinier Bernard Loiseau. Et aussi :
Guy Savoy, Patrick Fiori, la troupe des «Dix
commandements», Frédéric Lerner, Patrick
Bruel, Anne Roumanoff, Yannick Noah,
Mme Loiseau, Anabelle Buffet, Laure Adler,
Guy Roux, Philippe Labro, Henri Pescarolo
et Valérie-Anne Giscard d'Estaing.   7712442

15.35 La montagne perdue *Inédit.*   9785794
(S) Documentaire. Entre Amazone et Orénoque
s'élèvent d'étranges montagnes. Récem-
ment, des scientifiques y ont découvert un
monde animal et végétal insoupçonné.
16.35 Snoops *Inédit.* Série américaine.   8246442
(S) «Le chant du cygne». Glenn et Susan sont
chargés de veiller sur une star du rock.
17.25 Un agent très secret
(S) *Inédit.* Série américaine. «Le bon, la dinde
et les truands». Lisa et Heather passent les
fêtes de Thanksgiving sans Michael.   470404
18.15 Stade 2 Magazine.
Présenté par Christian Prudhomme. 6001317
19.25 Vivement dimanche prochain !
Divertissement. Invité : Bernard Loiseau.
Avec les chroniques de Bruno Masure,
Gérard Miller et Philippe Geluck.   603775
20.00 Journal Présenté par Béatrice Schönberg.
20.45 Météo
20.50 URGENCES
(S)(?) *Inédit.* Série américaine créée par Michael
Crichton. *Voir ci-contre.*   454201
22.25 LES SOPRANO
(S) *Inédit.* Série américaine créée par David
Chase. *Voir ci-contre.*   1515423
**23.20 BEAUCOUP, PASSIONNEMENT,
A LA FOLIE**
(S) *Inédit.* Documentaire. Dans le cadre des
«Documents du dimanche». Par Christophe
Hondelatte. *Voir ci-contre.*   2340268
0.40 Journal de la nuit, météo
1.05 Les résistants de l'ombre *Inédit.*
Documentaire de Goran Markovic.   3397621
2.00 Programme de la nuit
Vivement dimanche prochain ! • 2.30 Les
grandes énigmes de la science • 3.20 Thé
ou café • 4.10 Pour la vie • 4.15 Stade 2.

---

	oui	non		oui	non
1.	☐	☐	5.	☐	☐
2.	☐	☐	6.	☐	☐
3.	☐	☐	7.	☐	☐
4.	☐	☐	8	☐	☐

L'heure

CD3, Track 3

*7.2 Situation: Au bureau de renseignements. (p. 189) Monsieur Josserand calls the information office at **la Gare de Perrache** in Lyon to find out at what time the next train for Paris leaves. You will hear the conversation twice. Listen the first time as you hear it read, paying attention to intonation, tone, and pronunciation. During the second reading, repeat each line of the conversation after it is read to you.

CD3, Track 4

*7.3 Quelle heure est-il? (p. 190 A) Radio announcers give the time at various intervals. Use the clocks to tell what they say.

EXEMPLE You say: *Il est midi.* or *Il est minuit.*

1.  2.  3.  4.

5. 6. 7.  8.

CD3, Track 5

7.4 À la Gare de Lyon. While you are at a train station in Paris, you listen to the announcements of train departures. Write in the times you hear. You will hear each item twice.

EXEMPLE You hear: Le train pour Vintimille va partir à 17h15.
You write: *17h15*

1. Marseille _____ 4. Bâle _____

2. Lyon _____ 5. Rome _____

3. Genève _____ 6. Grenoble _____

Le passé composé

CD3, Track 6

*7.5 Situation: Vous avez été sages? (p. 195) Monsieur and Madame Lemoine spent the evening at their friends' home. Madame Lemoine is asking their children if they were good while they were out. You will hear the conversation twice. Listen the first time as you hear it read, paying attention to intonation, tone, and pronunciation. During the second reading, repeat each line of the conversation after it is read to you.

CD3, Track 7

*7.6 Activités et occupations. (p. 195 A) Sylviane is telling you what she did on her day off. Use the cues you hear to tell what she says.

> **EXEMPLE** You hear: 8h30 / téléphoner à Suzanne
> You say: *À huit heures et demie, j'ai téléphoné à Suzanne.*

CD3, Track 8

7.7 Nouvelles. Vanessa is telling her family what she and her roommates have been doing. For each of her statements, decide whether you hear an action in the present, the near future, or the past and mark the appropriate column. You will hear each item twice.

> **EXEMPLE** You hear: Le week-end dernier, mes amis et moi, nous avons fait une promenade à la campagne.
> You mark: *past*

	present	near future	past
1.			
2.			
3.			
4.			
5.			
6.			

Choisir et les verbes du deuxième groupe

CD3, Track 9

*7.8 Situation: On va au ciné? (p. 198) Valérie is inviting her sister Christine and brother-in-law Pierre to go to the movies tonight. You will hear the conversation twice. Listen the first time as you hear it read, paying attention to intonation, tone, and pronunciation. During the second reading, repeat each line of the conversation after it is read to you.

CD3, Track 10

*7.9 À quelle heure? (p. 199 A) You are planning to go to the movies with several friends and ask when they are free. They tell you when they finish for the day.

> **EXEMPLE** You hear: Marc / 6h
> You say: *Marc finit à six heures.*

CD3, Track 11

*7.10 Souvenirs d'enfance. (p. 199 B) A friend from the south of France is telling you where she and other members of her family grew up. What does she say?

> **EXEMPLE** You hear: ma grand-mère / Nice
> You say: *Ma grand-mère a grandi à Nice.*

CD3, Track 12

7.11 Tout va bien? Monsieur and Madame Brion have gone out for the evening, and Monsieur Brion has called the sitter to find out how things are going. In the space provided, jot down in English each of the sitter's comments. You will hear each item twice.

> **EXEMPLE**   You hear: Paul n'a pas encore fini son dîner.
>   You jot down: *Paul hasn't finished his dinner yet.*

1. _____
2. _____
3. _____
4. _____

Intégration et perspectives

CD3, Track 13

7.12 Programme du soir. One evening during your visit to Montreal, you and a friend watch TV. Listen as the announcer on a French-Canadian station talks about the evening's programs. Decide whether your friend has understood by marking the appropriate column. You will hear the passage twice.

vrai	faux

1. Tonight there is a great cartoon program for kids.
2. We'll be able to find out what an American program sounds like in French.
3. We're in luck, because there is a Canadian football game on tonight.
4. I'm glad there is a special program on music this evening.
5. *The Phantom Menace* is on tonight. The announcer doesn't think it's as good as the rest of the *Star Wars* series.

CD3, Track 14

7.13 Hier soir. Denise asks her roommate Hélène about what she did last night. Write their conversation in the space provided. Each line will be read twice, then the entire conversation will be read once again so that you can check your work.

DENISE: _____

HÉLÈNE: _____

DENISE: _____

HÉLÈNE: _____

CD3, Track 15

*7.14 Bien prononcer. (p. 208) When the letter **s** occurs between two vowels, it is pronounced /z/ as in **poison.** When there are two **s**'s, the sound is always /s/ as in **poisson.** The sound /s/ also corresponds to the following spellings: **c** with a **cédille, c** followed by **i** or **e,** and **t** in the **-tion** ending (**ça, ceci, nation**). An **x** is pronounced /z/ in a **liaison.** Compare and repeat.

Repeat the following sentences, paying special attention to the /z/ vs. /s/ contrast.

CD3, Track 16

*7.15 Petite conversation. Practice repeating the following conversation.

Chapitre huit ○○○○○○

La pluie et le beau temps

PARTIE ÉCRITE

Point de départ

A **La météo.** Use Friday's weather map to tell about the weather in Canada and around the world.

Montréal

Prévisions météo

AUJOURD'HUI	CE SOIR	SAMEDI	DIMANCHE	LUNDI
Possibilité de pluie ou neige faibles max 6	Pluie ou neige min -5	Pluie max 7, min 5	Ensoleillé max -1, min -5	Ensoleillé max 1, min -2

La météo en un clin d'œil

	Hier	Normales
Max.	9	0.0
Min.	2	-8.8
Precip.	2.0 mm	

Phases de la lune

3/6	3/13	3/20	3/28

Sept-Îles -4/-14
Val d'Or -1/4
Saguenay 0/-12
Québec 1/-9
Gatineau 7/1
Montréal 6/-2

Canada			Le monde		
St.John's		1\0	New York		12\6
Halifax		2\-4	Chicago		9\2
Ottawa		7\1	Atlanta		24\15
Toronto		7\1	Miami		28\23
Winnipeg		-2\-14	Los Angeles		20\13
Edmonton		-2\-14	Rio de Janeiro		28\22
Regina		-9\-14	Amsterdam		6\1
Vancouver		9\4	Moscou		2\-2
Whitehorse		-4\-14	Tokyo		13\5
Yellowknife		-23\-30	Sydney		25\19

Et aujourd'hui? Tell what the weather is like on Friday in the following cities. Use the map and the list of Canadian cities.

> **EXEMPLE** À Sept-Îles, *il pleut et il fait du soleil. Il fait moins quatre degrés.*

1. À Québec, _____

2. À Montréal, _____

3. À Halifax, _____

4. À Vancouver, _____

Prévisions à long terme pour Montréal. Using the long-term forecast for Montreal, tell what the weather is going to be like on the following days.

> **EXEMPLE** Lundi, *il va faire du soleil et il va faire un degré.*

5. Samedi, _____

6. Dimanche, _____

Et hier dans le monde? Imagine that it's Saturday and you're looking at the same weather report. Tell what the weather was like yesterday in the following cities around the world.

> **EXEMPLE** Hier à Chicago, *il a fait du soleil et il a fait neuf degrés.*

7. Hier à Amsterdam, _____

8. Hier à Sydney, _____

Ⓑ La pluie et le beau temps. In your opinion, what would be good weather conditions for each of the following situations? Begin each response with **j'espère** *(I hope)* and use a different weather expression each time.

> **EXEMPLE** Je voudrais faire une promenade en ville cet après-midi.
> *J'espère qu'il ne va pas faire trop froid.*

1. Nous avons un match de football important la semaine prochaine.

_____

2. Je vais passer le week-end à étudier pour mes examens.

_____

3. Mes amis et moi, nous allons faire du ski la semaine prochaine.

_____

4. J'ai un examen aujourd'hui en cours de sciences.

_____

5. Je suis fatigué(e) et je voudrais rester à la maison demain.

_____

6. Nous allons passer nos vacances à la plage.

_____

C Ça dépend du temps qu'il fait. Referring to your own experience, complete the following sentences with appropriate weather expressions.

1. On risque de prendre un coup de soleil quand _____.

2. On a besoin de mettre le chauffage quand _____.

3. Je ne quitte pas la maison quand _____.

4. Il y a souvent des accidents quand _____.

5. En général, on ne va pas à la plage quand _____.

6. Je préfère faire une promenade quand _____.

7. Les étudiants n'aiment pas aller en cours quand _____.

8. Je n'aime pas faire du camping quand _____.

Les verbes conjugués comme *partir* et comme *venir*

Êtes-vous prêts? Les verbes conjugués comme *partir* et comme *venir*

Indicate on a scale of 1 (not comfortable) to 5 (very comfortable) how well you can handle each of the following tasks and place the number in the box provided. If you answer 1 to 3 for any of the tasks, you should go back and review the explanations and exercises in your textbook.

☐ Conjugate **partir** and **venir** and give their English equivalents.

☐ List other verbs like **venir** and tell what they mean.

☐ Tell how to say that you have just done something; that you are in the process of doing something; that you are going to do something.

☐ Tell where you and people you know come from, at what time they leave for class, and when they come back in the evening.

A On part en vacances. Jacqueline Duval is making notes as she talks with her employees about when everyone is going on vacation. Using the information in the chart, tell when each person leaves and returns.

	départ	retour
1. moi	17/7	27/7
2. Paul et Richard, vous	21/8	4/9
3. toi, Hélène	10/7	14/7
4. Anne et Olivier	1/8	16/8
5. Madeleine	23/8	31/8

EXEMPLE Georges: départ 7/8; retour 28/8
Georges part le sept août et il revient le vingt-huit août.

1. _____

2. _____

3. _____

4. _____

5. _____

B À l'aéroport. Passengers on a flight from Paris to Algiers are getting acquainted and are discussing their vacation or business trips. Using the words and phrases provided, re-create their statements.

> **EXEMPLE** D'où est-ce que vous _Venez_ (venir), monsieur?

1. Moi, je _____ (venir) de Bruxelles.

2. À quelle heure est-ce que vous _____ (partir)?

3. Les avions de cette compagnie _____ (ne jamais partir) à l'heure.

4. Les touristes _____ (devenir) très impatients quand leur avion est en retard.

5. Nous _____ (venir de) visiter Versailles.

6. Ma femme et moi, nous _____ (revenir) de Genève.

C Dans une agence de voyages. You work for a travel agency in Montreal and are talking with a group of French tourists. How would you say the following in French?

1. Have you just arrived in Montreal?

_____

2. Are you going to leave Monday morning?

_____

3. Do you feel like going out this evening?

_____

4. We're in the process of looking for a hotel.

_____

5. Their plane just left, didn't it?

_____

6. We're going to come back to Montreal next summer.

_____

Le passé composé avec l'auxiliaire *être*

Êtes-vous prêts? Le passé composé avec l'auxiliaire *être*

Indicate on a scale of 1 (not comfortable) to 5 (very comfortable) how well you can handle each of the following tasks and place the number in the box provided. If you answer 1 to 3 for any of the tasks, you should go back and review the explanations and exercises in your textbook.

☐ List the verbs that use **être** as their auxiliary in the **passé composé.**

☐ Compare the formation of the **passé composé** with **avoir** and with **être.**

☐ Tell what you and people you know did yesterday, last week, last year, and so forth.

☐ Tell when you and people you know were born.

A Qu'est-ce qu'on a fait? Different people are talking about what they've done recently. Using the cues provided, tell what they say. Some verbs are conjugated with **avoir,** others with **être.**

EXEMPLE Aurélie / tomber malade / aller chez le médecin
Aurélie est tombée malade et elle est allée chez le médecin.

1. moi, je / inviter des amis à dîner / préparer un bon repas

_____

2. Paul / quitter la maison à 8h / arriver à son bureau à 8h45

_____

3. nous / aller au centre commercial / acheter de nouveaux vêtements

_____

4. vous / sortir ensemble / faire une promenade à vélo dans le parc

_____

5. notre ami / tomber de vélo / passer l'après-midi à l'hôpital

_____

6. nos cousins / aller au Mexique / revenir la semaine dernière

_____

B Bonnes et mauvaises nouvelles. A newscaster is reporting the day's events on the evening report. Complete her statements with the appropriate verbs from the following list: **arriver, devenir, monter, mourir, naître, partir, rester, revenir, tomber, venir.** Not all the verbs listed are used.

1. Deux hommes et une femme _____ dans un accident d'auto.

2. Les températures _____ stables pendant la journée, mais il a fait très froid pendant la nuit.

3. La championne de tennis, Sylvie Martin, _____ pour Genève où elle va participer aux championnats européens.

4. Selon les statistiques récentes, moins de touristes étrangers _____ en France pendant les deux dernières années.

5. Madame Claire Monet, envoyée spéciale du gouvernement du Québec, _____ à Paris hier.

6. En général, les prix _____ stables cette semaine.

7. Le président et sa femme _____ d'un voyage en Afrique du Nord.

8. Selon les experts, le crime et la violence _____ des problèmes très sérieux dans le pays.

C **Allées et venues.** Use the words provided (or other ideas of your own) to create a paragraph of five or more sentences telling what you and your friends have done recently. Be sure to add any necessary words (e.g., time expressions such as **hier** and **la semaine dernière** and connecting words such as **d'abord, ensuite,** and **après cela**), and vary your sentences as much as possible.

> **EXEMPLE** *Mes amis et moi, nous sommes allés au cinéma vendredi soir.*

Moi, je		avoir	cinéma
Mes ami(e)s et moi, nous		être	concert
Mes ami(e)s	(ne pas)	partir	cours
J'ai un(e) ami(e) qui		aller	sport
Mon / Ma camarade		rester	promenade
J'ai des amis qui		dîner	devoirs
		sortir	vélo
		arriver	plage
		faire	bibliothèque
		acheter	vacances
		?	maison
			?

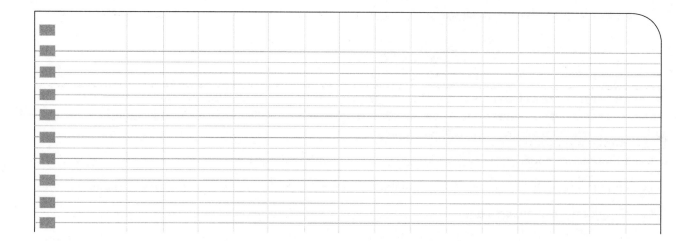

D **Alors, raconte.** Your friends have told you some of the things they've done recently, but you want to know more about what they did. In the space provided, write at least two questions you would ask to get more details about their activities. Vary your questions as much as possible; don't repeat any questions. Remember to use interrogative words (**où, pourquoi,** etc.). Depending on the information you're looking for, you will use some verbs conjugated with **avoir** and some with **être.**

1. Nous sommes allés en vacances.

> **EXEMPLE** *Où est-ce que vous êtes allés?*

_____

_____

2. Nous avons passé un week-end formidable.

_____

_____

3. J'ai mangé dans un bon restaurant hier.

_____

_____

4. Thibaut a eu une mauvaise note à son dernier examen de maths.

_____

_____

Depuis et autres expressions de temps

Êtes-vous prêts? *Depuis* et autres expressions de temps

Indicate on a scale of 1 (not comfortable) to 5 (very comfortable) how well you can handle each of the following tasks and place the number in the box provided. If you answer 1 to 3 for any of the tasks, you should go back and review the explanations and exercises in your textbook.

- [ ] Explain how to use **depuis** to express an action that began in the past and is still going on. Tell what verb tense is used in French.
- [ ] Ask people how long or since when they have been doing various activities.
- [ ] Tell how long you did certain things (e.g., how long you lived in a particular place).
- [ ] Tell how long ago you did certain things (e.g., "I traveled in France two years ago").

Ⓐ Au bureau d'immigration. An American exchange student is coming back to France after a trip to Italy. Using the cues in parentheses, write his answers to the officer's questions.

1. Depuis combien de temps avez-vous votre passeport? (four years)

_____

2. Depuis combien de temps étudiez-vous en France? (six months)

_____

3. Quand avez-vous quitté Rome? (two days ago)

_____

4. Quand avez-vous commencé à étudier le français? (five years ago)

_____

5. Pendant combien de temps allez-vous rester en France? (three months)

_____

6. Vous êtes déjà allé en Suisse et en Belgique, n'est-ce pas? Pendant combien de temps êtes-vous resté dans chaque pays? (two weeks)

_____

B À l'aéroport. While you wait for your flight, you strike up a conversation with a French tourist. Write what you would say in French to convey the following information.

1. Find out when he arrived at the airport.

_____

2. Say that you left your house three hours ago and that you've been here for an hour.

_____

3. Say that you looked for the parking lot for 15 minutes.

_____

4. Say that the last plane left 30 minutes ago.

_____

5. Ask how long he traveled in the United States.

_____

6. Tell him how long you've been studying French.

_____

Intégration et perspectives

A Chez nous en France: Destination la région de Bordeaux. Élise Martin, a winegrower's daughter from the Médoc who is currently studying oenology (the science of wine and wine making) at the **université de Bordeaux,** reflects on what the terrible heat wave of 2003 meant for France and for her region. Before you read the text, look for Bordeaux on the map at the front of the workbook.

> Pour la France qui a habituellement un climat doux et tempéré, cette année-là a été une année exceptionnelle. Mais selon les climatologues, dans un siècle, ces températures extrêmes vont devenir la norme si le réchauffement de la planète (*global warming*) continue au rythme actuel!...
>
> Après un hiver assez doux et pluvieux et un très beau printemps, la France a connu (*experienced*) des températures records et une terrible sécheresse (*drought*) pendant tout l'été. Plus de 14 000 personnes ont trouvé la mort pendant cette vague de chaleur et les incendies de forêt (*forest fires*) ont détruit plus de 50 000 hectares. Dans beaucoup de régions, les récoltes ont été perdues, et de nombreux animaux de ferme sont morts. (Par exemple, 75 000 porcs et 5 millions de poulets sont morts parce que les agriculteurs ne sont pas équipés pour faire face (*to face*) à des temperatures de 35° C pendant plus de vingt jours.)
>
> L'étude de l'évolution du climat fait partie de notre programme d'études ici à l'Institut d'œnologie. Je viens d'une famille de viticulteurs et j'ai l'intention de continuer à travailler dans notre entreprise familiale; c'est donc un sujet qui me passionne! La chaleur de cet été-là a été désastreuse pour beaucoup de gens, mais pour nous, les viticulteurs, la situation n'a pas été entièrement négative. En fait, dans certaines régions, les conditions ont été assez bonnes pour les raisins. La récolte (*harvest*) a été assez petite, mais les raisins ont eu tout le temps et le soleil nécessaires pour mûrir (*to ripen*) et les vendanges (*grape harvesting*) ont eu lieu (*took place*) dans d'excellentes conditions. Dans certains cas, le résultat de cet été exceptionnellement chaud et sec a donc été une récolte d'une très bonne qualité.

Avez-vous compris? How did this heat wave affect the farming industry in general and the wine industry in particular? In the space provided, list in French several of these effects for each.

Effets de la vague de chaleur sur...

l'agriculture française en général

_____

_____

_____

la viticulture en particulier

_____

_____

_____

B **À vous de lire: La météo.** The report on page 134 (July 24) gives the weather in France for the next day. Read the predictions and then in the space provided, jot down in English what the weather and temperatures will be for the regions indicated.

As you have learned, what you already know about a topic can help you understand a reading.

- For example, the weather map can be very helpful. When you encounter an area or province mentioned in the weather report, look up that area on the weather map. You may also want to check the map of France in your textbook to review these areas.
- Make sure you can interpret the temperatures, which are given in Celsius rather than in Fahrenheit. For example, 82°F = 28°C; 86°F = 30°C; 97°F = 36°C. You know the weather report is for July and that unless conditions are unusual, the temperature should be relatively warm.
- You will encounter some verb forms that may not be familiar. Because the article makes predictions, you can guess that the verbs will be in the future (e.g., **le ciel sera très nuageux** = *the sky will be very cloudy;* **elles pourront descendre** = *they [the temperatures] may go down*).

Avez-vous compris? Fill in the following chart in English with information from the weather report.

	le temps	la température
le Nord-Ouest		
la Bretagne		
la Normandie		
l'Île-de-France et la Picardie		
la Corse		
le Sud-Ouest		

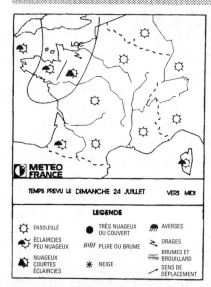

MÉTÉOROLOGIE

TEMPS PREVU LE DIMANCHE 24 JUILLET   VERS MIDI

LÉGENDE

☼ ENSOLEILLÉ   ● TRÈS NUAGEUX OU COUVERT   ☂ AVERSES

☼ ÉCLAIRCIES PEU NUAGEUX   ///// PLUIE OU BRUME   ⚡ ORAGES

☼ NUAGEUX COURTES ÉCLAIRCIES   ✳ NEIGE   ≡ BRUMES ET BROUILLARD

          ↗ SENS DE DÉPLACEMENT

TEMPÉRATURES
maxima – minima

FRANCE

AJACCIO	29/20
BIARRITZ	26/19
BORDEAUX	32/20
BOURGES	30/18
BREST	22/14
CAEN	23/17
CHERBOURG	24/17
CLERMONT-FER.	29/16
DIJON	30/20
GRENOBLE	33/19
LILLE	30/16
LIMOGES	28/18
LYON, BRON	30/19
MARSEILLE	33/21
NANCY, ESSEY	30/18
NANTES	27/18
NICE	29/24
PARIS-MONTS.	30/20
PAU	30/18
PERPIGNAN	32/20
POINTE-A-PITRE.	33/24
RENNES	24/15
ST-ÉTIENNE	30/17
STRASBOURG	31/17
TOULOUSE	31/20
TOURS	29/20

ÉTRANGER

ALGER	31/19
AMSTERDAM	28/15
ATHÈNES	34/25
BANGKOK	34/21
BARCELONE	30/22
BELGRADE	27/18
BERLIN	32/19
BRUXELLES	30/17
COPENHAGUE	27/17
DAKAR	30/25
GENÈVE	30/19
ISTANBUL	31/22
JÉRUSALEM	32/18
LE CAIRE	35/22
LISBONNE	24/19
LONDRES	28/16
LOS ANGELES	21/16
LUXEMBOURG	31/21
MADRID	36/15
MARRAKECH	43/22
MEXICO	21/12
MILAN	29/17
MONTRÉAL	29/22
MOSCOU	20/14
NAIROBI	17/13
NEW-DELHI	33/–
NEW-YORK	34/27
PALMA-DE-MAJ.	31/17
PÉKIN	33/25
RIO-DE-JANEIRO	–/–
ROME	31/20
HONGKONG	27/23
SÉVILLE	38/19
SINGAPOUR	32/27
STOCKHOLM	29/18
SYDNEY	14/ 7
TOKYO	32/26
TUNIS	32/20
VARSOVIE	27/14
VENISE	32/20
VIENNE	30/16

Dimanche : passages nuageux au Nord-Ouest, chaud et ensoleillé ailleurs. - Le matin, le ciel sera très nuageux par nuages moyens sur la Bretagne. Une averse ou un orage local n'est pas à exclure. A la mi-journée, cette zone nuageuse gagnera la Normandie et les Pays-de-Loire, puis en soirée l'Ile-de-France, la Picardie et le Nord. Les risques d'orage persisteront. Sur la Corse, on aura quelques résidus orageux en début de matinée, puis la journée sera bien ensoleillée. Sur le reste du pays, on aura des bancs de brume ou de brouillard au lever du jour. En général, ils laisseront rapidement place au soleil ; sur l'extrême Sud-Ouest, ils pourront persister jusqu'à la mi-journée. L'après-midi, des foyers orageux isolés pourront se développer sur les Pyrénées et sur les Alpes.
Les températures au lever du jour seront généralement comprises entre 18 et 20 degrés ; sur le Nord-Ouest, elles pourront descendre jusqu'à 16 degrés et sur le pourtour méditerranéen et la Corse elles seront comprises entre 20 et 22 degrés. L'après-midi, elles évolueront de 22 à 28 degrés du Nord au Sud sur la façade ouest du pays ; sur le reste du pays, elles resteront élevées, généralement comprises entre 30 et 32 degrés, voire localement 34 ou 36 degrés sur l'extrême Nord-Est et le Sud-Est.

(Document établi avec le support technique spécial de Météo-France.)

Ⓒ À vous d'écrire. Comment est la région où vous habitez? You have been corresponding with friends from Bordeaux. In this letter, you describe to your friends the town and region where you grew up, focusing particularly on the weather. Follow these four steps to develop your letter.

1. Préparation

In the space provided, jot down in French the things you want to say about the region where you grew up: weather (include all four seasons), geography (are there mountains? beaches? small or large towns? How far do you live from the ocean? from the mountains?), and typical activities of the region (people swim, ski, go to the theater, etc.).

climat	géographie	activités

2. Brouillon

Use these ideas to describe the town and the region where you grew up. Write this first draft (10–12 sentences) on a separate sheet of paper. Introduce your description by telling how long you've lived in the area (**J'habite ici depuis…**), or if you now live elsewhere when you left the region where you grew up (**J'ai quitté cette région il y a un an pour aller à l'université**). You might also want to mention how often you return (**Je reviens pour les vacances d'été et quelquefois je reviens pendant le week-end**). Then use the ideas you listed in the **Préparation** section to talk about the climate, geography, and typical activities of your town or region. When you begin your discussion about the climate of your region, you might want to start with a sentence such as **J'ai de la chance d'habiter dans une région où il fait beau toute l'année,** and when you talk about activities, you might use an introductory sentence such as **Si vous aimez le sport, vous allez probablement aimer la région où j'habite.** In each of these cases, you are helping your reader anticipate the content of the paragraph.

3. Révision

Now that you have finished writing your first draft, read through what you have written and check the following.

- Did you talk about how long you have lived in this area (or how long you've been gone) using the appropriate time expression?
- Did you describe the weather in all four seasons using a variety of vocabulary words?
- Did you describe the geography of the region where you live?
- Did you describe in enough detail the types of activities that people typically do?
- What else can you add to make your description complete?

4. Rédaction

Write the final draft of your description in the space provided here. Make the corrections and insert the additions you noted in step #3. Then reread your description to be sure you are satisfied with it.

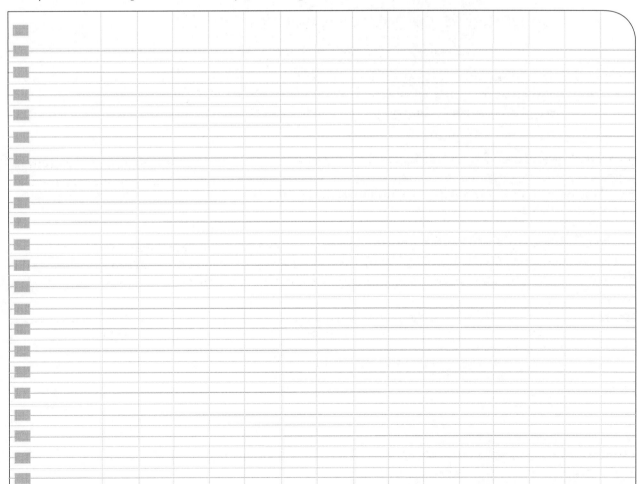

PARTIE ORALE

Point de départ

CD3, Track 17

8.1 Ouest Météo. As you listen to the weather forecast for various cities in western France, fill in the chart with the information you hear, using the abbreviations provided. You will hear each item twice.

> **EXEMPLE**   You hear: La température à Oléron est de vingt-neuf degrés et il pleut.
> You fill in: **29 P**

O = orage	N = neige	A = averse	C = couvert
S = soleil	V = vent	P = pluie	B = brouillard

Niort _____

St-Jean-de-Monts _____

Angers _____

Bordeaux _____

St-Malo _____

Les verbes conjugués comme *partir* et comme *venir*

CD3, Track 18

*8.2 Situation: Quoi de neuf? (p. 219) Mathieu meets his old friend Tamsir, and they exchange news. Tamsir is very busy. You will hear the conversation twice. Listen the first time as you hear it read, paying attention to intonation, tone, and pronunciation. During the second reading, repeat each line of the conversation after it is read to you.

CD3, Track 19

*8.3 D'où viens-tu? (p. 219 A) Students at the **université de Bordeaux** are telling each other where they are from. What do they say?

> **EXEMPLE**   You hear: Mounir / Tunisie
> You say: **Mounir vient de Tunisie.**

CD3, Track 20

*8.4 Que font-ils? (p. 220 C) A friend is bringing you up to date on the news of mutual friends. What does he say?

> **EXEMPLE**   You hear: Marc / partir en vacances
> You say: **Marc part en vacances.**

CD3, Track 21

8.5 Souvenirs de vacances. Alain is showing photos of his family's vacation. For each photo, you will hear two statements. Decide which of these statements correctly describes each photo and underline the appropriate letter. You will hear each pair of statements twice.

EXEMPLE

You hear: **a.** Benoît va faire une promenade sous la pluie.
 b. Benoît vient de faire une promenade sous la pluie.
You underline: *b*

1.

 a   b

2.

 a   b

3.

 a   b

4.

 a   b

Le passé composé avec l'auxiliaire *être*

CD3, Track 22

*8.6 Situation: Quel fiasco! (p. 223) Each year, a large number of French people as well as foreigners go skiing in the Alps. This year, Antoine and Céline, who are from Brussels, decided to go to Megève. Céline is explaining to her friend Béatrice why their trip wasn't very pleasant. You will hear the conversation twice. Listen the first time as you hear it read, paying attention to intonation, tone, and pronunciation. During the second reading, repeat each line of the conversation after it is read to you.

CD3, Track 23

*8.7 Il y a des gens qui travaillent… (p. 223 A) The driver of a sightseeing bus in Monaco is telling what happened earlier today. Using the cues you hear, tell what he says.

EXEMPLE   You hear: je / arriver / à l'hôtel à midi
 You say: *Je suis arrivé à l'hôtel à midi.*

CD3, Track 24

*8.8 Et des gens qui voyagent. (p. 224 B) Jean-Luc is telling about the trip he and his brother took to Canada this summer. Using the cues you hear, tell what he says.

  EXEMPLE   You hear: partir de Paris le 1ᵉʳ août
           You say: ***Nous sommes partis de Paris le 1ᵉʳ août.***

CD3, Track 25

8.9 Pendant les vacances. Estelle Duveau is talking about what happened when she and her husband, Pascal, took their vacation in England. Decide if what she says happened is **bon** or **mauvais** and check the appropriate box. You will hear each item twice.

  EXEMPLE   You hear: Il a fait beau le jour de notre départ.
           You check: ***bon***

	bon	mauvais			bon	mauvais
1.	☐	☐		5.	☐	☐
2.	☐	☐		6.	☐	☐
3.	☐	☐		7.	☐	☐
4.	☐	☐		8	☐	☐

Depuis et autres expressions de temps

CD3, Track 26

*8.10 Situation: À la plage. (p. 227) Laurence is on vacation on the Riviera. She is getting a suntan on the beach. A handsome young man tries to meet her. You will hear the conversation twice. Listen the first time as you hear it read, paying attention to intonation, tone, and pronunciation. During the second reading, repeat each line of the conversation after it is read to you.

CD3, Track 27

*8.11 Depuis quand? (p. 227 A) Using the cues you hear, ask other students how long they've been doing the following things.

  EXEMPLE   You hear: habiter dans une résidence universitaire?
           You say: ***Depuis quand habites-tu dans une résidence universitaire?***

CD3, Track 28

*8.12 J'ai le plaisir de vous présenter… (p. 228 C) You are an intern in a French company and have been asked to introduce an American representative at a company meeting. Using the facts you hear, introduce the visitor.

  EXEMPLE   You hear: graduated 20 years ago
           You say: ***Il a fini ses études il y a vingt ans.***

CD3, Track 29

8.13 Présentation. Lucien Forestier is telling you about himself. As you listen, fill in the chart with his activities and interests. You will hear each of his statements twice.

> **EXEMPLE**   You hear: J'ai acheté ma première voiture il y a six mois.
> You jot down: Voiture: *bought first car 6 months ago*

Langue	
Travail	
Voyage	
Études	
Intérêts	

Intégration et perspectives

CD3, Track 30

8.14 À Vanuatu. Listen to the following passage about Jean-Yves and Sylvie Duteuil's experiences in **Vanuatu**, a group of islands in the southwestern Pacific. Then answer the following questions. You will hear the passage twice.

1. Why did Jean-Yves and Sylvie go to **Vanuatu**?

_____

2. Which countries governed these islands until 1980?

_____

3. When did Jean-Yves and Sylvie arrive in Port-Vila?

_____

4. What is the weather like there?

_____

5. How do Jean-Yves and Sylvie feel about storms?

_____

CD3, Track 31

8.15 Opinions. Nadine is talking about the way her family feels about the local weather. During the pauses provided, write what Nadine says. Each line will be read twice, then the entire passage will be read once again so that you can check your work.

1. _____

_____

2. _____

_____

3. _____

_____

CD3, Track 32

*8.16 Bien prononcer (p. 238)

A. Vowels can be distinguished from one another not only by the shape of the lips (spread or rounded) and by the position of the tongue (front or back), but also by the degree of opening of the mouth. For example, the vowels **e, eu,** and **o** each have two pronunciations that differ only by the degree of opening of the mouth. First, note that the written forms may not differ.

Then note that in general, closed vowels tend to occur in syllables ending in a vowel sound, whereas open vowels are found in syllables ending in a consonant sound.

Study the following examples and repeat the pairs of words.

B. Practice repeating words containing the sound /e/, and note the different spellings associated with this sound.

C. Practice repeating words containing the sound /ɛ/, and note the different spellings associated with this sound.

D. Practice repeating words and phrases containing both the sound /e/ and the sound /ɛ/. Note the role of the contrast of the /e/ and /ɛ/ in distinguishing the masculine versus the feminine form of some nouns and adjectives.

CD3, Track 33

*8.17 Petite conversation. Practice repeating the following conversation.

Chapitre neuf ○ ○ ○ ○ ○ ○ ○

Le monde du travail

⑨

PARTIE ÉCRITE

Point de départ

Ⓐ Choix d'un métier. Based on the professions presented in the **Point de départ,** match jobs with the following logos.

EXEMPLE *Cela représente un agriculteur ou une agricultrice.*

1.  _____

2.  _____

3.  _____

4.  _____

5. 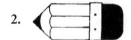 _____

6. _____

7. _____

8. _____

B **Catégories.** List the jobs that you believe belong in each of the following categories.

Faites une liste des professions ou des métiers…

1. où on a un bon salaire.

_____

_____

2. où on a la possibilité de voyager.

_____

_____

3. où on a des horaires flexibles.

_____

_____

4. où on travaille beaucoup avec les autres.

_____

_____

5. où on a de longues heures de travail.

_____

_____

ⓒ Professions et attributs. What qualities are necessary to succeed or be happy in different professions? In the space provided, choose six of the attributes listed and match them with the professions on page 243 of your text.

> **EXEMPLE** *Si vous désirez être médecin, il est important de ne pas avoir peur de travailler de longues heures.*

attributs:

ne pas avoir peur de travailler de longues heures	aimer travailler seul(e)
aimer les enfants	être doué(e) en sciences
être doué(e) en maths	être patient(e) avec les gens qui ont des problèmes personnels
désirer aider les gens	aimer travailler avec les gens
accepter de travailler pendant le week-end	aimer faire un travail manuel

Les verbes *vouloir, pouvoir* et *devoir*

Êtes-vous prêts? Les verbes *vouloir, pouvoir* et *devoir*

Indicate on a scale of 1 (not comfortable) to 5 (very comfortable) how well you can handle each of the following tasks and place the number in the box provided. If you answer 1 to 3 for any of the tasks, you should go back and review the explanations and exercises in your textbook.

- [ ] Conjugate the verbs **vouloir, pouvoir,** and **devoir** and tell what they mean in English.
- [ ] Know when to use polite as opposed to direct forms of requests.
- [ ] Talk about what you and other people want to do, are able to do, and have to do.

A Où est la vérité dans tout ça? Adèle Martin wants to know whether her employees are really unable to do certain things or simply don't want to do them. What does she say?

> **EXEMPLE**   Jean et Marie / arriver à l'heure
> ***Est-ce que Jean et Marie ne peuvent pas arriver à l'heure ou est-ce qu'ils ne veulent pas?***

1. vous / finir votre travail

_____

2. Caroline / comprendre la situation

_____

3. tu / aller à ce rendez-vous

_____

4. Gilles et Pauline / avoir une augmentation de salaire

_____

5. nous / trouver une solution à notre problème

_____

6. ces nouveaux employés / travailler à plein temps

_____

B Entretien d'embauche *(Job interview).* You work in a small company and are interviewing a candidate for an accounting position. Write what you say in French to convey the following information.

1. Say that you're late because you had to talk to your engineers.

_____

2. Say that you want to find a good accountant.

_____

3. Say that your accountant must be able to work alone.

_____

4. Find out why she wants to work here.

_____

5. Find out if she can sometimes stay at the office after 7 p.m.

_____

6. Find out if she can begin next Friday.

_____

C **Obligations, intentions et possibilités.** For each of the situations indicated, tell at least two of the following about yourself or people you know: (1) what you want or don't want to do; (2) what you can or can't do; (3) what you must or must not do.

> **EXEMPLE** *Quand on est malade, on doit rester à la maison; mais on peut regarder les feuilletons à la télé chaque après-midi.*

1. Quand il fait mauvais, _____

   _____

2. Quand mes amis n'ont pas d'argent, _____

   _____

3. Quand je vais chez des amis, _____

   _____

4. Quand nous ne comprenons pas nos leçons, _____

   _____

5. Quand c'est l'été, _____

   _____

6. Quand on a du temps libre, _____

   _____

Les pronoms compléments d'objet direct

Êtes-vous prêts? Les pronoms compléments d'objet direct

Indicate on a scale of 1 (not comfortable) to 5 (very comfortable) how well you can handle each of the following tasks and place the number in the box provided. If you answer 1 to 3 for any of the tasks, you should go back and review the explanations and exercises in your textbook.

☐ List the French direct object pronouns, then tell where they are placed in the sentence and what they mean in English.

☐ Explain what happens to the past participle of a verb in the **passé composé** when a direct object pronoun is used.

☐ Use direct object pronouns to replace nouns in talking about different topics or people.

A **Au bureau.** Anne Dupré is asking her secretary, Alain, questions about their office. Following the example, complete the secretary's answers. Be sure to use a direct object pronoun in each answer.

> **EXEMPLE** ANNE: Jean a-t-il fini son travail?
> ALAIN: *Non, il ne l'a pas fini.*

1. ANNE: Avez-vous préparé les documents nécessaires?

   ALAIN: Oui, _____ ce matin.

2. ANNE: Ces projets ne vous intéressent pas beaucoup, n'est-ce pas?

ALAIN: Non, à vrai dire, _____.

3. ANNE: Les autres secrétaires et vous, avez-vous pris votre leçon d'anglais commercial?

ALAIN: Oui, _____ à 9h30.

4. ANNE: Avez-vous confirmé mon rendez-vous pour cet après-midi?

ALAIN: Oui, _____.

5. ANNE: Le secrétaire de M. Thibaut a-t-il trouvé les adresses de nos clients de Londres?

ALAIN: Non, _____.

6. ANNE: Quand les agents publicitaires ont-ils fini notre nouveau programme de publicité?

ALAIN: _____ la semaine dernière.

7. ANNE: Où avons-nous acheté ces ordinateurs?

ALAIN: _____ dans un magasin d'équipement de bureau.

8. ANNE: Quand est-ce que vous pouvez m'aider avec ces documents?

ALAIN: _____ après trois heures.

B Travailler en équipe. A coworker is asking you questions to find out if you would be compatible as members of a work group. Using the appropriate forms of the direct object pronouns, answer your coworker's questions.

> **EXEMPLE** Est-ce que tu aimes ton bureau?
> ***Oui, je l'aime beaucoup.***

1. Est-ce que tu aimes le directeur?

_____

2. D'habitude, à quelle heure est-ce que tu commences ton travail?

_____

3. Et à quelle heure est-ce que tu finis ton travail?

_____

4. D'habitude, en quelle saison est-ce que tu prends tes vacances?

_____

5. Est-ce que tu aimes faire la comptabilité?

_____

6. Quand est-ce que tu vas finir tes projets?

_____

7. Où est-ce que tu aimes inviter les nouveaux clients à déjeuner?

_____

C **Pense-bête.** Gilles has made a list of tasks and chores he needs to accomplish today at work, and he has checked off the ones he has done. Following the example, answer the questions about his activities.

travail	✓
messages	✓
préparer / invitations	
ranger / affaires	✓
lettres	
vider / poubelle	✓
billets / avion	
programmes	

EXEMPLES Est-ce qu'il a préparé les invitations?
Non, il ne les a pas encore préparées.

Est-ce qu'il a fini son travail?
Mais oui, il l'a déjà fini.

1. Est-ce qu'il a envoyé ses messages?

_____

2. Est-ce qu'il a fini les dernières lettres?

_____

3. Est-ce qu'il a étudié les nouveaux programmes?

_____

4. Est-ce qu'il a réservé nos billets d'avion?

_____

5. Est-ce qu'il a rangé ses affaires?

_____

6. Est-ce qu'il a vidé la poubelle?

_____

Le subjonctif avec *il faut que* et *il vaut mieux que*

Êtes-vous prêts? Le subjonctif avec *il faut que* et *il vaut mieux que*

Indicate on a scale of 1 (not comfortable) to 5 (very comfortable) how well you can handle each of the following tasks and place the number in the box provided. If you answer 1 to 3 for any of the tasks, you should go back and review the explanations and exercises in your textbook.

☐ Explain how to form the subjunctive in French.

☐ Give the subjunctive of the regular and irregular verbs you know.

☐ Use the subjunctive to talk about what you and people you know must do and what you think is best to do.

Ⓐ Conseils. Xavier's friend Caroline doesn't always agree with the way Xavier and his family manage their lives. Following the example, complete Caroline's statements.

> **EXEMPLE**   XAVIER: Je vais toujours à mon travail en voiture.
> CAROLINE: Il vaut mieux que tu _ailles_ à ton travail à pied.

1. XAVIER: Mon fils a du travail à faire ce soir, mais il a envie de sortir avec ses amis.

    CAROLINE: Il vaut mieux qu'il ne _____ pas ce soir.

2. XAVIER: Je ne suis pas encore prêt; j'ai peur d'être en retard.

    CAROLINE: Il ne faut pas que tu _____ en retard.

3. XAVIER: Ma femme part à 8h30 pour aller à son travail.

    CAROLINE: Il vaut mieux qu'elle _____ à 8h.

4. XAVIER: Je n'ai pas envie de finir mon travail.

    CAROLINE: Il vaut mieux que tu le _____ tout de suite.

5. XAVIER: Mes enfants ne font jamais de sport.

    CAROLINE: Il vaut mieux qu'ils _____ quelquefois du sport.

6. XAVIER: Ma femme et moi, nous détestons marcher; nous préférons prendre notre voiture.

    CAROLINE: Il vaut mieux que vous _____ de temps en temps.

7. XAVIER: Nous n'avons pas d'argent en ce moment, mais nous avons envie d'acheter une nouvelle voiture.

    CAROLINE: Il vaut mieux que vous n'_____ pas de voiture.

8. XAVIER: Je n'ai pas envie d'aller travailler aujourd'hui; je pense que je vais rester à la maison.

    CAROLINE: Il faut que tu _____ à ton travail aujourd'hui.

Ⓑ Quelques jours de vacances. You have friends who are taking some time off from work. Choose six of the verbs provided and using **il faut que** followed by the subjunctive, give your friends advice on making good use of their vacation time. You can also add ideas of your own.

> **EXEMPLE**   bien dormir pendant vos vacances
> ***Il faut que vous dormiez bien pendant vos vacances.***

profiter de votre temps libre	réserver une chambre dans un hôtel
sortir tous les soirs	faire du camping
faire un petit voyage	envoyer des cartes postales à vos amis
aller au bord de la mer / à la plage	rencontrer de nouveaux amis
rester à la maison	?
prendre quelques jours de repos	

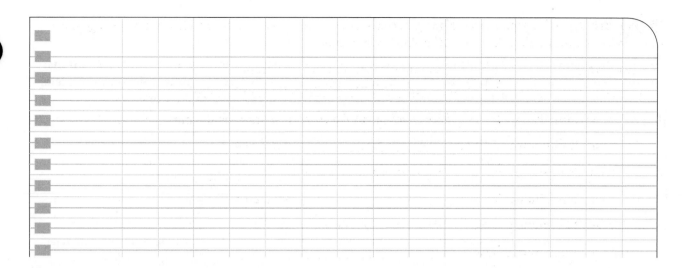

C **Et vous?** In the space provided and choosing ideas from the list, write at least six pieces of advice you would give a new intern on how to be successful in his internship.

EXAMPLES *Il faut que (Il vaut mieux que / Il vaudrait mieux que) vous arriviez tôt au bureau.*
Il ne faut pas que vous passiez trop de temps à la cafétéria.

être trop sûr de vous	comprendre votre rôle dans la compagnie
avoir peur de parler aux autres employés	finir votre travail
bien faire votre travail	faire très attention
arriver en retard	faire la connaissance des autres employés
réfléchir avant de parler	bien choisir vos horaires
être toujours très poli	partir avant l'heure de fermeture des bureaux
poser beaucoup de questions	?
prendre des notes	

Intégration et perspectives

Ⓐ Chez nous en France: Destination la Provence. Monsieur Chanet describes the tradition of **les santons,** an important custom in the south of France, and talks about the work that he and his wife do as **santonniers.** Before you read the text, look for **la Provence** on the map of France in the front of the workbook.

Si vous avez déjà eu l'occasion de passer les fêtes de Noël en France, vous avez peut-être remarqué les jolies petites «crèches» *(nativity scenes)* qu'on trouve dans beaucoup de familles françaises pendant cette période de l'année... C'est une vieille tradition qui a ses origines chez nous, en Provence.

La crèche est entourée de «santons», c'est-à-dire, de petites figurines qui représentent les animaux et les personnages *(characters)* traditionnels d'un village de Provence. Il y a, par exemple, le meunier *(miller)*, le boulanger, le berger *(shepherd)* avec ses moutons, le pêcheur *(fisherman)*, la vendeuse de poissons, les femmes qui viennent chercher de l'eau à la fontaine, la vieille femme qui porte un gros fagot de bois *(bundle of wood)* sur son dos, etc....

Les «santons» sont fabriqués en Provence par des artisans *(crafstmen)* appelés «santonniers», et nous, les Chanet, nous sommes santonniers de père en fils. C'est un métier passionnant parce qu'on est à la fois *(both)* artisan et artiste. Nous travaillons toute l'année dans l'atelier *(workshop)* que nous avons installé dans le garage de notre maison. Et en décembre, nous vendons nos santons pendant la grande foire *(fair)* annuelle des santons. Cette foire a lieu à Marseille, sur la célèbre avenue de la Canebière. C'est là que tous les santonniers de Provence exposent et vendent leurs créations, pour la grande joie des enfants—et des adultes—!

Avez-vous compris? Like a number of other **santonniers,** the Chanet family has decided to promote their business online. They have asked you to help them design their Web site. In the space provided, write a paragraph (about 50 words) in which you (1) describe the origin and tradition of the **santons,** and (2) discuss what you know about the Chanet family and their business.

B À vous de lire: Les gardians de Camargue. One of the most intriguing jobs in the Camargue area is that of **gardian** (or **manadier**), in which the work in training and herding horses and bulls is similar to the work of American cowboys. In fact, the **gardians** are sometimes called **les cowboys de Camargue.** The following is a synopsis of one of the episodes of a special series on France 5, *Les Cavaliers du mythe,* which explored different aspects of the life and work of the **gardians de Camargue.** Refer to the **lexique** that follows to help you understand some of the more technical vocabulary used in this synopsis.

Lexique

bouvier *(m) herdsman*
éleveur *(m)* de taureaux et de chevaux *bull and horse breeder*
monter *to ride (horse)*
dits amateurs *so-called nonprofessionals*
rémunérateur *lucrative*
il s'agit de *it's about, it's a question of*

parcours *(m) path, journey, route*
manade *(f) herd of bulls or horses*
dressage *(m) training (of an animal)*
ferrade *(f) branding; also, the celebration that takes place at branding time*
effréné *full speed, wild*

Le Gardian est loin de l'image d'Épinal véhiculée par les médias (*l'image d'Épinal* refers to a naive, rosy type of image; usually nostalgic of the good old days when everything was perfect)

Autrefois simple bouvier, il est aujourd'hui principalement éleveur de taureaux et de chevaux, qu'il soit Manadier ou Gardian salarié. C'est un métier moderne qui, pour survivre, doit combiner élevage, agriculture et accueil touristique. Le gardian est aujourd'hui plus sur son tracteur qu'à cheval, mais il doit toujours monter pour garder l'indispensable contact entre les chevaux et les taureaux. Il y a beaucoup plus de gardians dits amateurs que de gardians professionnels. Ils viennent donner un coup de main aux Manadiers en période chargée.

Mais cela reste un métier de passion et de tradition

Les places sont rares donc très chères et le travail est dur et peu rémunérateur. Il faut donc être passionné de chevaux pour choisir ce métier. On devient gardian et surtout manadier principale-

ment de père en fils. Il s'agit d'un parcours initiatique strict et long qui se commence jeune. En dépit de la modernisation technique du métier, les traditions sont scrupuleusement perpétuées, en particulier la façon de monter qui est spécifique aux Gardians.

Le travail du Gardian avec les chevaux et les taureaux

La reproduction des chevaux et des taureaux d'avril à juillet se fait en liberté dans la manade (technique autrefois critiquée, aujourd'hui réhabilitée).

Les naissances sont au printemps.

Le dressage des chevaux commence lorsqu'ils ont 3 ans, ils deviennent chevaux de taureaux à 6 ans.

La ferrade consiste à marquer les jeunes taureaux de l'année mais le terme désigne aussi les galops effrénés des chevaux, considéré comme un spectacle en soi.

Mais l'activité favorite des gardians reste le gardianage à cheval.

Avez-vous compris? Based on what you have read about the **gardians,** answer the following questions.

1. What are the three aspects of the **gardian**'s work listed in the first paragraph?

_____

2. How has the **gardian**'s work changed with the advent of modern agriculture?

_____

3. Who helps out the **gardians** during particularly busy times of the year?

_____

4. Why is it important that the **gardian** really like his work?

_____

5. How does one become a **gardian,** and what is the training like?

_____

6. When are the horses and bulls born?

_____

7. When does the training of the horses begin, and when are they ready to be used in work with the bulls?

_____

8. What ideas would you put in a travel brochure ad to encourage tourists to visit to **la Camargue**?

_____

_____

C À vous d'écrire: Choix d'une profession. Follow these four steps to write about the career you have chosen to pursue or are thinking about pursuing.

1. Préparation

As a first step, jot down your answers to the following questions in the space provided. As you brainstorm, think also of how to answer the questions. For example, you can't just answer the first question by mechanically saying **J'ai choisi la profession…**; you will need instead to say something like **J'ai envie d'être médecin** or **La médecine m'intéresse beaucoup.**

Quelle profession avez-vous choisie?

_____

Pourquoi avez-vous choisi cette profession?

_____

Est-ce que vous avez longtemps réfléchi à votre choix?

_____

Qu'est-ce qui compte le plus dans cette profession?

_____

Quelles aptitudes et qualités doit-on posséder pour réussir dans cette profession?

_____

Est-ce un travail où on peut accomplir des choses importantes? gagner un bon salaire? être son / sa propre *(own)* patron(ne)? avoir de bonnes possibilités de promotion?

_____

Quelles sont vos aptitudes personnelles (vous êtes doué[e] en maths, etc.)?

_____

Quand allez-vous finir vos études et quand espérez-vous commencer à travailler?

_____

2. Brouillon

Use these ideas to write two paragraphs (at least 12 sentences total). In the first paragraph, write a description of the profession you've chosen (qualities required for success, how well it pays, etc.), and in the second paragraph, write about yourself—why this profession interests you and why you believe you are suited to it. Write this first draft on a separate sheet of paper. Try to incorporate **pouvoir, vouloir,** and **devoir** (e.g., **Pour être un bon professeur, on doit avoir beaucoup de patience**) and **il faut que** and **il vaut mieux que** with the subjunctive (e.g., **Si vous voulez être professeur(e), il vaut mieux que vous aimiez les matières que vous allez enseigner**). In addition, you will want to use adverbs and connecting phrases to make your paragraph flow smoothly (e.g., **À mon avis, c'est vrai que, j'ai l'impression que**). You will also want to find an interesting way to begin and end your discussion. For example, you might want to start out with a sentence like this: **Être professeur(e) m'intéresse depuis très longtemps, surtout parce que j'ai beaucoup aimé certains de mes professeurs de lycée;** and to conclude, **Je suis impatient(e) de finir mes études et de commencer à faire le métier que j'ai choisi.**

3. Révision

Now that you have finished writing your first draft, read through what you have written and check the following.

- Did you answer all the questions listed in the **Préparation** section? Did you link them with adverbs and connecting phrases so that your sentences flow together?
- Did you use **vouloir, pouvoir,** and **devoir**? Were you able to include sentences with **il faut que / il vaut mieux que** and the subjunctive? If not, reread your paragraphs to find places where you can do so.
- Did you find an interesting way to begin and end your description?
- What else can you add to make your description of your career choice more complete?

4. Rédaction

Write the final draft of your description in the space provided here. Make the corrections and insert the additions you noted in step #3. Then reread your description to be sure you are satisfied with it.

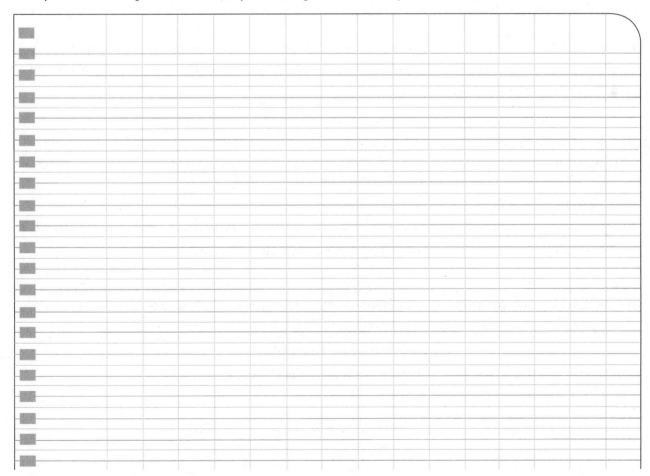

PARTIE ORALE

Point de départ

CD3, Track 34

9.1 Quelle est ma profession? Listen as some people talk about their jobs and then underline the name of each profession described. You will hear each item twice.

EXEMPLE   You hear: Quand les jeunes ne savent pas quels cours ou quel type d'études choisir, c'est à moi qu'ils viennent parler.
You underline: *conseiller pédagogique*

1. chef d'entreprise   professeur des écoles   psychiatre

2. mécanicienne   électricienne   infirmière

3. infirmier   technicien   comptable

4. kiné   chef d'entreprise   guide touristique

5. professeur des écoles   ingénieur   chirurgien

6. assistante dentaire   interprète   chercheuse

Les verbes *vouloir*, *pouvoir* et *devoir*

CD3, Track 35

*9.2 Situation: Un petit service. (p. 248) Emmanuel is looking for a job. He has an interview with the boss of a company, and he would like to borrow his sister's car to go to this interview. You will hear the conversation twice. Listen the first time as you hear it read, paying attention to intonation, tone, and pronunciation. During the second reading, repeat each line of the conversation after it is read to you.

CD3, Track 36

*9.3 C'est dommage. (p. 249 B) Your friends are talking about what they want to do this weekend, but unfortunately, can't do because they have to work. What do they say?

EXEMPLE   You hear: Laurent / aller au cinéma
You say: *Laurent veut aller au cinéma, mais il ne peut pas parce qu'il doit travailler.*

CD3, Track 37

*9.4 Un travail d'été. (p. 250 E) Richard would like to get a summer job. He is examining his preferences (**vouloir**), options (**pouvoir**), and obligations (**devoir**). Using the cues provided, tell what he says.

EXEMPLE   You hear: (option) faire un travail manuel
You say: *Je peux faire un travail manuel.*

CD3, Track 38

9.5 Pourquoi pas? Some people are talking about why they can't do certain things. Jot down what is said about each person. You will hear each item twice.

> **EXEMPLE**   You hear: Notre patron n'a pas pu partir en voyage d'affaires parce qu'il y a une grève des transports.
> You jot down: *couldn't go on trip; there's a transportation strike*

1. Anne et ses amis: _____

2. Jacqueline: _____

3. Moi: _____

4. Nous: _____

5. Jeanne et Paul: _____

6. Jacques: _____

Les pronoms compléments d'objet direct

CD3, Track 39

*9.6 Situation: Voyage d'affaires. (p. 252) Michel Maréchal's boss must go to the United States on business. He invites Michel to go with him. You will hear the conversation twice. Listen the first time as you hear it read, paying attention to intonation, tone, and pronunciation. During the second reading, repeat each line of the conversation after it is read to you.

CD3, Track 40

*9.7 Mais si! (p. 253 A) A friend scolds you for not listening to him. You try to reassure him.

> **EXEMPLE**   You hear: Tu ne m'écoutes pas.
> You say: *Mais si, je t'écoute!*

CD3, Track 41

*9.8 Réciprocité. (p. 253 B) Madame Dassin treats her employees with respect. What does she say about them?

> **EXEMPLE**   You hear: Je les écoute…
> You say: *Je les écoute, et ils m'écoutent.*

CD3, Track 42

9.9 Conflits. Marie Pascal is talking about the conflicts that working mothers face. Listen carefully to each of her statements. If you hear a direct object pronoun, write both the pronoun and the noun it refers to in the space provided. If you don't hear a direct object pronoun, write **non**. You will hear each statement twice.

> **EXEMPLE**   You hear: La vie d'une mère qui travaille est souvent compliquée, et je l'ai choisie sans penser à tous ces problèmes.
> You write: *l'; la vie*

1. _____   **5.** _____

2. _____   **6.** _____

3. _____   **7.** _____

4. _____   **8.** _____

Le subjonctif avec *il faut que* et *il vaut mieux que*

CD3, Track 43

*9.10 Situation: Une invitation. (p. 257) Georges Berger wants to invite Élise and Gilles Guérin to lunch, but they're busy right now. You will hear the conversation twice. Listen the first time as you hear it read, paying attention to intonation, tone, and pronunciation. During the second reading, repeat each line of the conversation after it is read to you.

CD3, Track 44

*9.11 Ils ne sont pas libres. (p. 258 B) Your friends want to go out with you, but they have other obligations. What do they say?

> **EXEMPLE**
> You hear: Mireille / aller chez le dentiste
> You say: ***Il faut que Mireille aille chez le dentiste.***

CD3, Track 45

*9.12 On cherche du travail. (p. 259 C) Marc Lemaître is looking for a job, and an employment counselor is giving him some advice. What does he say?

> **EXEMPLES**
> You hear: faire l'inventaire de vos talents
> You say: ***Il faut que vous fassiez l'inventaire de vos talents.***
>
> You hear: être en retard
> You say: ***Il ne faut pas que vous soyez en retard.***

CD3, Track 46

9.13 Agenda. Madame Audaire's secretary is going over the day's schedule with her. Decide if the secretary's statements agree with what you see on the schedule and check the appropriate column. You will hear each item twice.

> **EXEMPLE**
> You hear: Cet après-midi, il faut que vous alliez à la banque.
> You mark: *non*

	oui	non			oui	non
1.	☐	☐		5.	☐	☐
2.	☐	☐		6.	☐	☐
3.	☐	☐		7.	☐	☐
4.	☐	☐		8.	☐	☐

3 jeudi septembre

8 h. rendez-vous chef d'entreprise
9 h 30 - 11 h usine
rapport
déjeuner avec des clients
après-midi —
leçon de chinois
interviews : techs

Intégration et perspectives

CD3, Track 47

9.14 On embauche. Sylvie and Jean-Luc went to the same school. Sylvie now has a good job, but Jean-Luc isn't working. Listen to their conversation, and then decide if the following statements are **vrai** or **faux** and mark the appropriate column.

vrai	faux

1. Jean-Luc a trouvé du travail dans l'administration.
2. L'entreprise où Sylvie travaille va embaucher plusieurs ingénieurs.
3. Sylvie cherche un autre emploi.
4. Sylvie n'est pas satisfaite des conditions de travail dans son entreprise.
5. Sylvie fait de la recherche dans un laboratoire.
6. Jean-Luc aussi a envie de faire de la recherche.

CD3, Track 48

9.15 Mémorandum. Gérard Baudrier, the president of a small company, is dictating a memo to his department heads. During the pauses provided, write in French what Gérard says. Each line will be read twice, then the entire passage will be read once again so that you can check your work.

1. _____
2. _____
3. _____
4. _____
5. _____

CD3, Track 49

*9.16 Bien prononcer. (p. 268)

A. Certain French vowels are pronounced with the lips rounded and the tongue forward (i.e., resting against the back of the lower front teeth). These vowels in order of increasing openness are

/y/ as in **du**
/ø/ as in **deux**
/œ/ as in **jeune**

Because these vowels do not exist in English, learning to pronounce them requires special care. Make sure that your tongue is pressed against your teeth when you pronounce these sounds. Practice repeating the following sequences.

B. The sounds /ø/ and /œ/ are usually written as **eu**. Note the role of the /ø/ versus /œ/ contrast in distinguishing the singular and plural of certain verbs as well as the masculine and feminine of certain adjectives and nouns.

Repeat words containing the sound /ø/.
Repeat words containing the sound /œ/.

CD3, Track 50

*9.17 Petite conversation. Practice repeating the following conversation.

Chapitre dix ○ ○ ○ ○ ○ ○

On fait des achats

⑩

PARTIE ÉCRITE

Point de départ

Ⓐ Quelques achats. Before you return home from a trip to France, you decide to buy gifts and other items for at least eight friends and family members. In the categories provided on the following grid and using vocabulary from the **Point de départ** of this chapter, list the people you are shopping for and what you plan to buy for each person.

      EXEMPLE   Dans une librairie-papeterie: *Pour ma prof de français, un livre sur la France.*

Dans une pharmacie	Dans une droguerie	Dans une parfumerie

Dans une librairie-papeterie	Dans un magasin de vêtements	Dans une bijouterie

Dans un magasin de jouets	Dans une maroquinerie	Chez une fleuriste

B Où aller? You are spending time in Angers, and a friend who is new to the area wants to know where to go to buy different things. Using the information about shops that follows, write the answers you might give your friend; you can vary your answers by using the suggestions provided.

EXEMPLE Je dois acheter du pain.

Si tu veux du bon pain de campagne, tu peux aller à la Brioche d'or, au centre commercial Saint-Serge. Leur pain est excellent.

Suggestions: **Pour ça, je vais toujours… ; Tu peux toujours aller… ; Si tu veux… ; Tu peux acheter ça… ; Moi, j'achète mes… à… ; Il vaudrait mieux que tu ailles…**

Fleuristes

ALOES Créations Florales	14 rue Saint-Lazare 49100 ANGERS
ANNIE CLAIRE FLEURS	39 rue des Lices 49100 ANGERS
CAPRICE Fleurs	273 rue Saumuroise 49000 ANGERS
CHATAIGNER Fleurs	1 rue Plantagenêt 49100 ANGERS
JOSETTE Fleurs	139/141 rue de la Madeleine 49000 ANGERS
KARINE Fleurs	20 rue Marceau 49100 ANGERS
Le JARDIN d'AURÉLIE	C/C Grand Maine 49000 ANGERS
Les FLORALIES	C/C Saint-Serge 49100 ANGERS
Lycée Fleuri	1 place du Lycée 49100 ANGERS
Rose d'Anjou	223 ter av. Pasteur 49100 ANGERS
J. FLEURS	rue de Verdun 49124 ST-BARTHÉLÉMY D'ANJOU

Drogueries - Quincaillerie

Droguerie de la MADELEINE	176 rue de la Madeleine 49000 ANGERS
Droguerie des LICES	32 rue des Lices 49100 ANGERS
Droguerie SAINT JULIEN	24 rue Saint-Julien 49100 ANGERS
Droguerie TINON	70 rue Plantagenêt 49100 ANGERS
Quincaillerie FERRÉ	66 rue Jules Guitton 49100 ANGERS

Bijouteries

Bijouterie BRANGER	77 rue Bressigny 49100 ANGERS
Bijouterie des Fiancés	26 rue Saint-Aubin 49100 ANGERS
Bijouterie Joaillerie MINE D'OR	5 rue Sarret-Terrasse 49100 ANGERS
Bijouterie La Clé des Cœurs	39 rue Bressigny 49100 ANGERS
Bijouterie LARGEAU	28 bis av. Pasteur 49100 ANGERS
Bijouterie TRIANGLE D'OR	49 rue Saint-Aubin 49100 ANGERS
Bijouterie VIALLESOUBRANE	23 rue Lenepveu 49100 ANGERS
Bijoux ADELAIDE	bd Albert Camus 49100 ANGERS
FALBALA Bijoux fantaisie	31 rue Lenepveu 49100 ANGERS
FRANÇOIS-XAVIER	3 rue d'Alsace 49100 ANGERS
L'Atelier du Scarabée - bijoux fantaisies	7 rue Saint-Georges 49100 ANGERS
La PIERRE PRÉCIEUSE	50 bd Foch 49100 ANGERS
LES DIAMANTINES	45 rue Saint-Julien 49100 ANGERS

Chaussures

L'HYPER CHAUSSURE	5av. Besnardière 49100 ANGERS
PHILOMENE Chaussures	30 rue Lenepveu 49100 ANGERS

Maroquinerie et Accessoires

PASSEPORT	C/C Espace 49 49000 ANGERS
Maroquinerie CHOUANE	7 rue Saint-Étienne 49100 ANGERS
Maroquinerie DEPLAGNE Élégance	56 rue Saint-Julien 49100 ANGERS
Maroquinerie Françoise BIANNIC	3 rue Chaperonnière 49100 ANGERS
Maroquinerie SÉLECTION	31 rue Lenepveu 49100 ANGERS

Parfumeries

FEELING	C/C Espace 49 49100 ANGERS
Yves ROCHER	C/C Espace 49 49000 ANGERS

Librairie Papeterie

Librairie Papeterie ÉTUDES et LOISIRS	26 rue Saint-Julien 49100 ANGERS

Librairie Papeterie Presse

Librairie Presse Papet. GRAND MAINE	C/C Grand Maine 49000 ANGERS

Boulangeries

Boulangerie CADU	85 rue Létanduère 49000 ANGERS
Boulangerie DUMONTEIL	9 place de l'Academie 49100 ANGERS
Boulangerie La Maison du Pain	4 place de la Visitation 49100 ANGERS
Boulangerie PELHATRE	24 rue Boisnet 49100 ANGERS
Boulangerie THOUEILLE	83 bd Saint-Michel 49100 ANGERS
La BRIOCHE d'OR	C/C Saint-Serge 49100 ANGERS

Boulangeries-Patisseries

Boulangerie LE BROCH	124 rue Létanduère 49000 ANGERS
Boulangerie Patisserie GIRARD	21 rue Saint-Julien 49100 ANGERS
Boulangerie Patis. JEANNETEAU	17 rue de Brissac 49000 ANGERS
boulangerle Patisserie MINGOT	60 rue Saint-Lazare 49100 ANGERS
BOUTIQUE DU PAIN	27 rue Saint-Aubin 49100 ANGERS
boulangerle COMPAGNON	17 rue Victor Hugo 49130 Les PONTS-DE-CÉ

Boucheries - Charcuteries - Volailles

Boucherie charcuterie CHOVEAU	19 av. Patton 49000 ANGERS
Boucherie Charcuterie Volailles CLÉRAC	351 rue Saint-Léonard 49100 ANGERS

Banques

Caisse Fédérale de Crédit Mutuel	1 place Molière 49100 ANGERS
Caisse Régionale de Crédit Agricole	bd Pierre de Coubertin 49000 ANGERS
Crédit Industriel de l'Ouest	17 rue Voltaire 49100 ANGERS
Banque Populaire Anjou Vendée	chemin du Nid de Pie 49040 ANGERS Cédex

Supermarchés

INTERMARCHÉ	bd Jacques Millot 49000 ANGERS
SUPER M	C/C Chapeau de Gendarme 49000 ANGERS
INTERMARCHÉ	La Croix Cadeau 49240 AVRILLÉ
INTERMARCHÉ	C/C La Guillebotte 49130 Les PONTS-DE-CÉ
INTERMARCHÉ	C/C La Musardière 49460 MONTREUIL-JUIGNÉ

Disques et Livres d'Occasion

POLAR ET VYNIL	64 rue Jules Guitton 49100 ANGERS

Location de Voitures

A.D.A. Location véhicules	8 av. Patton 49000 ANGERS
AVIS	5 rue Max Richard 49100 ANGERS
EURO-RENT	30 rue Denis Papin 49100 ANGERS
EUROPCAR	26 bd Charles de Gaulle 49024 ANGERS
HERTZ	32 rue Denis Papin 49100 ANGERS

---

1. Il faut que j'achète du dentifrice, du savon et du shampooing.

_____

2. Je voudrais acheter une nouvelle montre et quelques bijoux pour mon amie.

_____

3. Où est-ce qu'on peut trouver des livres d'occasion?

_____

4. J'ai besoin de nouvelles chaussures. Où est-ce que je peux aller?

_____

5. Je ne sais pas où est passé mon sac à dos; je ne peux pas le trouver.

_____

6. J'ai envie de manger un gâteau ce soir; où est-ce qu'on peut acheter de bonnes pâtisseries?

_____

7. Je dois acheter un sèche-cheveux. Où est-ce que je peux aller?

_____

8. Où est-ce que je vais trouver des journaux et des revues?

_____

Les verbes comme *vendre*

Êtes-vous prêts? Les verbes comme *vendre*

Indicate on a scale of 1 (not comfortable) to 5 (very comfortable) how well you can handle each of the following tasks and place the number in the box provided. If you answer 1 to 3 for any of the tasks, you should go back and review the explanations and exercises in your textbook.

☐ List the verbs conjugated like **vendre** and tell what they mean in English.

☐ Explain how to conjugate these verbs in the present, the **passé composé,** and the subjunctive.

☐ Make up questions that you would ask using verbs like **vendre.**

A Les marchands parlent. Several shopkeepers are discussing business, the economy, and problems they are facing. Complete their statements by filling in the blanks with the appropriate form and tense of the following verbs: **attendre, entendre, perdre, rendre, répondre,** and **vendre.**

1. Hier j(e) _____ trois vélos.

2. L'année dernière, les affaires n'ont pas été bonnes, et les marchands de notre quartier

_____ de l'argent.

3. En général, les décisions du gouvernement ne _____ pas à nos besoins.

4. La situation économique de notre pays me _____ très triste.

5. Ma femme et moi, nous _____ tous les jours les critiques de nos clients. Nous ne

devons pas _____ à ces critiques.

6. Nous _____ les marchandises que nous avons commandées.

7. Nous traversons une période difficile, mais nous ne pouvons pas _____ patience.

8. Les marchandises que les marchands de ce quartier _____ sont d'une qualité excellente.

ⓑ Au centre commercial. You and your friend have just arrived at the shopping center where you plan to run some errands. Write what you would say in French to convey the following information.

1. Tell your friend that you are losing patience.

_____

2. Say that you have been waiting for him for an hour.

_____

3. Find out where they sell watches.

_____

4. Say that you lost your watch a week ago.

_____

5. Ask your friend why he is returning these shoes.

_____

6. Say that the employees at the shoe store never answer your questions.

_____

L'impératif

Êtes-vous prêts? L'impératif

Indicate on a scale of 1 (not comfortable) to 5 (very comfortable) how well you can handle each of the following tasks and place the number in the box provided. If you answer 1 to 3 for any of the tasks, you should go back and review the explanations and exercises in your textbook.

☐ Explain what the imperative means and how it is formed in French.

☐ Tell how to make an imperative negative; explain where direct object pronouns are placed in affirmative and negative imperatives.

☐ Use imperatives to instruct people on a variety of topics.

☐ Give several common expressions that use the imperative.

ⓐ Un homme tyrannique. Pierre Kelbrute is always giving orders and making suggestions to people around him. Using the cues provided and following the examples, re-create his commands.

— à sa fille

> **EXEMPLE** aller dans ta chambre
> ***Va dans ta chambre!***

1. faire tes devoirs _____

2. finir ton dîner _____

3. ne pas regarder la télé _____

4. écouter ton père _____

5. rendre visite à ta grand-mère _____

_____

— à ses employés

    EXEMPLE   arriver à l'heure chaque matin
                   Arrivez à l'heure chaque matin!

1. ne pas quitter le bureau avant cinq heures _____

_____

2. être plus polis quand vous parlez au téléphone _____

_____

3. avoir de la patience avec les clients _____

_____

4. finir ces lettres _____

5. ne pas perdre votre temps _____

— à sa femme et à lui-même

    EXEMPLE   regarder les informations
                   Regardons les informations!

1. acheter une nouvelle voiture _____

2. emmener les enfants chez leurs grands-parents _____

_____

3. aller au cinéma ce soir _____

4. ne pas inviter les Duvernet à dîner _____

_____

5. prendre nos vacances au mois de juillet _____

_____

B La publicité. Each of the following ads is missing a verb in the imperative. Using the verbs provided for each set of ads, fill in each blank with the **vous** form of the appropriate verb.

1. faire, venir, inviter

_____ COMME MOI !
ABONNEZ VOUS !
AU JOURNAL
DE LA MAISON

_____ passer **2** jours à VARAZUR
8 tennis × 2 piscines × 1 volley
× 1 parcours de santé × 4 ping-
pong × la pétanque...
       + le soleil et la mer !

_____ *L'ÉTÉ*

abonnez-vous = *subscribe*

2. être, perdre, apprendre

_____ plus Phosphore
que les autres...

NOM, PRÉNOM_____

AGE_____ CLASSE (SECTION)_____

ADRESSE COMPLÈTE_____

CODE POSTAL |__|__|__|__|__|

NUMÉRO DE TÉLÉPHONE_____

NOM ET ADRESSE DE MON ÉTABLISSEMENT SCOLAIRE_____

_____

NOMBRE DE FRÈRES (ÂGE)_____

NOMBRE DE SŒURS (ÂGE)_____

DEVENEZ
PHOSPHORE CONTACT

ETUDES
METIERS
AVENIR

**_____ efficacement
à votre rythme
par correspondance
avec**

L'ECOLE
UNIVERSELLE

Phosphore is a magazine for young people.

Ne _____ pas un temps précieux.

3. avoir, choisir, devenir

Le Web en direct

> _____ des
idées neuves

Encore plus simple, encore plus efficace avec,
maintenant, un accès direct au Web grâce
à la barre de navigation affichée en
permanence, et ultra-rapide
avec Internet Explorer.

neuves = *new*

Entre AoL
et Internet
les deux
_____
3 mois gratuits

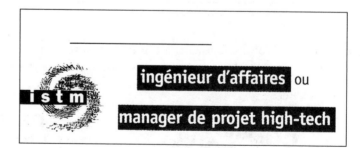

_____

ingénieur d'affaires ou

manager de projet high-tech

4. rester, prendre, changer

_____ en liaison permanente avec la France

Abonnez-vous

EDITION INTERNATIONALE

Votre 2ᵉ paire de lunettes pour 1 euro!

_____ de point de vue!

_____

le temps de vivre

ⓒ Vice versa. What advice would students and teachers give each other? In the first space provided, write three or four pieces of advice that students would give to teachers; in the second space, write three or four pieces of advice using the imperative that teachers would give to students. Vary your sentences as much as possible.

conseils pour les professeurs:

_____

_____

_____

_____

conseils pour les étudiants:

_____

_____

_____

_____

Le comparatif et le superlatif

A Rivalité. Guy Lacrème believes he is better than his friend Armand. Each time his friend makes a statement, Guy tries to outdo him. Re-create his statements by using the appropriate form of the comparative.

EXEMPLES   Je suis assez gentil.
                Je suis plus gentil que toi.

                Mes enfants travaillent bien à l'école.
                Mes enfants travaillent mieux à l'école que tes enfants.

1. En général, je suis très patient.

_____

2. Je suis doué en espagnol.

_____

3. Chez nous, nous mangeons très bien.

_____

4. Ma femme est très belle et très intelligente.

_____

5. J'ai un très bon travail.

_____

6. Nous habitons dans un beau quartier.

_____

7. Notre maison a coûté cher.

_____

8. J'ai beaucoup d'amis.

_____

ⓑ Opinions. Susan has asked a French friend about various aspects of French life. Using the cues provided and following the example, re-create her friend's answers to the following questions.

> **EXEMPLE** un bon restaurant à Lyon? (Paul Bocuse)
> ***À mon avis, Paul Bocuse est le meilleur restaurant de Lyon.***

1. un musée intéressant à Paris? (le Centre Pompidou)

À mon avis, _____.

2. une belle région dans le Sud-Ouest? (le Pays basque)

À mon avis, _____.

3. un bon vin rouge? (le Pommard)

À mon avis, _____.

4. une voiture très économique? (la 2CV)

À mon avis, _____.

5. une ville pittoresque en Alsace? (Riquewihr)

À mon avis, _____.

6. une bonne spécialité régionale? (la bouillabaisse)

À mon avis, _____.

7. une région où on mange bien? (la Bourgogne)

À mon avis, _____.

ⓒ Comparaisons. Using the suggestions provided here (or other ideas of your own) and the comparative, write a paragraph of at least five sentences in which you tell how university life is different from high school life. Vary your sentences as much as possible. Be sure to use the comparative of adjectives, nouns, and adverbs.

Sujets que vous pouvez mentionner: temps libre, cours, amis, responsabilités, intérêts, attitudes, professeurs

> **EXEMPLE** ***Maintenant que je suis à l'université, j'ai moins de cours, mais mes devoirs sont beaucoup plus difficiles!***

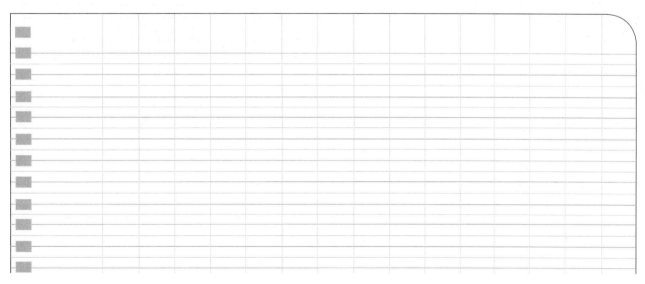

Intégration et perspectives

Ⓐ Chez nous en France: Destination la Bresse. Julien talks about his region, **la Bresse,** and his family's shoe retail business. Before you read, locate **la Bresse** on the map at the front of this book.

Ma région, la Bresse (située entre la Saône et le Beaujolais à l'ouest, le Rhône au sud et les montagnes du Jura au nord-est), est surtout connue pour ses produits agricoles comme la culture du maïs, l'élevage des bovins *(cattle)* et des volailles *(poultry)* et, en particulier, les célèbres «poulets de Bresse»!

Dans l'ensemble, la Bresse est une région assez plate *(flat)*, et dans la partie appelée la Dombes, il y a une multitude d'étangs *(small lakes)* qui font la joie des amoureux de la nature *(nature lovers)*. Pendant les week-ends, les Suisses et les Lyonnais aiment venir faire des promenades dans notre région, découvrir un charmant petit restaurant où on peut déjeuner sous les arbres, manger un bon poulet à la crème (une de nos nombreuses et délicieuses spécialités régionales!) et passer l'après-midi au bord d'un étang. Et n'oubliez pas que la Bresse a aussi longtemps été le domaine de Georges Blanc, le grand chef de réputation internationale!

Quant à moi, Julien, mon domaine, ce n'est pas la cuisine mais la vente des chaussures! J'ai fini mes études il y a quelques années et maintenant je partage avec mon père la gestion de notre entreprise familiale créée par mon arrière-grand-père *(great-grandfather)*. Nous avons une vingtaine de magasins situés dans les principales villes de la région, mais nos bureaux sont ici, à Châtillon. Le commerce, et en particulier le commerce des articles de mode, n'est pas une chose facile… En plus de tout le travail de gestion, il faut constamment faire des choix difficiles. Quels sont les modèles et les styles qui vont être à la mode *(in style)* cette année? L'économie du pays va-t-elle être bonne et les gens vont-ils avoir envie d'acheter? Et quel temps va-t-il faire?… Si on fait une grosse commande de sandales, et ensuite il pleut pendant tout l'été, il va falloir les solder *(put on sale)* pour presque rien à la fin de la saison!

Avez-vous compris? In the space provided, answer the questions about the region where Julien lives and about his profession.

1. Décrivez la région où habite Julien. Qu'est-ce qui fait le charme de cette région?

_____

_____

_____

_____

2. Décrivez la profession de Julien. Quelles sont les questions importantes à considérer dans ce métier?

_____

_____

_____

_____

B À vous de lire: On fait du shopping en ligne. You have gone online to look for high-tech products and discover Mistergooddeal.com, a company that specializes in such products. On the site, you find a description of Mistergooddeal's online offerings as well as those of several other high-tech Web sites. In the space below the description of each Web site, list three or more products sold and the types of special deals and discounts offered, and then explain in French why the site is (or is not) appealing to you.

Petit lexique
déstockage *(m) merchandise reduction, clearance*
logiciel *(m) software*
électroménager *(m) household appliances*
numérique *digital*

1 Rue Du Commerce

Le site leader de la vente en ligne de produits High-Tech en France. Les meilleurs produits au meilleur prix, avec le meilleur service. Notre offre couvre aujourd'hui l'Informatique, le Son Numérique et le Home Studio, la Photo et la Vidéo Numériques, les Logiciels CD-Rom, les Jeux Vidéo, la TV-HIFI-Vidéo, les Films DVD, la Téléphonie Mobile et Fixe.

_____

_____

_____

2 Surcouf, La foire permanente de l'informatique – matériels, logiciels et accessoires

La foire permanente de l'informatique et des nouvelles technologies vous présente sa boutique en ligne: matériel informatique, ordinateurs, périphériques, logiciels et accessoires.

_____

_____

_____

3 Mistergooddeal, leader du déstockage sur Internet

Déstockage en informatique, électroménager, hifi, téléphonie... Discount incroyable sur des milliers de produits: imprimantes, écrans, scanners, ordinateurs, téléviseurs, home cinéma, téléphones, fours...

_____

_____

_____

4 TopAchat.com

TopAchat.com est le leader de la vente sur Internet de produits High-Tech aux particuliers. TopAchat.com propose un choix de plus de 10 000 produits à des prix très compétitifs (jusqu'à – 40% sur des prix généralement constatés) en Micro, Home-Cinéma, Numérique, Téléphonie, Électroménager. Nombreuses offres exceptionnelles, promotions quotidiennes dans chaque catégorie permettent d'acheter au meilleur prix! La rubrique Déstockage permet de profiter d'une réduction atteignant jusqu'à 50% sur des produits moins récents!!

_____

_____

_____

5 Clust.com, le meilleur choix pour vos achats!

Bénéficiez de prix exceptionnels sur une vaste sélection de produits High-Tech. Informatique, Numérique, Image et son, Téléphonie, Électroménager: il y en a pour tous les goûts et tous les budgets! Clust.com propose également chaque semaine des coupons de réduction valables sur une sélection de produits.

_____

_____

_____

Ⓒ À vous d'écrire: Bienvenue sur le FORUM. Your university has set up a Web site for incoming French exchange students and visitors that includes information in French about the university and the town in which it is located. One part of the Web site is devoted to shopping. You have been asked to describe four shops or stores in your area (those that you like and at least one that you don't like). For each, indicate the name of the store, what is sold there, and your opinions (positive or negative) about the store.

1. Préparation

As a first step, make notes about the four stores you have selected: name of the store, products sold, your opinions.

Magasin #1: _____

  Produit(s) _____

  Opinion _____

Magasin #2: _____

  Produit(s) _____

  Opinion _____

Magasin #3: _____

  Produit(s) _____

  Opinion _____

Magasin #4: _____

  Produit(s) _____

  Opinion _____

2. Brouillon

Use these ideas and vocabulary you know to write your four 50-word descriptions. Write this first draft on a separate sheet of paper. Remember that you will need to get as much information as you can into these short descriptions so that readers have a good sense of what each store is like and why you recommend or don't recommend it. Be sure to use the imperative, and comparative and superlative expressions in your descriptions (**Dans votre ville, Vélorama est le meilleur magasin de ce type**).

3. Révision

Now that you have finished writing your first draft, read through what you have written and check the following.

• Did you include the required information in each description?
• Did you use the comparative and superlative as often as possible?
• Do your descriptions explain adequately why you liked or didn't like the store? If not, what else could you say?
• Did you find an interesting way to start and end each description?

4. Rédaction

Write the final draft of your entries in the space provided. Make the corrections and insert the additions you noted in step #3. Then reread your entries to be sure you are satisfied with them.

Bienvenue sur le FORUM

Ici, vous pouvez échanger vos opinions, partager vos impressions, vendre ou acheter, dialoguer... Dans cette partie de notre site, vous êtes invités à partager vos opinions sur les différents magasins et boutiques de votre ville.

PARTIE ORALE

Point de départ

CD4, Track 2

10.1 Où peut-on trouver ça? Joëlle wants to do some shopping while she visits some French relatives. Listen to each of the things she wants to buy and mark the name of the shop where she would go for each one. You will hear Joëlle's statements twice.

> **EXEMPLE** You hear: Je voudrais acheter du maquillage. Où est-ce que je peux aller?
> You mark: ***dans une parfumerie***

1. dans une bijouterie   dans un magasin de jouets   chez un marchand de journaux

2. dans une pharmacie   dans une boucherie   dans une librairie-papeterie

3. chez un marchand de journaux   dans un magasin de vêtements   dans une boulangerie

4. chez un opticien   dans une parfumerie   dans une pharmacie

5. dans une droguerie   dans une bijouterie   dans un magasin de chaussures

6. chez un marchand de journaux   dans une librairie   dans une maroquinerie

7. chez un opticien   dans une droguerie   dans un magasin de vêtements

8. chez un fleuriste   dans une pharmacie   dans une droguerie

Les verbes comme *vendre*

CD4, Track 3

*10.2 Situation: Au bureau des objets trouvés. (p. 280) Catherine has lost her purse. She has gone to the lost and found office to see if someone has found it. The employee there is very busy. Listen to their conversation. You will hear the conversation twice. Listen the first time as you hear it read, paying attention to intonation, tone, and pronunciation. During the second reading, repeat each line of the conversation after it is read to you.

CD4, Track 4

*10.3 Au marché aux puces. (p. 280 A) You are at the flea market where you listen to several merchants talk about what they are selling. What do they say?

> **EXEMPLE** You hear: Annette (livres)
> You say: ***Annette vend des livres.***

CD4, Track 5

*10.4 Confusion. (p. 281 D) You decided to go shopping with your friends, but you forgot where to meet them. Where did your friends wait for you?

> **EXEMPLE** You hear: Monique / devant le magasin de vêtements
> You say: ***Monique a attendu devant le magasin de vêtements.***

CD4, Track 6

10.5 Une mauvaise journée. This is one of those days when nothing is going right for some people. Listen to their complaints and decide which of the drawings each complaint describes. Write the number of the complaint by the appropriate drawing. Not all drawings will be described. You will hear each item twice.

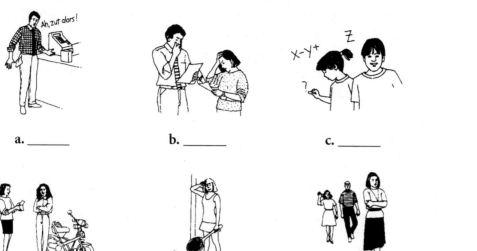

a. _____ b. _____ c. _____

d. _____ e. _____ f. _____ g. _____

L'impératif

CD4, Track 7

*10.6 Situation: Dans un grand magasin. (p. 283) Michel's job as a receptionist in a department store is to help people find what they're looking for. He is giving directions to a customer with an unruly little boy. Listen to their conversation. You will hear the conversation twice. Listen the first time as you hear it read, paying attention to intonation, tone, and pronunciation. During the second reading, repeat each line of the conversation after it is read to you.

CD4, Track 8

*10.7 Soldes de fin d'année. (p. 284 A) You work in the advertising department of a department store that is getting ready for year-end sales. You are proud of the quality of your products and your employees. What advice are you going to give customers so they will want to shop in your store?

EXEMPLES   You hear: ne pas manquer nos soldes de fin d'année
     You say: *Ne manquez pas nos soldes de fin d'année.*

   You hear: être les bienvenus chez nous
     You say: *Soyez les bienvenus chez nous.*

CD4, Track 9

*10.8 Mais non! (p. 284 C) Your friend Antoine is talking about what he intends to do. You're in a bad mood, and you say the opposite of everything he suggests.

EXEMPLES   You hear: Je vais rester à la maison.
     You say: *Mais non, ne reste pas à la maison.*

   You hear: Je n'ai pas envie de faire mes devoirs.
     You say: *Tant pis, fais-les quand même.*

CD4, Track 10

10.9 Conseils. Pierre has started out on his own and has a limited budget; his friends are advising him on how to manage his life. Decide whether their advice is **bon** or **mauvais** and check the appropriate boxes. You will hear each item twice.

EXEMPLE   You hear: Si tu empruntes quelque chose à quelqu'un, n'oublie pas de le rendre.
You check: *bon*

	bon	mauvais			bon	mauvais
1.	☐	☐		5.	☐	☐
2.	☐	☐		6.	☐	☐
3.	☐	☐		7.	☐	☐
4.	☐	☐		8	☐	☐

Le comparatif et le superlatif

CD4, Track 11

*10.10 Situation: Achat d'un cadeau. (p. 288) Mélanie wants to buy a gift for her best friend, who has just had her first baby. She asks her mother for advice. Listen to their conversation. You will hear the conversation twice. Listen the first time as you hear it read, paying attention to intonation, tone, and pronunciation. During the second reading, repeat each line of the conversation after it is read to you.

CD4, Track 12

*10.11 Qui dit mieux? (p. 289 A) You are convinced that Mademoiselle Villiers is an excellent teacher. You compare her to other teachers. One of your friends thinks Monsieur Martel is even better. For each of the cues you hear, give both your opinion of Mademoiselle Villiers and your friend's opinion of Monsieur Martel.

EXEMPLE   You hear: intéressant
You say: *Mlle Villiers est plus intéressante que les autres profs.*
À mon avis, M. Martel est encore plus intéressant!

CD4, Track 13

*10.12 Paris, ville lumière. (p. 290 G) A friend thinks that Paris is the most beautiful city in the world. What does he say?

EXEMPLE   You hear: des gens intéressants
You say: *C'est à Paris qu'on trouve les gens les plus intéressants.*

CD4, Track 14

10.13 Au marché aux puces. Monsieur Gérard, Madame Tournier, and Madame Thibault deal in secondhand furniture at the flea market in Saint-Ouen. The following chart shows what each of them sold today. Decide if each statement you hear about this information is **vrai** or **faux** and mark the appropriate column. You will hear each statement twice.

EXEMPLE   You hear: C'est Monsieur Gérard qui a vendu le plus de commodes.
You mark: *faux*

	M. Gérard		Mme Tournier		Mme Thibault	
	3 bureaux	330 €	2 bureaux	140 €	1 bureau	50 €
	1 buffet	150 €	1 buffet	160 €	1 buffet	125 €
	3 tables	100 €	4 tables	345 €	3 tables	300 €
	12 chaises	150 €	4 chaises	50 €	6 chaises	54 €
	2 commodes	100 €	2 commodes	90 €	3 commodes	140 €
	1 lampe	12 €	3 lampes	34 €	5 lampes	70 €
TOTAL	22 articles	842 €	16 articles	819 €	19 articles	739 €

	vrai	faux		vrai	faux
1.	☐	☐	6.	☐	☐
2.	☐	☐	7.	☐	☐
3.	☐	☐	8.	☐	☐
4.	☐	☐	9.	☐	☐
5.	☐	☐	10.	☐	☐

Intégration et perspectives

CD4, Track 15

10.14 Toutébo. You are at a market where a street vendor is selling a new product called Toutébo. Based on what the vendor says, decide if each statement is **vrai** or **faux** and mark the appropriate column. You will hear the passage twice.

vrai | **faux**

1. Toutébo peut vous aider à retrouver votre joie de vivre.
2. Ce produit peut vous aider si vous êtes souvent malade.
3. Une bouteille de Toutébo coûte moins de deux euros.
4. On a déjà vendu plus de six millions de bouteilles de ce produit.
5. Il faut boire un petit verre de Toutébo trois fois par jour.

CD4, Track 16

10.15 Au répondeur. Because Laure is going to be home late tonight, she leaves a message for her husband on their answering machine. During the pauses provided, write in French what Laure says. Each line will be read twice, then the entire message will be read once again so that you can check your work.

1. _____

2. _____

3. _____

4. _____

CD4, Track 17

*10.16 Bien prononcer. (p. 304)

The letter **e** (without an accent mark) is usually pronounced /ə/, as in the following words.

The **e** is not always pronounced, however. Whether it is pronounced depends on its position in a word or group of words and on its "phonetic environment."

A. It is not pronounced in the following situations.

1. At the end of a word.
2. When it is preceded by only one consonant sound.

Listen and repeat.

B. The letter **e** is pronounced when it is preceded by two consonants and followed by a third.

Listen and repeat.

CD4, Track 18

*10.17 Petite conversation. Practice repeating the following conversation.

Chapitre onze ○ ○ ○ ○ ○ ○ ○

Être bien dans sa peau

(11)

PARTIE ÉCRITE

Point de départ

Ⓐ Dans la salle d'attente du médecin. Some people in the doctor's waiting room have various problems. Using health-related vocabulary and ideas from pages 308–309 of your text, tell what is wrong with each person.

EXEMPLE   *Cet homme a mal au dos.*

1.  _____

2.  _____

3.  _____

4. _____

5. _____

6. _____

7. _____

B On fait du sport. Using vocabulary from the **Point de départ,** complete the following statements so that each describes the drawing beside it.

EXEMPLE Stéphanie et ses amies veulent *jouer au tennis.*

1. Mon fils apprend à _____.

2. Tous les matins, ma mère aime _____.

3. Mon ami et moi, nous _____ trois fois par semaine.

4. Hier je suis allé à la montagne et j(e) _____.

5. Quand allez-vous _____?

6. Le dimanche, mes parents aiment _____.

7. En été, nous aimons bien _____.

8. En ce moment, ma petite sœur fait un stage pour apprendre à _____.

9. Moi, je _____ depuis cinq ans.

10. Pendant les dernières vacances, mon frère _____.

⊙ Sportif(-ive) ou pro du canapé? Answer the following questions to find out if you tend to be the athletic type or the couch potato type.

1. Aimes-tu faire du sport?

_____

2. Si oui, quel(s) sport(s) pratiques-tu?

_____

3. Préfères-tu les sports d'équipe ou les sports individuels?

_____

4. Fais-tu régulièrement de l'exercice?

_____

5. Si oui, combien de fois par semaine fais-tu de l'exercice?

_____

6. Est-ce que tu regardes souvent des reportages sportifs à la télévision?

_____

7. Si oui, quel(s) sport(s) regardes-tu?

_____

8. Préfères-tu pratiquer une activité sportive ou bien être bien installé(e) dans ton canapé pour regarder ce même sport à la télévision?

_____

L'infinitif et le présent des verbes réfléchis

Êtes-vous prêts? L'infinitif et le présent des verbes réfléchis

Indicate on a scale of 1 (not comfortable) to 5 (very comfortable) how well you can handle each of the following tasks and place the number in the box provided. If you answer 1 to 3 for any of the tasks, you should go back and review the explanations and exercises in your textbook.

☐ Explain how reflexive verbs are different from nonreflexive verbs. Give the present tense forms of **se lever.**

☐ Explain how to make questions and negative statements using reflexive verbs

☐ List as many reflexive verbs as you can and tell what they mean in English.

☐ Use reflexive verbs and verbs you've learned previously to talk about what you do every day (e.g., I get up at 7:00; I get ready for school; I have my French class every day at 9:00).

☐ Use these verbs to ask others about their daily activities.

Ⓐ Narcissisme immodéré. Using the reflexive verbs provided, complete the following paragraph in which François Jemaime talks about his irresistible charms. Each verb is used only once.

Verbes à utiliser: **s'amuser, s'appeler, se coucher, se dépêcher, s'entendre, s'habiller, se laver, se lever, s'occuper, se peigner**

Je _____ François Jemaime. En général, je ne _____ pas tôt parce

que j'ai besoin de beaucoup de sommeil. Quand je _____ trop tard, je ne suis pas satisfait

de mon apparence le jour suivant et j'ai l'air fatigué. À mon avis, mes camarades de chambre ne

_____ pas assez de leur apparence. Moi, je _____ avec de l'eau bien

chaude et je _____ avec soin *(care)* parce que j'ai de jolis cheveux blonds que mes amis

adorent. Je _____ toujours avec beaucoup d'élégance. Souvent, je pars à neuf heures

moins cinq pour arriver en classe à neuf heures. C'est un peu juste, mais je ne _____ pas

parce que mes professeurs ne peuvent pas résister à mon charme. Mes professeurs et moi, nous

_____ très bien. Mes copains et moi, on _____ toujours bien quand

on sort ensemble. C'est pourquoi les autres étudiants sont souvent jaloux de moi: je suis irrésistible!

B Différences d'opinion. How do various people feel about the following aspects of daily life? Re-create their statements by giving the appropriate form of the infinitive.

1. se dépêcher tout le temps

Nous refusons de _____

Ils doivent _____

Tu n'as pas envie de _____

2. se lever tôt

J'ai besoin de _____

Nous n'avons pas l'intention de _____

Mes amis ont décidé de _____

3. se brosser les dents après chaque repas

Nous n'avons pas le temps de _____

Il faut essayer de _____

J'ai l'habitude de _____

4. s'arrêter de manger de la glace

Hélène a décidé de _____

Vous allez essayer de _____

Tu as besoin de _____

5. s'entendre avec tout le monde

Nous voulons _____

Je fais de mon mieux pour _____

Jacques ne peut pas _____

C Correspondance. You are writing to a French friend to find out about her habits and interests. Write the questions you would ask in French to find out the following information.

> **EXEMPLE** Ask her at what time she wakes up each morning.
> ***À quelle heure est-ce que tu te réveilles chaque matin?***

Ask her . . .

1. at what time she goes to bed.

_____

2. if she gets up early or late on the weekend.

_____

3. if she generally gets along well with her professors.

_____

4. if she gets along well in her courses.

_____

5. if she always remembers to do her homework.

_____

6. where she and her friends go to have a good time.

_____

7. if she is interested in sports.

_____

Le passé composé des verbes réfléchis

Êtes-vous prêts? Le passé composé des verbes réfléchis

Indicate on a scale of 1 (not comfortable) to 5 (very comfortable) how well you can handle each of the following tasks and place the number in the box provided. If you answer 1 to 3 for any of the tasks, you should go back and review the explanations and exercises in your textbook.

☐ What auxiliary verb do reflexive verbs use in the **passé composé**? How does the past participle change? Give the past tense forms of **se laver.**

☐ Where does **ne... pas** go in negative constructions?

☐ Use reflexive verbs and verbs you've learned previously to talk about what you and others did yesterday, last week, and so on (e.g., I got up at 7 o'clock; I got ready for school; my friends and I ate lunch together).

☐ Use these verbs to ask others about their activities yesterday, last week, and so on.

A Vous avez l'air fatigué. Hélène and a group of friends are talking about why they all look tired. Using the words and phrases provided and following the example, re-create their statements.

> **EXEMPLE** je / se coucher / très tard
> *Je me suis couché(e) très tard.*

1. Élise / se dépêcher / pour arriver / travail

_____

2. Marianne et Claude / bien s'amuser pendant le week-end

_____

3. Jacques / ne pas se peigner

_____

4. et toi, Anne, / tu / s'occuper / enfants de ta sœur hier soir?

_____

5. mes amis et moi, nous / ne pas se souvenir / examen

_____

6. Annette et Jeanne, vous / se coucher assez tôt? (use inversion)

_____

7. tout le monde / se retrouver / café

_____

8. nous / se réveiller tard

_____

B Le trimestre dernier. Using the words and phrases provided, create sentences telling what you and your friends did last term.

> **EXEMPLE** s'occuper d'un groupe d'enfants
> *Je me suis occupé(e) d'un groupe d'enfants.*
> *Mes amis et moi, nous nous sommes occupés d'un groupe d'enfants chaque samedi.*

1. s'amuser bien pendant les week-ends

_____

_____

2. faire du jogging

_____

_____

3. s'entendre bien avec ses professeurs

_____

_____

4. se lever tôt chaque jour

_____

_____

5. avoir des cours difficiles

_____

_____

6. s'intéresser beaucoup à ses cours

_____

_____

7. se débrouiller pour avoir de bonnes notes

_____

_____

8. se détendre un peu chaque soir

_____

_____

Ⓒ Ce matin. The drawings here show what Paul Vincent did this morning. Using the **passé composé** and vocabulary you know, write a sentence that describes each activity. Note that you will use both reflexive and nonreflexive verbs.

1. _____

2. _____

3. _____

4. _____

5. _____

6. _____

7. _____

8. _____

9. _____

10. _____

L'impératif des verbes réfléchis

> ### Êtes-vous prêts? L'impératif des verbes réfléchis
>
> Indicate on a scale of 1 (not comfortable) to 5 (very comfortable) how well you can handle each of the following tasks and place the number in the box provided. If you answer 1 to 3 for any of the tasks, you should go back and review the explanations and exercises in your textbook.
>
> ☐ What does the imperative mean? How is the imperative formed with regular verbs and with reflexive verbs?
>
> ☐ What happens to the reflexive pronoun in affirmative sentences? in negative sentences? when the **tu** form of the verb is used?
>
> ☐ Use reflexive and nonreflexive verbs to give others advice; for example, tell what people should do to stay in good health (go to bed early), what students should do to do well in school (study hard; don't go to bed too late, etc.).

Ⓐ Réponses. Pierre is asking his doctor what he needs to do to be in better physical shape. Using the appropriate imperative form of the reflexive verbs used and the cues in parentheses, give the doctor's answers.

> **EXEMPLE** Est-ce que je dois me reposer un peu? (oui)
> *Oui, reposez-vous un peu.*

1. Est-ce que je dois m'occuper de ma santé? (oui)

_____

2. Quand est-ce que je dois me coucher? (à 10h30)

_____

3. Est-ce que je dois me lever tôt tous les jours? (non)

_____

4. Est-ce que je dois m'arrêter de boire du café? (oui)

_____

5. Est-ce que je dois me souvenir de vos conseils? (oui)

_____

6. Est-ce que je dois me reposer après mon travail? (oui)

_____

B Oui ou non? Marianne is telling her friends Véronique and Gilles what she does not feel like doing. Véronique always agrees with what Marianne says; Gilles always disagrees. Give their reactions to Marianne's statements.

> **EXEMPLE**   Je n'ai pas envie de me lever.
> VÉRONIQUE: *Eh bien, si tu n'as pas envie de te lever, ne te lève pas!*
> GILLES: *C'est bien dommage, mais lève-toi quand même.*

1. Je n'ai pas envie d'aller à la bibliothèque.

VÉRONIQUE: _____

GILLES: _____

2. Je n'ai pas envie de me brosser les dents.

VÉRONIQUE: _____

GILLES: _____

3. Je n'ai pas envie d'être patiente.

VÉRONIQUE: _____

GILLES: _____

4. Je n'ai pas envie d'attendre mes amis.

VÉRONIQUE: _____

GILLES: _____

5. Je n'ai pas envie de m'arrêter à la boulangerie ce matin.

VÉRONIQUE: _____

GILLES: _____

6. Je n'ai pas envie de me dépêcher.

VÉRONIQUE: _____

GILLES: _____

Intégration et perspectives

ⓐ Chez nous en France: Destination les Alpes. Gilles, whose family owns and manages **le Relais des Alpes,** a small **hôtel-restaurant** in Lanslebourg-Val Cenis, one of the towns that line **la vallée de la Maurienne** in the center of the Alps, talks about the geography and the attractions of his region. Before you read, locate Lanslebourg on the map at the front of this book.

Lanslebourg-Val Cenis, la petite ville où j'ai grandi et où nous avons notre petit hôtel-restaurant, est située dans la vallée de la Haute Maurienne, en plein coeur des Alpes. En été, nos clients sont surtout des randonneurs *(hikers)* et des alpinistes *(mountain climbers)*. Il y a aussi des gens qui viennent simplement chercher ici le repos et le calme. Ils peuvent se promener tranquillement dans les alpages *(mountain meadows)* ou le long de la rivière, aller découvrir des chalets de montagne où on peut manger des fromages faits sur place ou bien monter jusqu'au village médiéval de l'Écot. Et pour les amateurs de sensations fortes, il y a les VTT *(vélos tout-terrain)*, le canyoning et le parapente *(paragliding)*!

En hiver, notre région est idéale pour tous les sports de neige. Vous avez ici le choix entre le ski alpin *(downhill skiing)*, le ski nordique *(cross-country skiing)*, la randonnée à ski *(back-country skiing)*, le patinage sur glace, les raquettes *(snowshoes)*, et même l'escalade des cascades de glace *(ice climbing)* et les chiens de traîneaux *(sled dogs)*!

De Lanslebourg, on peut facilement accéder à l'Italie par le tunnel du Fréjus, ou en été, par le col *(mountain pass)* du Mont Cenis à 2 081 mètres d'altitude. De l'autre côté de la vallée, la route du Col de l'Iseran donne accès à la vallée de l'Isère et à la célèbre station de ski de Val d'Isère. Cette route qui monte jusqu'à 2 764 mètres, est ouverte seulement quelques mois de l'année. Elle fait partie de la spectaculaire (et quelquefois terrifiante) Route des Grandes Alpes et c'est aussi une des plus dures et plus périlleuses étapes du Tour de France. Entre ces deux vallées se trouve le grand parc national de la Vanoise, paradis des alpinistes, des randonneurs et des amoureux de la nature qui sont charmés par la beauté des paysages et la richesse exceptionnelle de la faune et de la flore.

Alors, je suis sûr que maintenant vous comprenez pourquoi c'est ici que j'ai choisi de passer le reste de ma vie!

Avez-vous compris? A travel agent has asked you to briefly describe in English different aspects of the Lanslebourg area. Give the information requested in the space provided.

Location	
Summer activities and sports	
Winter activities and sports	
Parc national de la Vanoise	

Ⓑ À vous de lire: Le canyoning. You and several American friends have decided to go canyoning in the south of France. Because you know French, you looked on the Internet and found the following advertisement for a trip to the French **Alpes Maritimes.** You want to send essential information about the trip to your friends in an e-mail. Read the ad, and then fill out the form in the **Avez-vous compris?** section.

Stage canyoning 5 jours
Alpes Maritimes – 06
Eaux-Vives
À partir de 340 €
Les plus beaux canyons du sud-est de la France

Durée: 5 jours

Activité:

Partez à la découverte des plus beaux canyons des Alpes Maritimes.
Ce stage est destiné à tous les passionnés de sport et de nature qui désirent pratiquer une activité ludique et passionnante: le canyoning.

Vous découvrirez ainsi de façon exceptionnelle les paysages insolites et de toute beauté que cachent les cours d'eau de montagne des Alpes d'Azur…
Sensations garanties avec la pratique des toboggans naturels, des sauts, rappels sur corde et nage en eau vive…

Niveau du stage:

Stage évolutif à partir du niveau 1 à 5.

IMPORTANT: En fonction des conditions météorologiques et du niveau d'eau des rivières, certains canyons pourront être remplacés par d'autres offrant un intérêt équivalent. Sachez qu'il y a plus de 200 canyons praticables dans les Alpes du Sud!

Équipement à prévoir:

Maillot de bain, chaussures de sport pour marcher dans l'eau, gants de vélo.
Pour le retour: des affaires de rechange, pique-nique.
Prévoir une collation (pique-nique léger, barres énergétiques, fruits secs, etc…, 1 bouteille d'eau).

Équipement fourni:

Combinaisons néoprènes, casques, baudriers avec longe de sécurité, sacs, bidons étanches…

Encadrement:

Guides brevetés d'État possédant la qualification professionnelle "Canyon".

Le prix ne comprend pas:

L'hébergement (liste d'hébergement à disposition).

Dates:

Tous les jours du 1ᵉʳ avril au 31 octobre

Avez-vous compris? You have decided to send out the following form about each trip in your e-mail. Fill out the highlights of each part of the trip as indicated here.

Canyoning

Cost _____

Length of the trip _____

Location _____

_____

Equipment to bring _____

Special conditions _____

Dates _____

Ⓒ À vous d'écrire: Les Américains et le sport. A French friend has asked you to explain how Americans feel about sports, which sports are the most popular, and why. The questions that follow will help you organize your ideas into a composition of 125–150 words.

1. Préparation

Using the following questions as a guide, first jot down in French the information you want to include, then think about how you want to organize your description with a clear beginning, middle, and end.

- Quels sont les sports préférés de la plupart des Américains?
- Pourquoi les Américains s'intéressent-ils particulièrement à ces sports?
- À quel(s) sport(s) les Américains ne s'intéressent-ils pas?
- Quels sports peut-on pratiquer pour se détendre? être en forme? s'amuser? rencontrer des amis?
- Quelle importance le sport a-t-il dans les universités américaines? Quels sont les sports les plus populaires sur les campus américains?
- Quels sports les Américains regardent-ils à la télé, et quels sports préfèrent-ils pratiquer eux-mêmes?
- Qui sont les athlètes que les Américains admirent beaucoup (ou qu'ils n'admirent pas beaucoup)? Pourquoi?

2. Brouillon

Use these ideas and vocabulary you know to write your ideas about the importance of sports in American life. Write this first draft on a separate sheet of paper. Make sure you begin with a few sentences that will draw readers into your description. Be sure also that you don't simply stop at the end. Add a sentence or two that will bring your description to a close.

3. Révision

Now that you have finished writing your first draft, read through what you have written and check the following.

- Did you answer all the questions listed in the **Préparation** section?
- Did you discuss a variety of sports, and did you use **jouer à** and **faire de** appropriately with the names of sports?
- Did you use the correct forms of the reflexive verbs?
- Did you find an interesting way to begin and end your description? If not, go back to see if you can improve your introduction and/or your conclusion.

4. Rédaction

Write the final draft of your description in the space provided. Make the corrections and insert the additions you noted in step #3. Then reread your description to be sure you are satisfied with it.

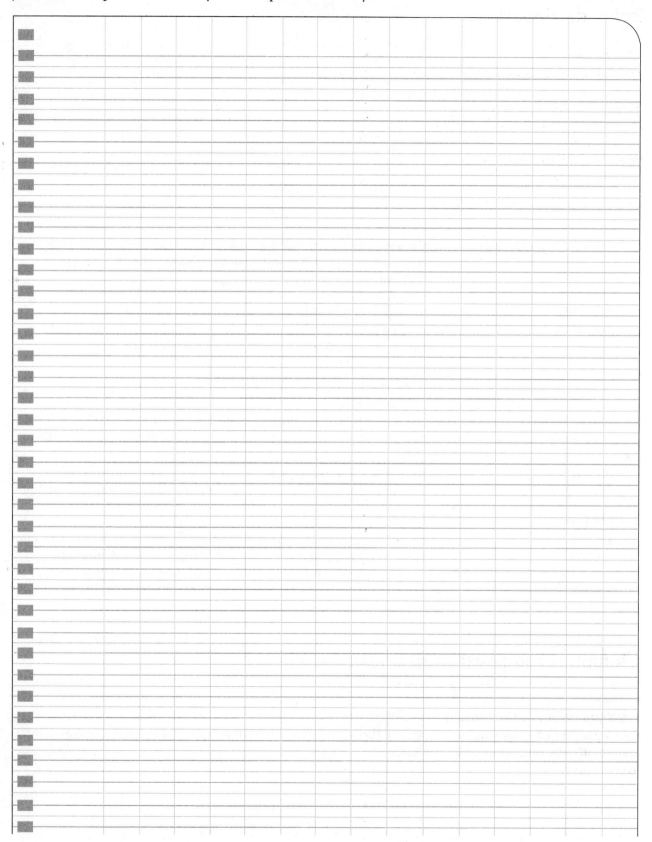

PARTIE ORALE

Point de départ

CD4, Track 19

11.1 Projets de vacances. Élise and Gilles Clébert are discussing where they might go during their vacation. Based on the information below, decide whether each of the statements Élise and Gilles make is **vrai** or **faux** and mark the appropriate column. You will hear each item twice.

EXEMPLE   You hear: On peut faire du ski nautique à Cros-de-Cagnes.

You mark: *vrai*

	vrai	faux
1.		
2.		
3.		
4.		
5.		
6.		

Sports de plein air

LA COTE	Piscine	Plongée sous-marine	Ski nautique	Voile	Tennis	Équitation	Sentiers de promenade	Golf et nombre de trous
Agay	–	–	✔	✔	✔	–	–	
Aiguebelle	✔							
Anthéor	–							
Antibes	✔	✔	✔	✔	✔			
Ayguade-Ceinturon	–	–	✔					
Bandol		✔	–		✔			
Beaulieu-sur-Mer	–	✔	✔	✔	✔		✔	
Beausoleil					✔			✔ 18
Beauvallon				–	✔	✔	–	✔ 19
Bendor (Ile de)			✔	✔				
Boulouris			✔	✔	✔			
Cannes	✔	✔	✔	✔		✔		
Cap d'Ail	–	–	–					
Cap d'Antibes			✔		✔			
Carqueiranne		✔			✔			
Cassis		✔	✔	✔	✔	✔	✔	
Cavalaire-sur-Mer		–	✔	✔	✔	✔	✔	
Cavalière		–			✔			
Ciotat (La)		–	✔	✔	✔	✔		
Croix-Valmer (La)		✔		✔	✔			
Cros-de-Cagnes	–	✔	✔	✔				
Èze-Bord-de-Mer		–			✔			
Fréjus-Plage		✔	✔		–		✔	
Garonne (La)						–	✔	

L'infinitif et le présent des verbes réfléchis

CD4, Track 20

*11.2 Situation: Chez le médecin. (p. 318) Monsieur Verdier doesn't feel good. Listen to his conversation with Dr. Dupas. You will hear the conversation twice. Listen the first time as you hear it read, paying attention to intonation, tone, and pronunciation. During the second reading, repeat each line of the conversation after it is read to you.

CD4, Track 21

*11.3 C'est l'heure! (p. 318 A) At what time do these students usually get up to go to the university?

EXEMPLE You hear: Paul
You say: ***Paul se lève à six heures et demie.***

1.

2.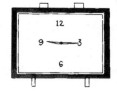

3.

4.

5.

6.

CD4, Track 22

*11.4 Couche-tôt ou couche-tard? (p. 320 C) Some people like to get up early, but other people don't. Use the suggestions you hear to describe each person's situation.

EXEMPLE You hear: Marc n'aime pas…
You say: ***Marc n'aime pas se lever tôt.***

CD4, Track 23

11.5 Problèmes. Some people are talking about the problems they are having. Jot down in English what each person says. You will hear each item twice.

EXEMPLE You hear: Ma grand-mère ne fait pas assez attention à sa santé. Elle ne mange pas bien et elle ne prend pas ses médicaments.
You jot down: *doesn't take care of her health; doesn't eat well or take medicine*

1. mes enfants: _____

2. mes parents et moi: _____

3. notre fille: _____

4. moi: _____

5. mes enfants: _____

Le passé composé des verbes réfléchis

CD4, Track 24

*11.6 Situation: Une histoire d'amour. (p. 323) Claude and Jocelyne just got married. Listen to Claude's conversation with his cousin Nathalie. You will hear the conversation twice. Listen the first time as you hear it read, paying attention to intonation, tone, and pronunciation. During the second reading, repeat each line of the conversation after it is read to you.

CD4, Track 25

*11.7 On va faire une cure à Évian. (p. 324 B) There are lots of things to do when you're leaving on vacation. Tell what the members of the Bertrand family did on the morning they left.

> **EXEMPLE** You hear: nous / se réveiller à 5 heures
> You say: ***Nous nous sommes réveillés à cinq heures.***

CD4, Track 26

*11.8 Au club de gymnastique. (p. 324 C) One of your friends works in a health club. She talks about what she did yesterday.

> **EXEMPLE** You hear: se lever très tôt
> You say: ***Je me suis levée très tôt.***

CD4, Track 27

11.9 Maman et papa se font du souci. André's parents tend to worry about him while he is away at the university, and so they often call to find out how he is. Decide whether they will be happy with what André says about his recent activities and check the appropriate boxes. You will hear each item twice.

> **EXEMPLE** You hear: Je me suis réveillé tard le jour de mon examen de maths.
> You check: ***non***

	oui	non			oui	non
1.	☐	☐		4.	☐	☐
2.	☐	☐		5.	☐	☐
3.	☐	☐				

L'impératif des verbes réfléchis

CD4, Track 28

*11.10 Situation: Allez, vite, lève-toi! (p. 326) It's seven in the morning. Stéphanie is still sleepy and wants to stay in bed a little longer, but her mother doesn't feel sorry for her and tells her to get up right away. Listen to their conversation. You will hear the conversation twice. Listen the first time as you hear it read, paying attention to intonation, tone, and pronunciation. During the second reading, repeat each line of the conversation after it is read to you.

CD4, Track 29

*11.11 Les jolies colonies de vacances. (p. 327 A) This summer, Gilbert is a camp counselor. The children don't feel like getting ready. What does he tell them?

> **EXEMPLE** You hear: se réveiller (à tout le monde)
> You say: *Réveillez-vous.*
>
> (à Julie)
> You say: *Réveille-toi.*

CD4, Track 30

*11.12 Comment vivre jusqu'à cent ans. (p. 327 B) Josette Lebrun is going to be 100 years old soon, and she is giving her recipe for a long life. What are her suggestions? (Note that some verbs you hear are not reflexive.)

> **EXEMPLE** You hear: se coucher tôt
> You say: *Couchez-vous tôt.*
>
> You hear: prendre le temps de s'amuser
> You say: *Prenez le temps de vous amuser.*

CD4, Track 31

11.13 Ordres. Monsieur Grandjean likes to tell people what to do. For each situation he describes, choose the command you hear that best completes his thought and circle the appropriate letter. You will hear each item twice.

> **EXEMPLE** You hear: Tu vas être en retard.
> **a.** Dépêche-toi! **b.** Ne te marie pas! **c.** Amuse-toi bien!
> You circle: *a*

1. a   b   c   **3.** a   b   c   **5.** a   b   c

2. a   b   c   **4.** a   b   c   **6.** a   b   c

Intégration et perspectives

CD4, Track 32

11.14 Chez le médecin. Listen to the conversation that takes place as Monsieur Vincent is examined by his doctor. Then answer the following questions in English. You will hear the conversation twice.

1. What problem does Monsieur Vincent have in the morning? at noon? and in the evening?

_____

_____

2. Name two pieces of advice the doctor gives him for these complaints.

_____

_____

3. Why does Monsieur Vincent have trouble sleeping?

_____

_____

4. What time does he get up in the morning?

_____

5. Where does Monsieur Vincent work?

_____

_____

CD4, Track 33

11.15 Recommandations. After Olivier's checkup, his doctor dictates a letter to him. During the pauses provided, write what the doctor says. Each sentence will be read twice, then the entire passage will be read once again so that you can check your work.

1. _____

2. _____

3. _____

4. _____

CD4, Track 34

*11.16 Bien prononcer. (p. 338)

Some consonant sounds are pronounced differently in French and in English. In particular, /p/, /t/, /k/ are not "exploded" or released with the same force as in English, especially at the beginning of a word. Compare the pronunciation of these English and French cognates.

The French pronunciation of these consonants is closer to their pronunciation in English when they follow an *s*. (Compare, for instance, these English words: *pair / spare; top / stop; kit / skit.*) Now practice repeating French words containing these sounds.

CD4, Track 35

*11.17 Petite conversation. Practice repeating the following conversation.

Chapitre douze ○ ○ ○ ○ ○ ○

Le passé et les souvenirs ⑫

PARTIE ÉCRITE

Point de départ

🅐 **Les sentiments et les rapports avec les autres.** Using vocabulary and structures from the **Point de départ** and other vocabulary you know, write three or four sentences that fit under each of the following categories.

> **EXEMPLE** les hauts de la vie quotidienne
> ***On s'amuse. On est de bonne humeur.***

la mauvaise entente

_____

_____

_____

la tristesse

_____

_____

_____

l'amitié et l'amour

_____

_____

_____

le plaisir et le bonheur

_____

_____

_____

B **La vie et les sentiments.** Using vocabulary from the **Point de départ** and other words you know, describe what is going on in each drawing and what the people shown are probably feeling.

EXEMPLE   *Elle est triste parce que son ami vient de partir. Elle a envie de pleurer.*

1. _____

_____

_____

2. _____

_____

_____

3. _____

_____

_____

4. _____

_____

_____

5. _____

_____

_____

C **Les étapes de la vie.** Each stage of life is characterized by certain joys, concerns, problems, and activities. Analyze the positive and negative aspects of the following stages of life.

EXEMPLE   l'enfance   *Quand on est enfant, on s'intéresse à tout. On a toujours envie de s'amuser. Mais les parents ne permettent pas toujours à leurs enfants de faire ce qu'ils veulent.*

1. l'enfance _____

_____

2. l'adolescence _____

_____

3. l'âge adulte _____

_____

4. la vieillesse _____

_____

L'imparfait et le passé composé

Êtes-vous prêts? L'imparfait et le passé composé

Indicate on a scale of 1 (not comfortable) to 5 (very comfortable) how well you can handle each of the following tasks and place the number in the box provided. If you answer 1 to 3 for any of the tasks, you should go back and review the explanations and exercises in your textbook.

- [ ] Explain how to form the imperfect.
- [ ] Contrast the uses of the imperfect and the **passé composé.**
- [ ] Use the imperfect and the **passé composé** appropriately to talk about things you and others used to do at various times in your lives.
- [ ] Use the imperfect and the **passé composé** appropriately to describe an event that took place in the past.
- [ ] Use the imperfect and the **passé composé** appropriately to describe the lives of well-known people or people that you or others know.

A **Souvenirs.** Claudine is reminiscing about her childhood on a farm. Complete her story by giving the appropriate form of the imperfect for the verbs in parentheses.

Quand j' _____ (**être**) petite, nous _____ (**habiter**) dans une ferme qui

_____ (**se trouver**) à quelques kilomètres d'un petit village. C'_____ (**être**) un tout

petit village où il n'y _____ (**avoir**) pas beaucoup d'habitants. Mon père _____ (**être**)

assez satisfait de cette situation mais ma mère _____ (**s'ennuyer,** *to get bored*) un peu. Mon frère

et moi, nous _____ (**être**) très contents et nous _____ (**s'amuser**) beaucoup. Moi,

j'_____ (**adorer**) l'été. Le matin j'_____ (**aider**) maman dans la maison et l'après-

midi, mon père nous _____ (**emmener**) travailler dans les champs *(fields)*. Le dimanche, nous

_____ (**aller**) à la messe *(mass)* le matin et l'après-midi, nous _____ (**faire**) souvent un pique-nique au bord de la rivière. Mon père _____ (**choisir**) toujours un endroit agréable. Après le déjeuner, mon frère et moi, nous _____ (**pouvoir**) jouer dans l'eau pendant que mes parents _____ (**se reposer**). Maintenant, j'habite dans une grande ville et je regrette beaucoup notre petit village tranquille.

B Interruptions. Some people are talking about what they were doing when they were interrupted by someone or something else. Using the example as a guide, tell what they say.

> **EXEMPLE** les enfants / jouer / leurs grands-parents / arriver
> *Les enfants jouaient quand leurs grands-parents sont arrivés.*

1. Martine / laver la voiture / il / commencer à pleuvoir

_____

2. nous / regarder des DVD / des amis / venir nous rendre visite

_____

3. je / aller à Dijon / la voiture / tomber en panne

_____

4. papa / finir de préparer le dîner / maman / rentrer à la maison

_____

5. Jeanne et Sabine / être au centre commercial / Sabine / perdre son sac à main

_____

6. tout le monde / chercher notre chien égaré *(lost)* / Jacques / le trouver au sous-sol

_____

7. moi, je / se reposer / des amis / téléphoner

_____

C Un mauvais souvenir. André Moreau is talking about a bad day he remembers all too well. Complete his story by filling in the blanks with the appropriate forms of the imperfect or the **passé composé**.

C'était le jour où j'allais partir en vacances, je _____ (**se réveiller**) trop tard. En plus de cela, il _____ (**faire**) mauvais. Le ciel _____ (**être**) couvert et il _____ (**pleuvoir**). Plus tard on _____ (**annoncer**) à la radio qu'il _____ (**aller**) neiger. Ça _____ (**commencer**) bien! J(e) _____ (**décider**) de me préparer et j(e) _____ (**faire**) mes valises. J(e) _____ (**essayer**) de téléphoner pour appeler un taxi, mais toutes les lignes _____ (**être**) occupées. Finalement, après une demi-heure d'attente, j(e) _____ (**pouvoir**) trouver un taxi. Le chauffeur de taxi _____ (**ne pas être**) prudent et j(e) _____ (**avoir**) très peur d'avoir un accident. Heureusement, nous

_____ (**avoir**) de la chance et nous _____ (**arriver**) à l'aéroport sans

incident. Quand j(e) _____ (**finalement trouver**) le guichet (*ticket counter*), il y

_____ (**avoir**) déjà cinquante autres personnes qui _____ (**attendre**)

pour acheter leur billet. Pendant que j(e) _____ (**attendre**), j(e) _____

(**faire**) la connaissance d'un autre voyageur qui _____ (**aller**) aussi à Rome. Nous

_____ (**décider**) de voyager ensemble. Finalement, notre tour (*m*) (*turn*)

_____ (**arriver**) et nous _____ (**acheter**) nos billets. Mais à ce moment-là,

un employé nous _____ (**expliquer**) que nous _____ (**ne pas pouvoir**)

partir parce que les pilotes _____ (**venir de***) décider de faire la grève.

*When **venir de** is used in the sense of *to have just,* only the imperfect can be used to express a past action.

D Un souvenir. Describe a first day of school you remember well (the first day of kindergarten, first grade, high school, college, etc.). Tell what the weather was like, what you were wearing, what happened, what the teachers were like, where you went, what you ate, and so on. Be sure to use the appropriate forms of the **imparfait** or the **passé composé** as required by the context of your story.

Les pronoms *y* et *en*

Êtes-vous prêts? Les pronoms *y* et *en*

Indicate on a scale of 1 (not comfortable) to 5 (very comfortable) how well you can handle each of the following tasks and place the number in the box provided. If you answer 1 to 3 for any of the tasks, you should go back and review the explanations and exercises in your textbook.

☐ Tell what the pronouns **y** and **en** mean in English and what they replace in a sentence.

☐ Tell which pronoun should be used in these sentences and why: **Je pense à mon ami. Je pense à mes problèmes. Je réponds à la lettre. Je réponds au professeur. Qu'est-ce que tu penses de mon cousin? Qu'est-ce que tu penses de ce livre?**

A Tout change. Several people are talking about things that are now different. Following the examples, re-create their statements.

EXEMPLES Autrefois, nous allions en vacances en Suisse.
Mais maintenant, ***nous y allons rarement.***

Mais l'année dernière, ***nous n'y sommes pas allés.***

Mais l'année prochaine, ***nous n'allons pas y aller.***

1. L'année dernière, Paul a travaillé dans un restaurant.

Mais l'année prochaine, _____.

2. Autrefois, tu allais chez tes parents tous les dimanches.

Mais l'année dernière, _____.

3. Le trimestre dernier, j'ai passé tout mon temps à la bibliothèque.

Mais maintenant, _____.

4. Il y a deux ans, nous sommes restés à l'Hôtel du Mont Blanc.

Mais l'été prochain, _____.

5. Autrefois, je pensais tout le temps à mes problèmes.

Mais maintenant, _____.

B Nous sommes tous dans la même situation. Several friends have decided that they have many of the same problems. Following the example, re-create their statements.

EXEMPLE Le mois dernier, nous avons eu beaucoup de visites. Et vous?
Nous en avons eu beaucoup aussi.

1. L'année dernière, vous aviez beaucoup de problèmes financiers. Et Paul?

_____

2. Vos amis ont eu des difficultés pendant leur voyage à l'étranger. Et vous?

_____

3. La semaine dernière, les étudiants ont eu un peu trop de travail. Et les professeurs?

_____

4. Paul a bu trop de bière vendredi soir. Et les autres invités?

_____

5. Sylviane a plusieurs camarades de chambre. Et toi?

_____

6. Autrefois, il y avait beaucoup de gens pauvres en France. Et aux États-Unis?

_____

7. J'ai beaucoup de problèmes en ce moment. Et Nadine?

_____

8. La plupart des étudiants ont un cours de maths chaque jour. Et toi?

_____

G Activités et intérêts. A French friend wants to know what American college students are like. Using **y** or **en** and the cues provided, describe yourself or people you know. Vary your statements as much as possible.

> **EXEMPLES** aller à la plage
> ***Autrefois, j'y allais souvent.***
>
> avoir du temps libre
> ***Malheureusement, nous n'en avons pas beaucoup.***

1. penser aux problèmes sociaux

_____

2. aller au cinéma

_____

3. avoir beaucoup d'examens

_____

4. prendre des vacances

_____

5. se souvenir de mon premier jour à l'école élémentaire

_____

6. penser à mes années au lycée

_____

La négation

Êtes-vous prêts? La négation

Indicate on a scale of 1 (not comfortable) to 5 (very comfortable) how well you can handle each of the following tasks and place the number in the box provided. If you answer 1 to 3 for any of the tasks, you should go back and review the explanations and exercises in your textbook.

☐ List the negative expressions you've learned and give their English equivalents.

☐ Explain where negative expressions are placed in a sentence in the present tense and in the **passé composé.**

☐ Use negative expressions to tell what you and other people never or no longer do, what no one does, and so forth.

☐ Complain about various topics and activities using negative expressions.

Ⓐ Le choc du futur! Pierre Vieujeu is concerned about the rapid changes taking place in society. Using the cues provided, re-create his complaints. Be sure to use both parts of the negative expression in each sentence.

> **EXEMPLE**   les gens / plus / avoir envie / aider les autres
> *Les gens n'ont plus envie d'aider les autres.*

1. rien / simple / de nos jours

_____

2. pour beaucoup / jeunes / mariage / avoir / plus / importance

_____

3. jeunes / plus / respecter / parents

_____

4. personne / vouloir / avoir / enfants

_____

5. jeunes / rien / vouloir / faire

_____

6. on / jamais / penser / avenir

_____

7. la famille / plus / être / importante

_____

B **Différences d'opinion.** Jean-Paul, who has an optimistic outlook, is talking with his more pessimistic friend Roger. Following the example and using the appropriate negative expressions, re-create Roger's comments.

> **EXEMPLE**   Tout est simple dans la vie.
> ***Rien n'est simple dans la vie.***

1. Tout le monde est content de nos jours.

_____

2. On peut toujours changer son attitude.

_____

3. On peut encore espérer que les choses vont s'arranger.

_____

4. On peut tout contrôler.

_____

5. Tout marche bien dans notre pays.

_____

6. Tout le monde m'aide quand j'ai des problèmes.

_____

7. Notre société a toujours respecté tout le monde.

_____

8. J'ai toujours tout compris.

_____

C **Personne, rien, jamais.** You are in a particularly bad mood today. Using negative expressions and vocabulary you know, write at least six sentences in which you complain about people, events, and so on in your life. Vary your sentences as much as possible. Your complaints can be real or imagined.

> **EXEMPLE**   *J'ai envie de sortir avec mes amis ce soir, mais personne n'est libre.*

Intégration et perspectives

Ⓐ Chez nous en France: Destination la Lorraine. In the text that follows, Damien evokes the painful history of his region plagued by war no fewer than three times in the course of a century, the attachment of its inhabitants to their land and identity, and their pride in its being the birthplace of the great French heroine Joan of Arc. Before you read, locate **la Lorraine** on the map at the front of this book.

La région d'où je viens est une région lourdement marquée par l'histoire… En moins d'un siècle, nous avons non seulement connu *(experienced)* trois guerres, comme le reste de la France, mais notre situation géographique nous a placés au cœur même des combats. Notre identité elle-même a été menacée car *(because)* pendant plus de quarante ans nous avons été privés *(deprived of)* de notre nationalité française! Après la guerre de 1870, la France a dû céder la Lorraine et l'Alsace à la Prusse. Ces deux provinces ont été annexées par l'Allemagne et on nous a imposé la nationalité et la langue allemandes. C'est seulement après la Première Guerre mondiale de 1914–18 et la victoire des alliés que la Lorraine et l'Alsace sont redevenues françaises. Au cours de la Deuxième Guerre mondiale, la Lorraine et l'Alsace ont de nouveau été annexées par l'Allemagne et sont restées sous le contrôle allemand jusqu'à la Libération en 1944.

Ce passé tourmenté est largement dû au fait que notre région est située dans le nord-est de la France, près de la frontière avec l'Allemagne, le Luxembourg et la Belgique. C'est une région de collines *(hills)*, avec de nombreux lacs et étangs *(ponds)* et de belles forêts. C'est aussi une très importante région industrielle, surtout dans le domaine de la sidérurgie *(steel industry)* et des industries chimiques grâce à *(thanks to)* nos mines de fer *(iron ore)* et de sel.

Savez-vous aussi que c'est en Lorraine, dans le petit village de Domrémy, que Jeanne d'Arc, notre grande héroïne nationale, est née en 1412? C'est là, qu'à l'âge de 13 ans, elle a entendu les voix qui lui disaient de partir libérer la France ravagée par les Anglais. Quant au *(As for)* reste de son histoire, vous le connaissez probablement…

Avez-vous compris?

1. Pourquoi peut-on dire que la Lorraine est «une région qui a été lourdement marquée par l'histoire»?

_____

2. Pourquoi les Lorrains ont-ils perdu plusieurs fois leur nationalité française?

_____

3. Quelles sont les principales caractéristiques des paysages de cette région?

_____

4. Quelles sont les principales industries de cette région?

_____

5. Où et quand Jeanne d'Arc est-elle née?

_____

B À vous de lire: Jeanne d'Arc. You are doing research on Jeanne d'Arc in French and have come across the following entry on a French online encyclopedia at *asinah.net*. Although there may be vocabulary, dates, and historical references that you don't understand and can reference later, you should be able to find the information to the basic questions that are listed after each segment of text. There is also space for you to include additional information that you found interesting.

> Jeanne affirme avoir entendu des voix divines lui demandant de libérer la France de l'envahisseur et de ramener le Dauphin sur le trône. À 16 ans, elle se met en route. Arrivée à la ville voisine, elle demande à s'enrôler dans les troupes du Dauphin. Sa demande est rejetée, mais elle revient un an plus tard et est autorisée à voir le Dauphin Charles à Chinon. Portant des habits masculins (ce qu'elle fera jusqu'à sa mort), elle se rend à Chinon. L'anecdote raconte qu'elle est capable de reconnaître Charles, dissimulé parmi ses courtisans et lui parle de sa mission. Après l'avoir fait interroger par les autorités ecclésiastiques, Charles donne son accord sur son plan de libération d'Orléans assiégée.

1. Jeanne d'Arc heard voices; what did these voices tell her to do?

   _____

2. What happened when she asked to be in the **Dauphin**'s army?

   _____

3. What kind of clothing did she start wearing during this period of time?

   _____

> Ses frères la rejoignent, et on l'équipe d'une armure et d'une bannière blanche frappée de la fleur de lys. Avec sa foi, sa confiance et son enthousiasme, elle parvient à insuffler aux soldats français désespérés une énergie nouvelle, et à contraindre les Anglais à lever le siège de la ville en 1429. Après cette victoire célébrée chaque année le 9 mai, elle prend le nom de pucelle d'Orléans. Après une autre victoire remportée face aux Anglais, elle décide Charles à aller à Reims pour s'y faire sacrer roi de France. Le 17 juillet 1429, dans la cathédrale de Reims, en la présence de Jeanne d'Arc, Charles VII est couronné.

4. What was inscribed on her banner, and what name did she assume at this time?

   _____

5. What enabled her to energize the French troops?

   _____

6. What event took place in the cathedral in Reims on July 17, 1429?

   _____

> Dans la foulée, Jeanne tente de convaincre le roi de reprendre Paris aux Bourguignons, mais il hésite. Une attaque est menée par Jeanne sur Paris mais doit être rapidement abandonnée. Elle est capturée lors de la tentative de reprise de Compiègne le 23 mai 1430 par les Bourguignons. Elle essaye de s'échapper par deux fois mais elle échoue. Elle tombe ensuite entre les mains de Pierre Cauchon, évêque de Beauvais et allié des Anglais.

7. What happened to the plan to retake Paris?

_____

8. Who finally captured Jeanne d'Arc?

_____

> *Elle est accusée d'hérésie et soumise à la question à Rouen. Le procès débute le 21 février 1431. Des aveux sont finalement obtenus, dans lesquels Jeanne reconnaît avoir menti à propos des voix et admet l'autorité de l'Église. Cependant, elle se rétracte deux jours plus tard. Le 30 mai 1431, elle meurt brûlée vive sur le bûcher en criant «Jésus».*

9. Where did her trial take place, when did it start, and when was she put to death?

_____

> *Lorsque Charles reprit Rouen, un second procès, décrété par le pape Callixte III, cassa en 1456 le premier jugement. L'Église catholique canonisa Jeanne d'Arc le 16 mai 1920.*

10. What honor did the Catholic Church bestow upon Jeanne d'Arc in 1920?

_____

Other information:

_____

_____

_____

_____

Ⓒ À vous d'écrire: Rétrospective. Imagine that 20 years from now, you are reminiscing about what life was like when you were a student. You will want to touch on different topics to give your readers an idea of what student life was like back then.

1. Préparation

Use the following categories and the related questions as a guide, but make sure to include other ideas of your own; depending on the meaning you wish to convey, you will need either the **imparfait** or the **passé composé**. Note the line added for the title of your description; you may want to decide beforehand the title you want to use, or you might find it useful to write your description and then identify a title. Remember that a title is used for a variety of purposes: to give an overview, to pique the curiosity of the reader, or to pose a question or problem.

Titre: _____

- **Les étudiants:** Comment étaient les étudiants en général? Quelles sortes de cours avaient-ils? À quelles sortes d'activités pouvaient-ils participer pendant leur temps libre?
- **Vos amis:** Est-ce que vous aviez de bons amis? Que faisaient-ils dans la vie? Parmi vos amis ou connaissances *(acquaintances)* de cette époque-là, est-ce qu'il y a une personne qui vous a beaucoup influencé(e)? Comment?
- **Vos activités et vos intérêts:** Qu'est-ce que vous aimiez faire pour vous amuser quand vous sortiez avec vos amis?
- **Les événements:** Quels sont les événements importants qui ont marqué cette époque de votre vie? Décrivez quelques-uns de ces événements.
- **Vos réactions et vos sentiments:** Quels étaient vos sentiments et vos réactions vis-à-vis de la situation où vous vous trouviez—ou des événements qui se sont produits—à cette époque? Est-ce que vos sentiments ont changé depuis?

Vos idées:

2. Brouillon

Write your first draft on a separate sheet of paper. Remember to include as many of the categories from **Préparation** as you need to make your description interesting and evocative of that point in time. You should think about a length of approximately 200 words so that you can adequately describe the categories you are including in your paragraph(s). Don't forget to include a title that will attract the attention of your readers: **Que la vie était belle! Comme on s'amusait bien! Un petit retour dans le passé.**

3. Révision

Now that you have finished writing your first draft, read through what you have written and check the following.

- Did you include information from the categories given or from your selection of the categories?
- Did you use the imperfect and the **passé composé** correctly to convey different past-tense meanings?
- Did you find an interesting title for your work?
- Did you find an interesting way to start and end each description?

4. Rédaction

Write the final draft of your description in the space provided here. Make the corrections and insert the additions you noted in step #3. Then reread your description to be sure you are satisfied with it.

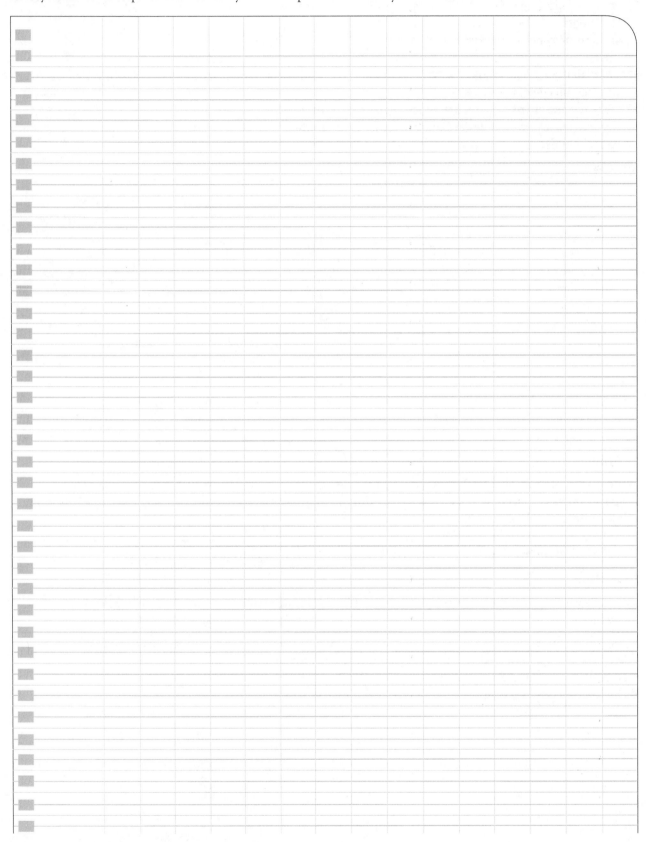

PARTIE ORALE

Point de départ

CD5, Track 2

12.1 Sentiments. Some people are talking about their lives or what has happened recently. As you listen, jot down what each person says in English, and then decide which emotion is being expressed by circling the word that best completes the description of the emotion. You will hear each item twice.

> **EXEMPLE**   You hear: Je n'ai pas de problèmes dans ma vie: je réussis bien dans mes études, et je m'entends bien avec mes parents. Tout va bien pour moi.
> You jot down: *no problems; doing well in school; gets along well with parents*
> You circle: Il éprouve… ***du bonheur***

1. _____
   Elle est…   **a.** surprise   **b.** inquiète   **c.** fière

2. _____
   Elle…   **a.** est contente   **b.** en a marre   **c.** est jalouse

3. _____
   Il…   **a.** est jaloux   **b.** a le cafard   **c.** a honte

4. _____
   Il éprouve…   **a.** de la tristesse **b.** de l'inquiétude **c.** du bonheur

L'imparfait et le passé composé

CD5, Track 3

*12.2 Situation: Je me souviens. (p. 350) Catherine Gagnon, a young woman from Quebec, is talking with her 90-year-old great-grandmother. They are discussing the past. Listen to their conversation. You will hear the conversation twice. Listen the first time as you hear it read, paying attention to intonation, tone, and pronunciation. During the second reading, repeat each line of the conversation after it is read to you.

CD5, Track 4

*12.3 Quand j'étais petit… (p. 351 A) During a visit to old Lyon, Monsieur Berger recalls some childhood memories. What does he say?

> **EXEMPLE**   You hear: je / jouer souvent dans cette rue
> You say: ***Je jouais souvent dans cette rue.***

CD5, Track 5

*12.4 Pourquoi? (p. 351 B) Bertrand always asks his friends for explanations. What do his friends answer?

> **EXEMPLE**   You hear: Pourquoi est-ce que tu as téléphoné à Mireille? (s'ennuyer)
> You say: ***J'ai téléphoné à Mireille parce que je m'ennuyais.***

CD5, Track 6

12.5 Souvenirs. André Fournier is telling his grandchildren what life was like when he was growing up. Decide whether each of his memories is **bon** or **mauvais** and mark the appropriate column. You will hear each item twice.

EXEMPLE   You hear: Mon grand-père nous racontait ses souvenirs de voyage. J'aimais bien ça.
You mark: *bon*

	bon	mauvais		bon	mauvais
1.	☐	☐	5.	☐	☐
2.	☐	☐	6.	☐	☐
3.	☐	☐	7.	☐	☐
4.	☐	☐	8	☐	☐

Les pronoms *y* et *en*

CD5, Track 7

*12.6 Situation: Souvenirs d'enfance. (p. 355) Catherine Gagnon continues her conversation with her great-grandmother. You will hear the conversation twice. Listen the first time as you hear it read, paying attention to intonation, tone, and pronunciation. During the second reading, repeat each line of the conversation after it is read to you.

CD5, Track 8

*12.7 Fêtes de famille. (p. 356 A) Your cousin wants to know who is going to different family celebrations that are taking place soon. What does he find out?

EXEMPLE   You hear: Est-ce que Serge va au mariage de Véronique? (oui)
You say: *Oui, il y va.*

CD5, Track 9

*12.8 À quoi pensez-vous? (p. 356 B) Who or what do you think about often?

EXEMPLES   You hear: vos études (oui)
You say: *Oui, j'y pense souvent.*

You hear: vos amis du lycée (oui)
You say: *Je pense souvent à eux.*

CD5, Track 10

*12.9 Habitudes et activités. (p. 357 D) Use the suggestions you hear to answer questions about your leisure activities and what you do to stay healthy. Don't forget to use **y** or **en** in your answers.

EXEMPLES   You hear: Est-ce que tu vas souvent au cinéma? (oui)
You say: *Oui, j'y vais souvent.*

You hear: Est-ce que tu bois souvent du café? (non, rarement)
You say: *Non, j'en bois rarement.*

CD5, Track 11

12.10 Discussion. Some people are talking about their lives. Listen carefully to each of their statements and decide if you hear either the pronoun **y** or the pronoun **en.** Check the appropriate box, and then write the words the pronoun refers to. You will hear each item twice.

EXEMPLE   You hear: Ma cousine m'a invité à lui rendre visite à Montréal, mais je ne peux pas y
aller parce que je n'ai pas assez de temps maintenant.
You check: *y*
You write: *à Montréal*

	y	en	
1.	☐	☐	_____
2.	☐	☐	_____
3.	☐	☐	_____
4.	☐	☐	_____
5.	☐	☐	_____
6.	☐	☐	_____
7.	☐	☐	_____
8.	☐	☐	_____

La négation

CD5, Track 12

*12.11 Situation: Il y a eu un cambriolage! (p. 359) When they got home from vacation, the Perrettis were surprised to discover that their house had been broken into. They are talking to their neighbors, the Darmons. Listen to their conversation. You will hear the conversation twice. Listen the first time as you hear it read, paying attention to intonation, tone, and pronunciation. During the second reading, repeat each line of the conversation after it is read to you.

CD5, Track 13

*12.12 Que la vie est cruelle! (p. 360 A) Jean feels abandoned and neglected by his friends. What does he answer when his friends ask him questions?

EXEMPLE   You hear: Est-ce que tes amis viennent souvent te voir? (non… jamais)
You say: ***Non, ils ne viennent jamais me voir.***

CD5, Track 14

*12.13 Mais non, ne t'inquiète pas. (p. 360 B) Bernadette is worried about her friend Christian and his family. Try to reassure her.

EXEMPLE   You hear: Tout le monde est malade en ce moment.
You say: ***Mais non, personne n'est malade.***

CD5, Track 15

12.14 Réactions. Jean-Pierre is talking about how he feels about fitness. Decide whether he is happy about the things he says and check the appropriate box. You will hear each item twice.

EXEMPLE   You hear: Je ne comprends pas les gens qui ne font jamais de sport.
           You check: *non*

	oui	non			oui	non
1.	☐	☐		4.	☐	☐
2.	☐	☐		5.	☐	☐
3.	☐	☐		6.	☐	☐

Intégration et perspectives

CD5, Track 16

12.15 Souvenirs. Listen as Moboudou Dialot talks about his life in Africa. Then answer these questions in English. You will hear the passage twice.

1. How is Moboudou's life different now from the way it was in the past?

_____

_____

2. Describe his family.

_____

_____

3. What are some of Moboudou's worries?

_____

_____

4. What did the villagers think of his grandfather? Why?

_____

_____

5. What did Moboudou's grandfather advise him to do?

_____

_____

6. Do Moboudou's relatives still live in the village?

_____

_____

CD5, Track 17

12. 16 Mauvais souvenirs. Georges is recalling a less-than-memorable vacation that he and his wife, Brigitte, took. Write what he says during the pauses provided. You will hear each line twice; then the entire passage will be read a third time so that you can check your work.

1. _____

2. _____

3. _____

4. _____

5. _____

CD5, Track 18

*12.17 Bien prononcer: Le système vocalique français (p. 370)

Vowels can be classified according to several criteria. Although there are several nasal vowels (/$\tilde{\epsilon}$/, /$\tilde{\oe}$/, /$\tilde{a}$/, /$\tilde{ɔ}$/), most French vowels are oral vowels, that is, air passes through the mouth only. Oral vowels can be differentiated according to the following characteristics.

- The **point of articulation** (i.e., the position of the tongue along the vocal tract). Front vowels (**voyelles antérieures**) are articulated near the front of the mouth; back vowels (**voyelles postérieures**) are articulated toward the back of the mouth. Repeat the following pairs of words, paying attention to the position of your tongue.

- The **degree of aperture** (i.e., how open the mouth is while pronouncing the vowel). The following three series of vowels go from most closed (**voyelles fermées**) to most open (**voyelles ouvertes**). Repeat these words, paying attention to your jaw opening progressively, as you move from closed vowels to open ones.

- The **shape of the lips.** The lips may be spread (**voyelles écartées**), as in **la vie,** or rounded (**voyelles arrondies**), as in **la vue.** Repeat the following pairs of words (that differ only by this one characteristic), paying close attention to the contrast in the shape of your lips.

CD5, Track 19

*12.18 Petite conversation. Practice repeating the following conversation.

Chapitre treize ○ ○ ○ ○ ○ ○ ○

Des goûts et des couleurs ⑬

PARTIE ÉCRITE

Point de départ

Ⓐ Faites vos valises. What types of clothing and other items would you pack for each of the following trips?

EXEMPLE un week-end au bord de la mer
un maillot de bain, des tee-shirts, un jean, un short et un sweat

1. un week-end de ski dans les Alpes

_____

_____

2. une semaine dans l'état d'Hawaï

_____

_____

3. une croisière *(a cruise)* élégante dans la mer des Caraïbes *(Caribbean)*

_____

_____

4. une semaine de camping

_____

_____

5. un week-end tranquille chez de bons amis

_____

_____

B Défilé de mode. You are the moderator at a style show. Using vocabulary from the **Point de départ** and colors and adjectives you know, describe what the people shown are wearing. Because the drawings are black and white, you need to use your imagination for the colors.

EXEMPLE *Ce jeune homme porte un joli costume gris avec une chemise blanche et une cravate rouge et blanche. C'est très élégant, n'est-ce pas?*

1. _____
   _____

2. _____
   _____

3. _____
   _____

4. _____
   _____

5. _____
   _____

6. _____
_____

7. _____
_____

Les compléments d'objet indirect

Êtes-vous prêts? Les compléments d'objet indirect

Indicate on a scale of 1 (not comfortable) to 5 (very comfortable) how well you can handle each of the following tasks and place the number in the box provided. If you answer 1 to 3 for any of the tasks, you should go back and review the explanations and exercises in your textbook.

☐ List the French indirect object pronouns and tell what they replace; list verbs that require indirect objects.

☐ Explain where indirect object pronouns are placed in the present tense, in the **passé composé,** in commands, and with an infinitive.

☐ Use indirect object pronouns to tell what gifts you are going to give to different people.

☐ Talk about whether an article of clothing looks good on your friends (e.g., **ce tee-shirt te va bien; cette chemise ne lui va pas bien**).

Ⓐ Suggestions. A friend wants to know what to give different people for their birthdays. Using the example as a guide, write what you tell him.

    EXEMPLE à Pierre / chaîne stéréo / CD
        Tu peux lui offrir une chaîne stéréo, mais ne lui offre pas de CD.

1. à moi / pull-over / sweat

_____

2. à David et Martine / petit téléviseur / lecteur DVD

_____

3. à Sabine / sac à main / parapluie

_____

4. à nous / argent / livres

_____

5. à moi / portefeuille / chaussures

_____

6. aux enfants / jouets / vêtements

_____

B La vie de famille. Madame Monot and a friend are talking about their relationships with their children and with their own parents. Using the cues provided and following the example, re-create their answers to the following questions. Be sure to use the appropriate indirect object pronoun in each response.

EXEMPLE   Est-ce que tes enfants te téléphonent quand ils vont être en retard? (oui)
Oui, ils me téléphonent quand ils vont être en retard.

1. Est-ce qu'ils t'achètent toujours quelque chose pour ton anniversaire? (oui)

_____

2. Est-ce que Paul et toi, vous téléphonez souvent à votre fils? (oui, très souvent)

_____

3. Et votre fils, est-ce qu'il vous téléphone quelquefois? (non, pas souvent)

_____

4. Est-ce que tes enfants te posent beaucoup de questions? (oui)

_____

5. Est-ce que tes enfants te parlent de leurs problèmes? (non, pas toujours)

_____

6. Et toi, est-ce que tu peux parler franchement à tes parents? (oui)

_____

7. Est-ce que tu rends très souvent visite à tes parents? (non)

_____

8. Est-ce que vos enfants vous obéissent toujours? (non, pas toujours)

_____

C Au grand magasin. While you're shopping in your town with a French friend, you tell him what some of the clerks and customers say. Write the French equivalent of each sentence in the space provided, being sure to use the appropriate direct or indirect object pronouns.

1. I showed her this dress, but she didn't like it.

_____

2. Buy me these shoes; I think they're pretty.

_____

3. The clerk (**Le vendeur**) showed him a necktie.

_____

4. Some customers are telephoning you. Can you speak to them?

_____

5. We just bought a new CD. Let's listen to it tonight.

_____

Les verbes conjugués comme *mettre*

Êtes-vous prêts? Les verbes conjugués comme *mettre*

Indicate on a scale of 1 (not comfortable) to 5 (very comfortable) how well you can handle each of the following tasks and place the number in the box provided. If you answer 1 to 3 for any of the tasks, you should go back and review the explanations and exercises in your textbook.

☐ List the verbs conjugated like **mettre** and tell what they mean in English.

☐ Explain how to conjugate these verbs in the present and in the **passé composé.**

☐ Use **mettre** to talk about what you and other people wear for different occasions.

☐ Use **promettre** to tell the resolutions you and people you know usually make for the new year.

Ⓐ Résolutions. Several students are talking about resolutions they are making to improve their study habits. Using the words and phrases provided, re-create their statements.

EXEMPLE   je / ne pas promettre / être parfait / mais / je / promettre / essayer
Je ne promets pas d'être parfait(e) mais je promets d'essayer.

1. Geneviève / promettre / ne pas parler en classe

_____

2. nous / promettre / téléphoner / plus souvent / parents

_____

3. tu / promettre / aller en classe / tous les jours

_____

4. vous / me / promettre / ne pas remettre / travail / dernier / minute?

_____

5. camarades de chambre de Suzanne / promettre / se coucher / plus tôt

_____

_____

6. hier, mon professeur de géo / promettre / étudiants / être moins sévère

_____

_____

B À prendre ou à laisser. Madame Critique is talking with her daughter Brigitte about the permissive way Brigitte is raising her children and running her life. Complete her statements by filling in the blanks with the appropriate form and tense of the verbs provided. Verbs can be used more than once.

Verbes à utiliser: **admettre, mettre, permettre, promettre, remettre, se mettre**

J(e) _____ que les temps ont changé, mais tu vas trop loin, Brigitte. Par exemple, ton mari et

toi, vous _____ à Mathilde de faire ce qu'elle veut. L'autre soir, par exemple, tu lui

_____ de porter une jupe trop courte avec un anorak. Ce n'est pas une tenue pour une

adolescente!

Et Nicolas qui _____ un short et un tee-shirt pour venir à table dimanche dernier. Il

m' _____ de ne pas recommencer mais en réalité, il a refait la même chose hier. C'est parce

que Denis et toi, vous lui _____ d'avoir trop de liberté. Quand est-ce qu'il va

_____ à être responsable?

Et puis, Denis et toi, vous ne savez pas économiser. Si vous n'avez pas assez d'argent en ce moment, il

faut _____ à plus tard l'achat d'un nouveau magasin. Tu es aussi trop gentille avec tout le

monde, surtout avec tes enfants. _____ en colère de temps en temps! Ne leur

_____ pas d'avoir tant de liberté. Demande-leur de _____ la table de

temps en temps. Et s'ils ne sont pas à la maison à l'heure pour le dîner, Denis et toi, _____

à table sans eux. _____-moi de faire un effort pour ne pas me faire honte.

Le subjonctif avec les verbes de volition, d'émotion et de doute

---

Êtes-vous prêts? Le subjonctif

Indicate on a scale of 1 (not comfortable) to 5 (very comfortable) how well you can handle each of the following tasks and place the number in the box provided. If you answer 1 to 3 for any of the tasks, you should go back and review the explanations and exercises in your textbook.

☐ List the verbs of emotion, wishing, and doubt that are followed by the subjunctive and tell what they mean in English.

☐ Explain when **croire** and **penser** are and are not followed by the subjunctive.

☐ Use the subjunctive to tell what you and others are surprised about, what you want others to do, and what you are happy about.

☐ Use the subjunctive and the indicative appropriately to tell what you are sure will happen and things that you doubt will take place.

A **Tous les goûts sont dans la nature!** Two friends, Anne and Natasha, are talking about what they and people they know wear or have purchased lately. Using the cues in parentheses, complete the responses that Anne gives to each of Natasha's questions and statements. Note that some expressions will be followed by the subjunctive, others by the indicative.

     EXEMPLE   NATASHA: Est-ce que Jacques va aller aux Galeries Lafayette aujourd'hui?
                ANNE: ***Je doute qu'il y aille aujourd'hui!***
                        or
                Je doute qu'il aille aux Galeries Lafayette.

1. NATASHA: Est-ce que Pierre a toujours cette horrible coupe de cheveux *(haircut)*?

     ANNE: J'ai peur _____!

2. NATASHA: Est-ce que Samira et Omar suivent toujours autant la mode?

     ANNE: Je suis sûre _____!

3. NATASHA: Est-ce que ta sœur choisit des modèles pratiques et bon marché quand elle achète des chaussures?

     ANNE: Je doute _____!

4. NATASHA: Je peux trouver une jolie paire de lunettes de soleil dans ce catalogue.

     ANNE: Je ne suis pas sûre _____!

5. NATASHA: Caroline ne porte plus de pantalon ces jours-ci.

     ANNE: Je pense _____!

6. NATASHA: Est-ce que Jacques porte des verres de contact maintenant?

     ANNE: J'espère _____!

7. NATASHA: Jérémie a beaucoup de goût pour s'habiller.

     ANNE: Je ne suis pas d'accord avec toi. Moi, je ne crois pas _____!

B **Un week-end gâché *(spoiled)*!** The children in the Dupont family are looking forward to a fun weekend, but their parents have a different idea. Using the cues provided, tell what their parents want them to do.

     EXEMPLE   nous / regarder la télé / papa / passer l'aspirateur
                Nous voulons regarder la télé, mais papa veut que nous passions l'aspirateur.

1. nous / aller au cinéma / maman / ranger nos affaires

    _____

2. je / téléphoner à mes amis / papa / finir mes devoirs de chimie

    _____

3. Jeanne et toi, vous / aller au centre commercial / papa / laver la voiture

    _____

4. je / rester au lit jusqu'à onze heures / maman / aller au supermarché avec elle

    _____

5. André / voir ses amis / nos parents / rendre visite à notre grand-mère

_____

6. toi, tu / écouter de la musique / maman / faire la vaisselle

_____

Intégration et perspectives

🅐 Chez nous en France: Destination la Corse. Xavier, a forest ranger in Corsica, talks about what makes that island so special to him—and to the many tourists who like to vacation there. Before you read, locate **la Corse** on the map at the front of this book.

Ma région n'est pas seulement une des vingt-deux régions de France, c'est aussi une île. Et pour certains, la Corse devrait même être un pays indépendant de la France!... À mon avis, c'est seulement une petite minorité de Corses qui veulent cette indépendance, mais ils font beaucoup parler d'eux et ils emploient quelquefois des moyens assez violents pour arriver à leurs fins. Heureusement, j'ai l'impression que depuis quelque temps, les choses se calment un peu...

La Corse est située à 160 km des côtes françaises et à 80 km de l'Italie. Comme le disait l'écrivain Guy de Maupassant, la Corse est une sorte de «montagne dans la mer». Il y a de nombreux sommets de plus de 2 000 mètres, y compris *(including)* le Monte Cinto (2 710 m) qui est à seulement 30 kilomètres de la mer et qui reste couvert de neige toute l'année! Nous avons aussi 1 000 km de côtes, avec de belles plages de sable dans les golfes et de nombreux petits ports de pêche nichés *(nestled)* entre les falaises *(cliffs)*. Ajoutez à cela le beau soleil méditerranéen, de grandes forêts de pins et de châtaigniers *(chesnut trees)*, le fameux «maquis» *(thick brush)* corse, des villages pittoresques et accueillants, et vous comprenez pourquoi la Corse est souvent appelée «l'île de Beauté»!

Moi, je suis d'Ajaccio, la ville où l'empereur Napoléon est né (en 1769), mais je travaille comme garde forestier dans le grand parc régional qui couvre un cinquième de l'île. C'est un travail très intéressant et, en plus, j'ai la chance de vivre en plein milieu de la nature et dans des sites d'une très grande beauté. À part les randonneurs qui font le GR20 (sentier *[trail]* de grande randonnée de 170 km qui suit la ligne de partage des eaux au centre de l'île), je ne vois presque jamais personne... Mais ça ne me dérange pas parce que je préfère la solitude et le calme.

Avez-vous compris? Que pouvez-vous dire au sujet...

1. de la situation politique en Corse?

_____

2. de la position géographique de la Corse?

_____

3. de la géographie de la Corse?

_____

4. des raisons pour lesquelles la Corse est souvent appelée «l'île de Beauté»?

_____

5. de la ville d'Ajaccio?

_____

6. du travail de Xavier et des raisons pour lesquelles il aime tant son travail?

_____

7. du tempérament de Xavier?

_____

B **À vous de lire: Parcourir le GR20.** Read the following information about the hiking trail GR20 taken from a Web site for the **Parc naturel régional de Corse,** where the GR20 is located. Using the information in the **Introduction** and **Pratique** sections and the questions in **Avez-vous compris?,** write a description of the GR20. Looking over the questions first will help focus your reading. (You will need the information in the **Dix commandements** section for the **À vous d'écrire** that follows.) As you read, don't worry about the words you don't understand; you will still be able to complete the task.

INTRODUCTION

Le **GR20** est le fleuron de la montagne Corse; il est le sentier d'altitude réputé pour être le plus difficile d'Europe.

Nombreux sont ceux qui en rêvent. Quant à ceux qui l'ont parcouru, ils s'en souviennent comme d'un challenge réussi et comme l'un des plus beaux moments de leur vie.

Ce sentier de 200 kilomètres suit la ligne de partage des eaux de la partie ouest la plus septentrionale de l'île vers l'extrême sud-est, épousant le relief montagneux de Calenzana vers Conca.

Nous vous proposons maintenant de rêver un peu et de le parcourir virtuellement sans vous fatiguer avant de l'affronter véritablement un jour ou l'autre.

PRATIQUE

La Grande Randonnée n° 20 est un itinéraire très sportif, réservé aux randonneurs expérimentés. Le Parc propose d'autres randonnées, Mare a Mare et Mare e Monti, randonnées sportives mais sans difficultés particulières.

Ce parcours, considéré comme de haute montagne, nécessite une très bonne condition physique et une bonne pratique. Il se parcourt en 14 jours, uniquement en montagne avec une moyenne quotidienne de marche de 7 heures.

Le sentier est praticable de la mi-juin jusqu'à la mi-octobre. Le reste de l'année, il est enneigé et se parcourt en partie à ski; c'est une des plus belles randonnées hivernales: L'Alta Strada, ou Haute Route à ski, est réservée aux skieurs et aux montagnards chevronnés.

Des refuges de montagne accueillent les randonneurs à chaque étape.

Les refuges du Parc naturel régional offrent les services suivants: un dortoir avec une cuisine équipée d'ustensiles, une gazinière pour vous permettre de préparer votre repas; une salle commune avec tables et bancs, un point d'eau courante à l'intérieur et à l'extérieur du refuge, toilettes et douches (chauffage solaire), un service de sécurité radio pendant les périodes de gardiennage.

LES DIX COMMANDEMENTS POUR BIEN PRÉPARER LE GR20

1. Être en très bonne condition physique: le randonneur doit aborder le GR20 comme un itinéraire à caractère alpin accusé. Le parcours se déroule en partie à des altitudes supérieures à 2000 mètres avec des dénivelés à la montée, souvent supérieurs à 600 mètres et des étapes quotidiennes de 7h de marche en moyenne.
2. Prendre des chaussures à semelle Vibram. Le sol, essentiellement composé de rocailles et d'éboulis, constitue une difficulté essentielle pour le randonneur non aguerri.
3. Consulter la météo montagne (08.92.68.02.20) et ne pas hésiter à annuler un départ si le temps vire au mauvais: les orages et les crues peuvent être violents et dangereux.
4. Prévoir une base de lyophilisé dans le sac. Les points de ravitaillement se multiplient mais restent aléatoires. Avoir toujours un ravitaillement de secours à base de glucides et de l'eau.

> **5.** Bien gérer le poids du sac avant le départ. Certes la chose n'est pas aisée, mais très importante. Ne pas partir avec plus de 18 kg pour les hommes et 14 kg pour les femmes.
> **6.** Attention, le camping sauvage est interdit en Corse. Par mesure de sécurité, il est conseillé de rejoindre un refuge à chaque étape. Des aires de bivouac sont aménagées aux abords des refuges où vous pourrez planter votre tente.
> **7.** Attention, il est interdit d'allumer des feux.
> **8.** Se méfier des cochons. Ils adorent manger les tissus et les victuailles des randonneurs.
> **9.** Photographier les fleurs, sans les cueillir.
> **10.** Laisser la nature propre.

Avez-vous compris? You have been hired by an online travel company for students to write in French a description of the GR20 and to give advice to future hikers. As a first step, use the following questions to prepare your description of the GR20.

Où le sentier GR20 est-il situé?

Quelle est la longueur de ce sentier?

Quel est le niveau de difficulté de ce sentier?

Pendant quelle époque de l'année ce sentier est-il ouvert?

Qu'est-ce que les randonneurs peuvent trouver dans les refuges?

_____

_____

_____

_____

_____

_____

_____

_____

⊙ À vous d'écrire: Conseils pour le GR20. Now that you have prepared your brief description of the GR20, you also need to give hikers advice on what to take to wear, what kind of physical shape to be in, when to go, etc. You have space for 12 pieces of advice and any information you need to include with the advice. Use information from the **Chez nous** reading and the **À vous de lire** selection to prepare your advice.

1. Préparation

In the space provided, first list the topics that you might want to cover, and then under each, include the piece(s) of advice you would give. Use the following suggestions to introduce your advice.

Sujets possibles: **vêtements, condition physique, difficulté des étapes, météo, équipement, refuges, saison(s) préférée(s), aliments (nourriture) à emporter** *(to take)*, **précautions à prendre, interdictions à respecter,** etc.

Structures à utiliser: **Il faut que vous...** (+ subjonctif)
                      Il vaut mieux que vous... (+ subjonctif)
                      Il est bon que le randonneur... (+ subjonctif)
                      Vous devez... + infinitif
                      Il faut... + infinitif

2. Brouillon

Using the ideas you have prepared, write a first draft on a separate sheet of paper. Be sure to use a variety of expressions to begin each piece of advice as given in the suggestions in **Préparation,** and then elaborate as necessary on each. For example, you might want to talk about the need to be in good physical condition or have proper equipment.

> **EXEMPLES** *Il faut que vous soyez en excellente condition physique pour faire le GR20 qui est un challenge même pour les randonneurs qui ont beaucoup d'expérience.*
>
> *Il ne faut pas que vous oubliiez d'emporter de bonnes chaussures de montagne parce que le sentier est très mauvais.*

Think of a way to introduce your list (e.g., **Le GR20 n'est pas un parcours pour ceux qui aiment les petites promenades faciles et reposantes.**) and a way to end your list of advice that perhaps reminds the hiker of the joys of this particular route (e.g., **Même si le GR20 pose de sérieuses difficultés pour le randonneur, ceux qui ont réussi à le faire s'en souviennent avec le plus grand plaisir.**).

3. Révision

Now that you have finished writing your first draft, read through what you have written and check the following.

- Did you include the advice that you brainstormed in the **Préparation** section?
- Did you use a variety of expressions to introduce your advice, and did you use the subjunctive or the infinitive as required by the introduction phrase?
- Did you add brief explanations and elaborations to each piece of advice so that the reader would have a clear idea of what you meant?
- Did you find an interesting way to begin and end your list?
- What else can you add to make your discussion more complete?

4. Rédaction

Write the final draft of your advice for GR20 hikers in the space provided here. Make the corrections and insert the additions you noted in step #3. Then reread your description to be sure you are satisfied with it.

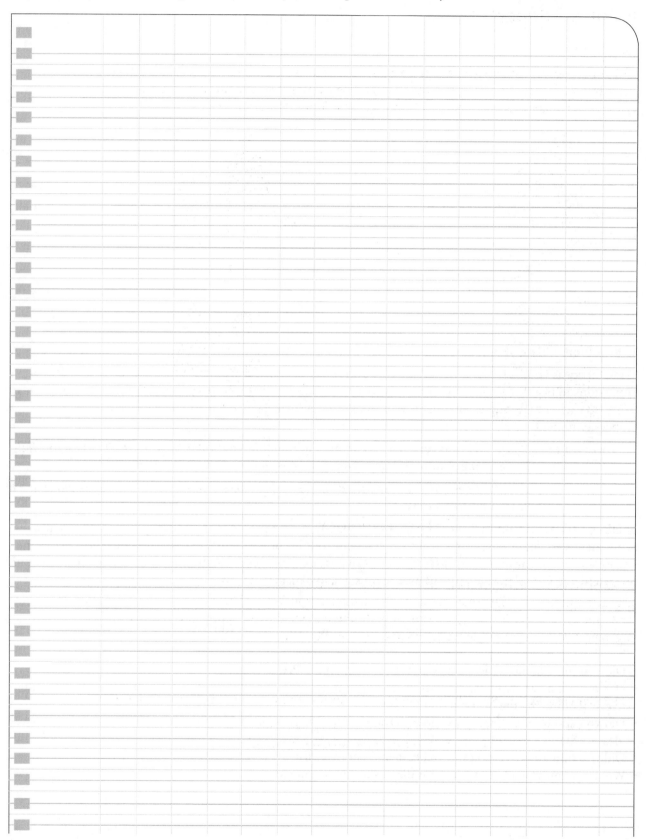

PARTIE ORALE

Point de départ

CD5, Track 20

13.1 À l'aéroport. You are going to the airport to pick up a couple you've never met, although you have a description of them and you know what they will be wearing. Based on the description you hear, pick out the couple you are going to meet from the drawings here. You will hear the description twice.

1.

2.

3.

4.

Les compléments d'objet indirect

CD5, Track 21

*13.2 Situation: Noël approche. (p. 380) Madame and Monsieur Humbert are wondering what they should get their children for Christmas. Listen to their conversation. You will hear the conversation twice. Listen the first time as you hear it read, paying attention to intonation, tone, and pronunciation. During the second reading, repeat each line of the conversation after it is read to you.

CD5, Track 22

*13.3 Générosité. (p. 380 A) Robert bought gifts for his family and friends. What did he give them?

    EXEMPLE   You hear: à ses parents / un magnétoscope
                          You say: *Il leur a donné un magnétoscope.*

CD5, Track 23

*13.4 J'ai changé d'avis. (p. 381 C) Some people change their minds as often as they change shirts. Jean-Luc is one of those people. What does he say?

> **EXEMPLE** You hear: Explique-lui ta situation.
> You say: *Ne lui explique pas ta situation.*

CD5, Track 24

13.5 Dans l'autobus. While you are riding on a bus, you overhear the conversations of people around you. Each person speaking uses a pronoun. Decide whether the pronoun you hear is a direct object, an indirect object, or a stress pronoun and write it in the appropriate column. You will hear each item twice.

> **EXEMPLE** You hear: Nous avons des CD de musique classique, mais les enfants ne les écoutent jamais.
> You write: *les* in the *direct object* column

direct object	indirect object	stress
1. _____	_____	_____
2. _____	_____	_____
3. _____	_____	_____
4. _____	_____	_____
5. _____	_____	_____
6. _____	_____	_____
7. _____	_____	_____
8. _____	_____	_____

Les verbes conjugués comme *mettre*

CD5, Track 25

*13.6 Situation: Un compromis acceptable. (p. 384) Martine wants to go out tonight, but Sébastien has other plans. Fortunately, they find a solution. Listen to their conversation. You will hear the conversation twice. Listen the first time as you hear it read, paying attention to intonation, tone, and pronunciation. During the second reading, repeat each line of the conversation after it is read to you.

CD5, Track 26

*13.7 Qu'est-ce qu'on va mettre? (p. 384 A) Danielle is talking to you about what her friends are going to wear to the concert tonight. What does she say?

> **EXEMPLE** You hear: Philippe / pantalon gris
> You say: *Philippe met son pantalon gris.*

CD5, Track 27

*13.8 Chose promise, chose due. (p. 385 C) One of your friends just made some good resolutions. What has she promised the following people?

> EXEMPLE   You hear: à ses parents… de ranger ses affaires
> You say: *Elle leur a promis de ranger ses affaires.*

CD5, Track 28

13.9 Réponses. Céline is asking people some questions. Decide whether the answers she gets are appropriate and check the corresponding box. You will hear each item twice.

> EXEMPLE   You hear: —Est-ce que nous allons bientôt manger?
> —Oui, nous allons nous mettre à table dans vingt minutes.
> You check: *oui*

	oui	non			oui	non
1.	☐	☐		4.	☐	☐
2.	☐	☐		5.	☐	☐
3.	☐	☐		6.	☐	☐

Le subjonctif avec les verbes de volition, d'émotion et de doute

CD5, Track 29

*13.10 Situation: Différences d'opinion. (p. 387) Catherine is upset because she and her parents don't agree about her future. She confides in her grandfather and asks his advice. Listen to their conversation. You will hear the conversation twice. Listen the first time as you hear it read, paying attention to intonation, tone, and pronunciation. During the second reading, repeat each line of the conversation after it is read to you.

CD5, Track 30

*13.11 Ça dépend du temps qu'il va faire. (p. 387 A) Thierry and Sandrine are getting married on Saturday and all their friends are invited. But what is the weather going to be like? Everyone has an opinion.

> EXEMPLES   You hear: je crois
> You say: *Je crois qu'il va faire beau.*
>
> You hear: je ne crois pas
> You say: *Je ne crois pas qu'il fasse beau.*

CD5, Track 31

*13.12 Confidences. (p. 388 B) Your friends are sharing their joys and their worries with you. You listen sympathetically, and you react to what they say.

> EXEMPLE   You hear: Je ne me sens pas très bien. (Je regrette)
> You say: *Je regrette que tu ne te sentes pas bien.*

CD5, Track 32

13.13 Réunion de famille. Different members of the Blanchard family are talking at their family reunion. In the space provided, jot down in English what each person says. You will hear each item twice.

EXEMPLE   You hear: Crois-tu que Marie vienne avec ses parents?
You jot down: *wondering if Marie will come with parents*

1. _____

2. _____

3. _____

4. _____

5. _____

Intégration et perspectives

CD5, Track 33

13.14 À mon avis... Madame Lemoine is talking about what she thinks college students should wear. After you listen, decide whether Madame Lemoine might have made the statements listed here and mark the appropriate column. You will hear the passage twice.

oui	non	
		1. Les étudiants ne s'intéressent pas assez à leur apparence.
		2. Les jeunes filles d'aujourd'hui ne sont pas assez féminines.
		3. Les tee-shirts sont peut-être confortables, mais ils coûtent trop cher.
		4. Quand on est jeune, on peut s'habiller comme on veut; ça n'a pas d'importance.
		5. Il faut essayer de faire bonne impression sur les gens qu'on rencontre.

CD5, Track 34

13.15 Soirée. Some friends are talking about their evening out tonight. During the pauses provided, write what they say. Each line will be read twice, then the entire passage will be read once again so that you can check your work.

1. _____

_____

2. _____

_____

3. _____

_____

4. _____

_____

CD5, Track 35

*13.16 Bien prononcer. (p. 398)

Basic phonetic differences between French and English

The French phonetic system contrasts in several important ways with the English system.

1. Predominance of front vowels

The majority of French vowels are pronounced in the front of the mouth, whereas English vowels tend to be articulated toward the middle or the back. This difference becomes problematic for English speakers when combined with the rounded shape of the lips, a combination that does not exist in English. Thus, many English speakers have problems with the following series of front, rounded vowels: /y/ as in **du,** /ø/ as in **deux,** and /œ/ as in **peur.**

To help with these sounds, combine the shape of the lips as in the English word *you* and the front position of the tongue as in *see.* You can also produce the French **u** by saying **i** with rounded lips. Repeat the following words ending with front, rounded vowels.

Now repeat and contrast these pairs of words that differ only by the position of the tongue.

2. Muscular tension

This aspect of French pronunciation contrasts sharply with the more relaxed articulation of English sounds. Lack of muscular tension produces diphthongs, as in the English word *oil,* and diphthongized vowels as in *row.* French has neither diphthongs nor diphthongized vowels. To produce a French vowel, the lips do not move during the production of the sound, and the same degree of muscular tension is maintained throughout. Repeat the following words, being careful to produce a pure vowel instead of a diphthong as you would when saying the English words in parentheses.

CD5, Track 36

*13.17 Petite conversation. Practice repeating the following conversation.

Chapitre quatorze ○ ○ ○ ○ ○ ○ ○

Le monde d'aujourd'hui et de demain

(14)

PARTIE ÉCRITE

Point de départ

Ⓐ Actualités. The following headlines have been taken from French-language magazines and newspapers and from the Internet. Using vocabulary from the **Point de départ** as a guide, decide into which category each headline fits.

EXEMPLE ## Les lessives lavent plus vert

> **Quels produits remplacent les phosphates dans les lessives?**
> **Des produits qui menacent la vie aquatique.**

C'est un article sur la pollution.

1. **Nouvelle menace de grève**

_____

2. **Le chômage baisse encore**

_____

3. **La lutte des classes existe**

_____

4. **TROUBLES SOCIAUX: la tension monte**

_____

5. *Le «Parlement des enfants» dénonce l'injustice*

_____

6. **Le tremblement de terre de San-Francisco a fait plus de deux cent cinquante morts**

_____   _____

7. **La police municipale d'Aix visée par un attentat à l'explosif**

_____

8. *Transition politique en Afrique de l'Ouest*

_____

B **Journaliste.** You are a writer for a newspaper, and you have been assigned to write several articles on current events. Choose a topic from at least four of the categories in the **Point de départ** and then, for each topic, write the first two sentences of the article.

EXEMPLE   les grèves
          Les ouvriers de plusieurs usines sont en grève en ce moment. Ils veulent une augmentation de salaire et de meilleures conditions de travail.

Le futur et le futur antérieur

Êtes-vous prêts? Le futur et le futur antérieur

Indicate on a scale of 1 (not comfortable) to 5 (very comfortable) how well you can handle each of the following tasks and place the number in the box provided. If you answer 1 to 3 for any of the tasks, you should go back and review the explanations and exercises in your book.

☐ Explain how to form the future and the **futur antérieur** for regular verbs and for the irregular verbs you've learned.

☐ Use the future to make predictions about yourself, people you know, and future events.

☐ Use the future and the **futur antérieur** to tell what you and others will do when you finish your studies, when you are old, and so forth.

Ⓐ Prédictions. Claire Voillante has had a dream in which she saw the future course of her life and that of her friends. She is sharing her dream with them. Fill in the blanks in Claire's statements with the correct forms of the future tense of the verbs in parentheses.

EXEMPLE Je _ne serai pas_ (ne pas être) riche, mais je _____serai_____ (être) assez heureuse.

1. J(e) _____ (habiter) dans une jolie petite maison.

2. Mon futur mari et moi, nous _____ (avoir) une vie longue et heureuse.

3. Mon mari _____ (s'occuper) des enfants et moi, je _____ (travailler).

4. Et toi, Christophe, tu _____ (faire) de brillantes études et tu _____ (devenir) très célèbre.

5. Madeleine et André _____ (ne pas finir) leurs études, mais je suis sûre qu'ils

    _____ (réussir) à trouver du travail.

6. Et vous, Anne et Marc, vous _____ (attendre) quelques années pour vous marier.

7. Il _____ (falloir) être courageux parce que nous _____ (rencontrer) beaucoup de difficultés.

8. Mais heureusement nous _____ (pouvoir) rester en contact et nous

    _____ (être) contents de passer de bons moments ensemble.

Ⓑ Problèmes et solutions. Jean Marin is the manager of a factory that has been having personnel difficulties. To solve the problem, he has called in an efficiency expert. Following the example, re-create the statements Jean Marin and the expert made. Begin each sentence with **dès que, aussitôt que, quand,** or **lorsque.**

EXEMPLE nous / étudier la situation / nous préparer notre rapport
Dès que nous aurons étudié la situation, nous préparerons notre rapport.

1. les experts / arriver à l'usine / ils / consulter le personnel

    _____

    _____

2. vous / se mettre au travail / vous / pouvoir accomplir beaucoup de choses

_____

_____

3. nous / examiner le problème / nous / savoir s'il y a une solution ou non

_____

_____

4. vous / visiter l'usine / vous / mieux comprendre la situation

_____

_____

5. les employés / discuter la situation entre eux / ils / ne pas hésiter à vous parler

_____

_____

6. nous / finir notre rapport / nous / vous communiquer nos conclusions

_____

_____

⊙ Qu'est-ce que l'avenir nous réserve? Complete the following sentences to indicate what you think will happen to you or other people in the future.

1. Dans vingt ans, je _____

_____.

2. Le nouveau président ou la nouvelle présidente des États-Unis _____

_____.

3. Quand nous serons âgés, _____

_____.

4. Dès que j'aurai fini mes études, _____

_____.

5. Dans dix ans, mon (ma) professeur(e) de français _____

_____.

6. Quand je gagnerai ma vie, _____

_____.

7. Lorsque mes amis auront quitté l'université, _____

_____.

Le conditionnel et la phrase conditionnelle

Êtes-vous prêts? Le conditionnel et la phrase conditionnelle

Indicate on a scale of 1 (not comfortable) to 5 (very comfortable) how well you can handle each of the following tasks and place the number in the box provided. If you answer 1 to 3 for any of the tasks, you should go back and review the explanations and exercises in your book.

☐ Explain how to form the conditional and tell what it means in English.

☐ For sentences containing a **si** clause, tell what tenses are used in the **si** clause and in the result clause.

☐ Use the conditional and the imperfect in **si** clauses to make predictions about what would happen in certain situations.

☐ Use the conditional to tell what you and people you know would do if you had more time or more money, if you were someone else, and so forth.

☐ Use the conditional to relate in indirect style what other people said would happen.

Ⓐ Action solidarité. Élise is talking about what she, her family, and her friends have said they would do to help create a better world. Following the example, re-create her statements.

> **EXEMPLE** Monique va recycler les bouteilles.
> ***Monique a dit qu'elle recyclerait les bouteilles.***

1. Roger va participer à l'opération anti-gaspillage samedi.

_____

2. Je vais lire un article sur les animaux en voie d'extinction.

_____

3. Angèle et Marion vont assister à une conférence sur l'environnement.

_____

4. Tu vas voter dimanche, n'est-ce pas?

_____

5. Nous allons faire partie d'une association contre le racisme.

_____

6. Ma mère va être volontaire dans l'opération contre la faim.

_____

7. Mes camarades de chambre vont organiser un débat sur les inégalités sociales.

_____

8. Vous allez choisir seulement des produits recyclés.

_____

ⓑ À votre place… Some of your friends at Laval University are talking about what they are doing. Using the example as a guide, write what you would do in each situation.

> **EXEMPLE** Les expériences en laboratoire sont très ennuyeuses; mes amis et moi, nous n'y allons presque jamais.
> *À votre place, j'irais tous les jours au laboratoire.*

1. Paul remet toujours son travail à la dernière minute.

_____

_____

2. Ma camarade de chambre, Natasha, me demande tout le temps de l'aider à faire ses devoirs.

_____

_____

3. Je n'aime pas aller à la bibliothèque pour étudier.

_____

_____

4. Mon amie Claire ne prend pas de notes, et après elle ne sait pas ce qu'elle doit étudier.

_____

_____

5. Chaque semaine, j'ai un compte rendu *(report)* à faire pour mon cours de littérature. Je déteste ça et j'attends toujours la dernière minute pour le commencer.

_____

_____

6. Au début de chaque trimestre, Sébastien doit emprunter de l'argent pour payer ses frais d'inscription *(registration fees)*.

_____

_____

7. Je ne sais pas quels cours je vais choisir le trimestre prochain.

_____

_____

8. Hélène n'est pas allée à son cours de comptabilité pendant deux semaines.

_____

_____

G Suggestions. Monsieur Dubois, the president of a small company in Montreal, wishes his employees did things differently. Knowing that they respond better to tactful suggestions, he rephrases his statements. Following the example, re-create what he says.

> **EXEMPLE** Prenez seulement une heure pour le déjeuner. Vous aurez plus de temps pour finir votre travail.
> *Si vous preniez seulement une heure pour le déjeuner, vous auriez plus de temps pour finir votre travail.*

1. Regardez ce rapport avant d'aller à la réunion. Vous serez mieux préparés.

   _____

   _____

2. Étudiez l'anglais commercial. Cela vous aidera beaucoup.

   _____

   _____

3. Donnez moins de travail à votre secrétaire. Il sera content.

   _____

   _____

4. Ne quittez pas le bureau sans me dire où vous allez. Je saurai où vous trouver.

   _____

   _____

5. Faites un effort pour être à l'heure. Vous aurez peut-être une augmentation de salaire.

   _____

   _____

6. Téléphonons à M. Gillet maintenant. Il comprendra mieux notre position.

   _____

   _____

7. Faisons moins de voyages en avion. Nous économiserons de l'argent.

   _____

   _____

8. Venez parler à ces clients. Cela leur fera plaisir.

   _____

   _____

D Point et contrepoint. People in different interest groups don't always agree on things. Using the example as a guide, re-create statements these people might make. Remember to use the imperfect in the **si** clause and the conditional in the result clause.

> **EXEMPLE** les loisirs *(leisure activities)*
>
> UN ADOLESCENT: *Si je me couchais plus tard, j'aurais plus de temps à passer avec mes amis.*
>
> SA MÈRE: *Si tu passais moins de temps avec tes amis, tu pourrais te coucher plus tôt.*

1. les autos

LE PUBLIC: _____

L'INDUSTRIE AUTOMOBILE: _____

2. les vêtements

LES JEUNES: _____

LEURS PARENTS: _____

3. les grèves

LES EMPLOYÉS: _____

LES PATRONS: _____

4. l'argent

VOUS: _____

VOS PARENTS: _____

5. l'étude du français

VOUS: _____

VOTRE PROFESSEUR(E): _____

6. les prix

LES CLIENTS: _____

LES MARCHANDS: _____

Les pronoms relatifs

Êtes-vous prêts? Les pronoms relatifs

Indicate on a scale of 1 (not comfortable) to 5 (very comfortable) how well you can handle each of the following tasks and place the number in the box provided. If you answer 1 to 3 for any of the tasks, you should go back and review the explanations and exercises in your textbook.

☐ List the French relative pronouns, tell what they refer to, and explain what they mean in English.

☐ Make up a sentence using each of the following relative pronouns: **qui, que, dont, ce qui, ce que, ce dont.**

☐ Use relative pronouns to combine simple sentences into more complex ones, using one or several of your own writing samples.

☐ Describe a person you know or an event, using as many relative pronouns as you can in your description.

Nom _____ Date _____ Classe _____

Ⓐ L'environnement. Maryse is talking about ecology and the environment. Complete her statements with the appropriate relative pronouns.

Je participe à un groupe écologique _____ s'intéresse à la protection de l'environnement. _____ nous inquiète, c'est le manque de ressources et d'espaces verts pour les générations _____ viendront après nous. Il y a beaucoup de problèmes _____ nous avons besoin de résoudre. Je voudrais croire que les gens _____ jettent des ordures *(garbage)* n'importe où *(anywhere)* ne comprennent pas _____ ils font, mais ce serait naïf. Les personnes _____ gaspillent l'énergie doivent savoir qu'elles ne peuvent pas faire tout _____ elles ont envie. Personne ne sait _____ va arriver, mais une chose _____ je suis certaine, c'est que tous les pays du monde seront obligés de travailler ensemble pour trouver des solutions.

Ⓑ Le savez-vous? You are asking some French friends their opinions on environmental issues. Complete the following questions with the appropriate relative pronouns.

    EXEMPLE   Savez-vous _ce qu'_ on doit faire pour protéger l'environnement?

1. Savez-vous quelles sont les ressources _____ nous avons besoin de conserver?
2. Savez-vous quels sont les animaux _____ nous devons protéger?
3. Savez-vous quels sont les groupes _____ travaillent pour la protection de l'environnement?
4. Savez-vous _____ inquiète les groupes écologiques?
5. Savez-vous _____ les groupes écologiques veulent faire?
6. Savez-vous expliquer ce problème _____ beaucoup de gens ne comprennent pas?

Ⓒ Tu devrais lire ça. Marine is telling Florian about a book on ecology she thinks he should read. Using appropriate relative pronouns, combine each pair of statements into one longer sentence.

    EXEMPLE   Je viens de lire un livre. Ce livre décrit la vie des insectes.
               Je viens de lire un livre qui décrit la vie des insectes.

1. Tes parents t'ont donné un livre. Est-ce que c'est ce livre-ci?

_____

2. Non, c'est un autre livre. Un ami m'a parlé de ce livre.

_____

3. C'est un livre intéressant. Tu devrais lire ce livre.

_____

4. Pourquoi lire un livre? Le sujet est si ennuyeux.

_____

5. Parce que c'est un livre important. Mon prof d'écologie nous a conseillé de lire ce livre.

_____

D Futurologie. A Web page on **la futurologie** has asked individuals to contribute ideas about what the future holds for them. What would you write about yourself? In the space provided, write at least 10 simple sentences using the future tense that tell what you think will happen (e.g., **J'achèterai une voiture**). Then write your paragraph, incorporating relative pronouns, adjectives, conjunctions, and other vocabulary you know to make the paragraph lively (**Quand j'aurai fini mes études, j'achèterai la belle nouvelle voiture dont je rêve**).

Vos idées

Intégration et perspectives

Ⓐ Chez nous en France: Destination la vallée de la Loire. In the following text, Ariane talks about the beautiful **châteaux** for which the Loire valley is famous, and some of its modern-day problems. Before you read, look for the Loire valley on the map at the front of this book.

Bonjour, je m'appelle Ariane et je suis de Tours, dans la vallée de la Loire. Pour beaucoup de gens, cela évoque automatiquement les somptueux châteaux de la Loire construits pendant la Renaissance par les rois de France et les grands seigneurs *(noblemen)* de leur cour. Attirés par les paysages verdoyants, le climat doux et agréable de notre région, souvent surnommée «le jardin de France», et aussi par la proximité de grandes réserves de chasse *(hunting)*, ils ont fait construire là de magnifiques châteaux sur les bords de la Loire et de ses nombreux affluents *(tributaries)*. Vous avez sans doute vu des photos, ou entendu parler, des châteaux les plus connus comme Chenonceaux, Chambord, Blois ou Azay-le-Rideau.

Mais il n'y a pas seulement des châteaux dans la vallée de la Loire. Il y a aussi un grand nombre de centrales nucléaires, surtout entre Blois et Saumur! Ces centrales ont été construites pendant la grande crise de l'énergie des années 70. On croyait alors que l'énergie nucléaire était la réponse à tous nos problèmes... La vallée de la Loire, ainsi que la vallée du Rhône, semblaient réunir les conditions idéales pour l'implantation de ces centrales: abondance d'eau pour refroidir *(cool down)* les réacteurs, et proximité des grands centres urbains ou industriels qui ont besoin de l'électricité ainsi produite *(produced in this way)*.

Malheureusement, ces centrales ont maintenant vieilli et on se préoccupe beaucoup de leurs effets possibles sur la santé des habitants, en particulier à cause du radon. Il y a aussi le problème du recyclage des déchets radioactifs, et celui de plus en plus sérieux des dangers de sabotage ou d'actes de terrorisme!... Mais la France possède très peu de pétrole *(crude oil)*, les sources d'énergie hydro-électrique sont déjà exploitées presque au maximum, et nous consommons de plus en plus d'électricité... Alors, où est la solution?

Avez-vous compris? Ariane has described both the beauty and the problems of the **vallée de la Loire.** In the space provided, describe in French what you have learned about each of these aspects of this area of France.

Ce qui fait le charme de la vallée de la Loire

Ce qui présente des problèmes

B À vous de lire: La Charte de l'environnement. The following text describes **la Charte de l'environnement** passed in 2004 by France's **Assemblée nationale.** The first section outlines the rationale for **la Charte,** and the second presents the rights and responsibilities of both the citizens and the government. Answer the questions that are given before each section.

1. Read **Article 2** and then in English give three reasons why the authors of **la Charte** felt that this document was important.

   a. _____

   b. _____

   c. _____

Article 2

La Charte de l'environnement de 2003 est ainsi rédigée: «Le peuple français considérant

- que les ressources et les équilibres naturels ont conditionné l'émergence de l'humanité;
- que l'avenir et l'existence même de l'humanité sont indissociables de son milieu naturel;
- que l'environnement est le patrimoine commun des êtres humains;
- que l'homme exerce une influence croissante sur les conditions de la vie et sur sa propre évolution;
- que la diversité biologique, l'épanouissement de la personne et le progrès des sociétés humaines sont affectés par certains modes de consommation ou de production et par l'exploitation excessive des ressources naturelles;
- que la préservation de l'environnement doit être recherchée au même titre que les autres intérêts fondamentaux de la Nation;
- qu'afin d'assurer un développement durable, les choix destinés à répondre aux besoins du présent ne doivent pas compromettre la capacité des générations futures et des autres peuples à satisfaire leurs propres besoins proclame:

---

2. *Articles:* In the section on the next page, specific charges are given to citizens and to the government regarding their rights and responsibilities in maintaining an ecologically sound society. As you read, indicate in the space provided the letter of the category in which each article belongs: a) responsibilities of individuals to support the environment; b) responsibilities of the government and other organizations to support environmental efforts; c) individual rights such as access to information and living in an environmentally safe world.

_____ Art. 1ᵉʳ – Chacun a le droit de vivre dans un environnement équilibré et favorable à sa santé.

_____ Art. 2 – Toute personne a le devoir de prendre part à la préservation et à l'amélioration de l'environnement.

_____ Art. 3 – Toute personne doit, dans les conditions définies par la loi, prévenir ou, à défaut, limiter les atteintes qu'elle est susceptible de porter à l'environnement.

_____ Art. 4 – Toute personne doit contribuer à la réparation des dommages qu'elle cause à l'environnement, dans les conditions définies par la loi.

_____ Art. 5 – Lorsque la réalisation d'un dommage, bien qu'incertaine en l'état de connaissances scientifiques, pourrait affecter de manière grave et irréversible l'environnement, les autorités publiques veillent, par application du principe de précaution, à l'adoption de mesures provisoires et proportionnées afin d'éviter la réalisation du dommage ainsi qu'à la mise en œuvre de procédures d'évaluation des risques encourus.

_____ Art. 6 – Les politiques publiques doivent promouvoir un développement durable. À cet effet, elles prennent en compte la protection et la mise en valeur de l'environnement et les concilient avec le développement économique et social.

_____ Art. 7 – Toute personne a le droit, dans les conditions et les limites définies par la loi, d'accéder aux informations relatives à l'environnement détenues par les autorités publiques et de participer à l'élaboration des décisions publiques ayant une incidence sur l'environnement.

_____ Art. 8 – L'éducation et la formation à l'environnement doivent contribuer à l'exercice des droits et devoirs définis par la présente Charte.

_____ Art. 9 – La recherche et l'innovation doivent apporter leur concours à la préservation et à la mise en valeur de l'environnement.

_____ Art. 10 – La présente Charte inspire l'action européenne et internationale de la France.»

⊙ À vous d'écrire: Éditorial. Write a letter to the editor (approximately 200 words) about an environmental issue that is important to you or to your community (e.g., recycling, creating a park instead of a parking lot).

1. Préparation

In the space provided, first list topics that might be of interest to you along with a brief note about why each is important. You can find ideas (and vocabulary) in the Chapter 14 **Intégration et perspectives** section in your textbook and in the preceding **Chez nous** and **À vous de lire** activities. Then pick the topic you would like to discuss in your letter to the editor. As a next step, write down in French as many ideas as you can that you might include in your letter; then choose three or four of the most important ones to develop more fully in your rough draft.

Sujets possibles:

Vos idées:

2. Brouillon

Write a rough draft of your letter on a separate sheet of paper. Begin your letter with a phrase such as **Ce qui m'inquiète particulièrement en ce moment, c'est…** End your letter with a forceful concluding statement such as **Le problème est sérieux, mais si tout le monde se mettait d'accord, on arriverait à le résoudre.** The main ideas that you identified in **Préparation** can be developed into separate short paragraphs. As you write your letter, emphasize and strengthen your ideas with the future tense and sentences in the conditional (e.g., **Si on ne commence pas à recycler maintenant, on aura beaucoup plus de problèmes dans les années qui viennent; Si on ne fait rien maintenant, c'est plus tard qu'il faudra payer; Pensez à vos enfants et à vos petits-enfants: aimeriez-vous qu'ils soient obligés de vivre dans un monde complètement pollué?**). Be attentive also to combining simple statements with relative pronouns (**qui, que, dont**).

3. Révision

Now that you have finished writing your first draft, read through what you have written and check the following.

- Did you incorporate all of the important ideas you listed in **Préparation**? Are there others that should be included?
- Did you use the future tense and conditional phrases in your letter?
- Are there sentences in your letter that you could combine using relative pronouns?
- Did you end your letter with a forceful concluding sentence that summarizes your thoughts on the topic you selected? If not, think about another way to end your letter.

4. Rédaction

Write the final draft of your letter in the space provided here. Make the corrections and insert the additions you noted in step #3. Then reread your letter to be sure you are satisfied with it.

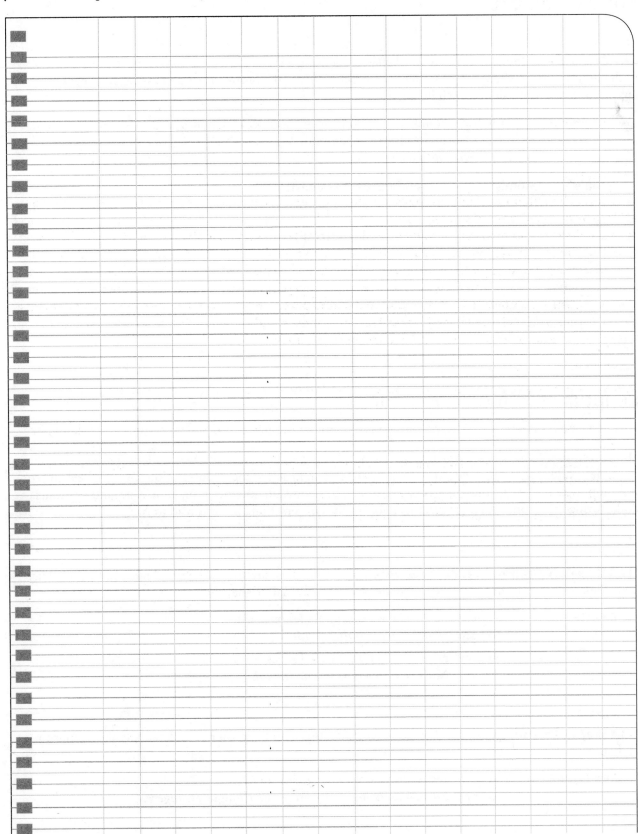

PARTIE ORALE

Point de départ

CD6, Track 2

14.1 Points de vue. Students in Madame Lafleur's sociology class are discussing what events might take place in the future. Decide whether each student's comment is generally **optimiste** or **pessimiste** and check the appropriate box. You will hear each item twice.

> **EXEMPLE**   You hear: À mon avis, les gens vont travailler ensemble pour mettre fin au racisme et au sexisme dans le monde.
>   You check: *optimiste*

	optimiste	pessimiste			optimiste	pessimiste
1.	☐	☐		5.	☐	☐
2.	☐	☐		6.	☐	☐
3.	☐	☐		7.	☐	☐
4.	☐	☐		8.	☐	☐

Le futur et le futur antérieur

CD6, Track 3

*14.2 Situation: Ne sois pas si pessimiste! (p. 409) Patrick and Régine have two children. They are wondering what their children's lives will be like when they are grown. Listen to their conversation. You will hear the conversation twice. Listen the first time as you hear it read, paying attention to intonation, tone, and pronunciation. During the second reading, repeat each line of the conversation after it is read to you.

CD6, Track 4

*14.3 Il y a des optimistes… et des pessimistes. (p. 410 A) You have friends who are fairly optimistic when they think about the future and others who are pessimistic. What do they say?

> **EXEMPLES**   You hear: nous / trouver du travail; les optimistes
>   You say: *Nous trouverons du travail.*
>
>   You hear: nous / trouver du travail; les pessimistes
>   You say: *Nous ne trouverons pas de travail.*

CD6, Track 5

*14.4 Projets d'avenir. (p. 410 B) What do other students intend to do later in life? Ask them questions to find out.

> **EXEMPLE**   You hear: apprendre une autre langue étrangère
>   You say: *Est-ce que tu apprendras une autre langue étrangère?*

CD6, Track 6

14.5 Quand ça? Several friends are talking about past, present, and future vacations. Listen to what each says; then jot down in French the trip each refers to and mark when it takes place or took place.

> **EXEMPLE**   You hear: Mes parents feront un long voyage aux États-Unis au mois de juillet.
> You write: *voyage aux États-Unis;* you mark the *futur* column

	voyage	passé	présent	futur
1.				
2.				
3.				
4.				
5.				
6.				
7.				
8.				

Le conditionnel et la phrase conditionnelle

CD6, Track 7

*14.6 Situation: Si on allait lui rendre visite? (p. 413) André and Robert are making travel plans. They get the idea to visit their friend Liliane in Quebec. Listen to their conversation. You will hear the conversation twice. Listen the first time as you hear it read, paying attention to intonation, tone, and pronunciation. During the second reading, repeat each line of the conversation after it is read to you.

CD6, Track 8

*14.7 Je me suis trompée. (p. 414 A) Monique has misunderstood what people have told her, and she is surprised to find out that she was wrong. What does she say?

> **EXEMPLE**   You hear: Il viendra demain. (aujourd'hui)
> You say: *Ah oui? Moi, je croyais qu'il viendrait aujourd'hui.*

CD6, Track 9

*14.8 À chacun ses responsabilités. (p. 414 B) Several friends have decided to travel to Canada. Here is what each person has promised to do.

> **EXEMPLE**   You hear: Luc va choisir l'itinéraire.
> You say: *Luc a dit qu'il choisirait l'itinéraire.*

CD6, Track 10

14.9 Écoutez bien. Listen to different members of a political candidate's election committee, and decide whether you hear them use the imperfect, the future, or the conditional. Check the appropriate column. You will hear each item twice.

> **EXEMPLE**   You hear: Je parlais à des reporters quand vous êtes entrés.
> You mark: the *imperfect* column.

	imperfect	future	conditional		imperfect	future	conditional
1.	☐	☐	☐	5.	☐	☐	☐
2.	☐	☐	☐	6.	☐	☐	☐
3.	☐	☐	☐	7.	☐	☐	☐
4.	☐	☐	☐	8	☐	☐	☐

Les pronoms relatifs

CD6, Track 11

*14.10 Situation: Elle te plaît? (p. 417) During an ecology demonstration, Guillaume met a girl who interests him. He's talking to his friend Jonas about her. Listen to their conversation. You will hear the conversation twice. Listen the first time as you hear it read, paying attention to intonation, tone, and pronunciation. During the second reading, repeat each line of the conversation after it is read to you.

CD6, Track 12

*14.11 Un amoureux bien malheureux. (p. 418 A) Your friend Bruno is unlucky. He likes Natacha, but they don't have the same tastes. What does he say?

> **EXEMPLE**   You hear: J'ai écrit des chansons.
> You say: *Elle n'aime pas les chansons que j'ai écrites.*

CD6, Track 13

*14.12 J'ai suivi tes conseils. (p. 419 E) You followed the advice your friend Camille gave you. What do you say?

> **EXEMPLE**   You hear: écouter les CD
> You say: *J'ai écouté les CD dont tu m'as parlé.*

CD6, Track 14

*14.13 On invite des copains. (p. 419 G) You've decided to invite some friends over, and you ask a friend for advice. Unfortunately, she doesn't have any suggestions. How does your friend answer?

> **EXEMPLE**   You hear: Qu'est-ce qu'on va faire s'il pleut?
> You say: *Je ne sais pas ce qu'on va faire s'il pleut!*

CD6, Track 15

14.14 Qu'est-ce qui m'est arrivé? Adèle got hurt and was taken to the hospital emergency room. Jot down in English what Adèle says. You will hear each item twice.

> **EXEMPLE**   You hear: Je ne sais pas ce qui m'est arrivé.
> You jot down: *doesn't know what happened to her*

1. _____

2. _____

3. _____

4. _____

5. _____

6. _____

Intégration et perspectives

CD6, Track 16

14.15 Comment sera la vie? Listen to the following interview with Professeure Vision, in which she tells her views on what life will be like 50 years from now. After you listen to the interview, decide whether the statements you see correctly describe what she predicts and mark the appropriate column. You will hear the interview twice.

oui	non	
		1. Il y aura de nouvelles écoles pour les enfants.
		2. On continuera à regarder la télévision pour s'amuser.
		3. On travaillera beaucoup plus, et on aura moins de temps pour s'amuser.
		4. On prendra des vitamines spéciales pour être plus fort.
		5. Les ordinateurs feront tout le travail à la maison.
		6. On pourra visiter les autres planètes sans problème.

CD6, Track 17

14.16 Et si je gagnais? André is thinking about what his life could be like if he won the lottery. During the pauses provided, write what he says. You will hear each line twice; then the entire passage will be read once again so that you can check your work.

1. _____

2. _____

3. _____

4. _____

*14.17 Bien prononcer: Le français familier (p. 430)

In French, as in English, circumstances determine how things are said. You might hear casual, fast speech—or even slang—typical of many young people, or the extremely formal, stylized speech of classical poetry or theater. Casual speech (**le français familier**) affects vocabulary (colloquial or even slang words), syntax (word order revealing the feelings of the speaker), and pronunciation. You do not need to speak in this manner (a more careful form of language has a better chance of being acceptable no matter where you are), but it is useful to be able to understand French as it may be spoken by native speakers.

Some of the ways in which casual speech may affect your understanding are:

1. Casual speech implies a degree of familiarity, shared knowledge, and freedom to express emotions in a spontaneous way. As a result, there is a deterioration of the traditional syntax, and word order tends to reflect what comes to speakers' minds first, or what they feel a need to emphasize.

   Parts of speech that are not essential to the meaning are often dropped, especially the **ne** part of the negative.

2. There is a heavier reliance on intonation (exclamations, laughter, irony, annoyance, etc.), rhythm (faster tempo, groups of words rushed together, false starts), pauses (hesitations and fill-in words), and unfinished sentences. Intonation, for example, rather than syntax may signal a question.

3. Because of the need for speed and facility, phonology is characterized by a careless articulation of many sounds and the dropping of some—particularly the mute **e,** which is dropped whenever the articulatory difficulty is not too great.

   This elision often decreases the number of syllables in a word, or in a breath group.

   Dropping the mute **e** can also result in devoicing (no vibration of the vocal cords) of consonants thus brought together.

   Other sounds that can be dropped in fast speech are the **u** in **tu,** the **l** in the pronouns **il** and **ils,** and **l** and **r** when they are at the end of a word.

Because you do not need to speak in this manner, it is not necessary to practice repeating a **petite conversation.**

Chapitre quinze ○ ○ ○ ○ ○ ○ ○

Les arts et la vie

15

PARTIE ÉCRITE

Point de départ

Ⓐ Après le concert. You write a music review column for your newspaper, and you are describing a concert you just attended. In the space provided, write the instrument each member of the group plays.

EXEMPLE André Duchemin _joue du violon_.

1. Georges Bert _____.

2. Martine Laurent et François Soulard _____.

3. Véronique Perrineau _____.

4. Catherine Valo _____.

5. Robert Héroult _____.

ⓑ Activités artistiques. The following drawings show people engaged in various artistic activities. In the space provided, write a sentence describing what the people shown are doing. Then, using vocabulary you know, write two or three additional statements explaining your own interests in each activity (for example, whether you've already done the activity, if a friend or relative does it, whether you'd like to do it and why or why not). Vary your sentences as much as possible.

EXEMPLE

Ces personnes font du théâtre. Moi, je faisais du théâtre quand j'étais plus jeune, mais maintenant je n'ai plus le temps d'en faire.

1. _____

_____

_____

_____

2. _____

_____

_____

_____

3. _____

_____

_____

_____

4. _____

_____

_____

_____

5.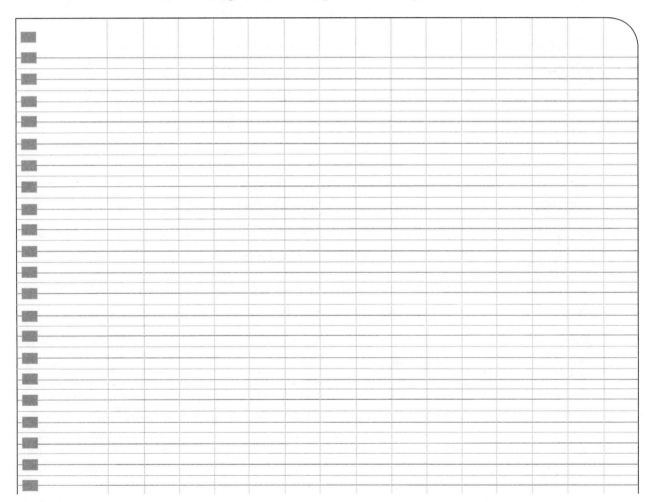

_____

_____

_____

_____

6.

_____

_____

_____

_____

⊙ Où aller et que faire? A French exchange student has asked you to tell him about different cultural activities that are taking place on or near campus. Using vocabulary you know, describe some of these activities. Base your descriptions on activities listed in your university or town newspaper.

EXEMPLE   *Ce week-end, vous pouvez voir une pièce de Shakespeare au théâtre de l'université.*

Les pronoms démonstratifs

Ⓐ Snobisme. Janine, who has simple, practical tastes, is talking with her friend Marie-Chantal, who has expensive tastes. Following the model and using the cues provided, re-create Marie-Chantal's statements. Replace the underlined words in each sentence with the appropriate demonstrative pronoun.

> **EXEMPLE** J'aime <u>les tableaux</u> qu'on achète dans la rue. (dans une galerie d'art)
> ***J'aime mieux ceux qu'on achète dans une galerie d'art.***

1. J'aime <u>les objets</u> qui sont simples et utiles. (élégants et artistiques)

   _____

2. <u>La voiture</u> que je viens d'acheter est assez ordinaire. (très belle)

   _____

3. Je préfère <u>les restaurants</u> simples et bon marché. (où on sert des spécialités régionales)

   _____

4. <u>Les peintures</u> que je préfère sont assez bon marché. (coûtent très cher)

   _____

5. <u>L'appartement</u> où j'habite est situé dans le Quartier latin. (dans le 16ᵉ)

   _____

6. <u>La nouvelle robe</u> de ma sœur vient des Galeries Lafayette. (chez Dior)

   _____

7. <u>Les amis</u> de mon frère sont assez sympathiques. (très cultivés)

   _____

8. C'est ma mère qui a fait <u>les dessins</u> que j'ai dans ma chambre. (c'est un artiste bien connu)

   _____

B Le présent ou le passé? Do you prefer things of the present or things of the past? Indicate your preferences by using the appropriate form of the demonstrative pronoun in each response.

> **EXEMPLE** la musique de notre époque / la musique de l'époque classique
> *Je préfère celle de l'époque classique.*

1. le style de vie d'aujourd'hui / le style de vie des années cinquante

_____

2. les films en couleur / les films en noir et blanc

_____

3. la musique d'aujourd'hui / la musique des années soixante

_____

4. les amis que vous avez maintenant / les amis que vous aviez quand vous étiez enfant

_____

5. les vêtements qu'on porte maintenant / les vêtements qu'on portait pendant les années soixante-dix

_____

6. les chansons d'aujourd'hui / les chansons qui étaient populaires il y a cinq ans

_____

Le plus-que-parfait et le conditionnel passé

Êtes-vous prêts? Le plus-que-parfait et le conditionnel passé

Indicate on a scale of 1 (not comfortable) to 5 (very comfortable) how well you can handle each of the following tasks and place the number in the box provided. If you answer 1 to 3 for any of the tasks, you should go back and review the explanations and exercises in your book.

☐ Explain how to conjugate the **plus-que-parfait** and the **conditionnel passé** and tell what each means in English.

☐ Use the **plus-que-parfait** to talk about events that had already taken place before another past event, for example, what a relative or friend had already done by a certain age **(Quand mon grand-père a rencontré ma grand-mère, il avait déjà fait son service militaire).**

☐ Use these forms appropriately in sentences with **si** clauses to tell what you and others would have done if certain conditions or situations had happened (e.g., what your life would have been like if you had been born in France, if you hadn't come to this university).

A Je suis arrivé en retard. Antoine is telling his friend about being late for an exam. Using the example as a guide, write what he says.

> **EXEMPLE** le prof / fermer la porte
> *Le prof avait déjà fermé la porte.*

1. tous les autres étudiants / arriver

_____

2. le prof / distribuer les examens

_____

3. il / répondre à plusieurs questions

_____

4. tout le monde / se mettre à travailler

_____

5. plusieurs étudiants / finir

_____

6. les plus rapides / partir

_____

B À ta place. Maryse has returned from vacation, and she is asking some friends what they would have done in certain circumstances. Using the example as a guide, tell what they say.

> **EXEMPLE** J'ai pris le train. (nous / prendre l'avion)
> ***Nous aurions pris l'avion.***

1. Je suis restée dans un hôtel de luxe. (nous / chercher quelque chose de moins cher)

_____

2. J'ai pris des centaines de photos. (nous / prendre moins de photos)

_____

3. J'ai pris tous mes repas dans des restaurants trois étoiles. (moi, je / chercher un petit café sympa)

_____

4. Je n'ai pas visité de monuments. (nous / aller voir les monuments les plus célèbres)

_____

5. J'ai téléphoné à mes parents. (moi, je / envoyer des cartes postales à tout le monde)

_____

6. Je suis revenue au bout d'une semaine. (nous / rester plus longtemps)

_____

C Si... Imagine what would have happened if the following events had taken place. Be sure to vary your sentences as much as possible.

1. Si la guerre de Sécession (la guerre civile américaine) avait été gagnée par le Sud plutôt que par le Nord,

_____

_____ .

2. Si Christophe Colomb n'avait pas découvert l'Amérique, _____

_____

_____ .

3. Si on n'avait pas inventé l'automobile, _____

_____

_____ .

4. Si je n'avais pas décidé de faire mes études ici, _____

_____

_____ .

5. Si j'avais été totalement libre de choisir mes cours, _____

_____

_____ .

6. Si j'étais né(e) il y a deux cents ans, _____

_____

_____ .

Le participe présent et l'infinitif

Êtes-vous prêts? Le participe présent et l'infinitif

Indicate on a scale of 1 (not comfortable) to 5 (very comfortable) how well you can handle each of the following tasks and place the number in the box provided. If you answer 1 to 3 for any of the tasks, you should go back and review the explanations and exercises in your book.

☐ Explain how to form the present participle and tell what it means when used with the preposition **en.**

☐ Explain when the infinitive and the past infinitive are used after prepositions.

☐ Use the present participle to talk about activities that you and others are able to do simultaneously.

☐ Use the infinitive and the past infinitive to talk about what you will do before and after doing certain activities.

A Vous êtes interprète. Some American artists are going to France to participate in an international art exhibit. Give the French equivalents of the following English sentences so that some newspaper reporters can write an article about them.

1. They will come to Paris after leaving New York.

_____

_____

2. Before arriving in Paris, they will stop in London.

_____

_____

3. They will probably be tired upon arriving in Paris.

_____

_____

4. After resting a little, they will go to the museum.

_____

_____

5. After seeing the exhibit, they will go back to the hotel.

_____

_____

6. They won't leave Paris without visiting the Louvre.

_____

_____

ⓑ Et vous? In the space provided, write at least three statements about your daily or weekly routine for each of the following: activities you do simultaneously, activities you do before doing something else, and activities you do after doing other activities. Vary your statements as much as possible.

EN MÊME TEMPS:

    EXEMPLE *Je regarde la télé en me préparant le matin.*

_____

_____

_____

_____

AVANT:

    EXEMPLE *Avant de partir le matin, je prends toujours un café.*

_____

_____

_____

_____

APRÈS:

    EXEMPLE *Après être rentré(e) le soir, je me repose un peu.*

_____

_____

_____

Intégration et perspectives

Ⓐ Chez nous en France: Destination la région Champagne-Ardennes. Isabelle, a modern-day puppeteer, tells us about the region of Champagne-Ardenne, where she grew up and where she learned this art form. She also expresses what her art means to her and why this region is well known for **l'art de la marionnette.** Before you read, locate Champagne-Ardenne on the map at the front of this book.

«Chez nous», c'est bien sûr en Champagne où j'ai grandi, et dans les Ardennes, à Charleville-Mézières où j'ai fait mes études. C'est là que j'ai suivi mes premiers cours de théâtre, et que j'ai appris les rudiments du métier que j'ai choisi: celui de marionnettiste (puppeteer)... Mais maintenant, pour moi, «chez nous», c'est aussi partout où nous rencontrons le regard émerveillé des enfants, partout où il y a de la joie et du rire (laughter) sur leur visage quand ils viennent voir notre spectacle de marionnettes (puppet show). Les enfants sont les meilleurs spectateurs du monde: ils savent rire aux éclats (laugh out loud), battre des mains (clap their hands), crier de joie–ou de peur–, et se laisser transporter dans le monde de l'imaginaire.

Comme les troubadours d'autrefois qui allaient de château en château pour amuser les seigneurs (noblemen), nous allons de ville en ville pour présenter notre spectacle. Le plus souvent, nous sommes invités par des Maisons de la Culture ou des écoles, d'autres fois, nous donnons notre spectacle en plein air dans un parc ou dans un jardin public, ou même sur les marches (steps) d'un théâtre romain vieux de plus de 2 000 ans! Nous avons même fait des tournées (went on tour) en Russie, en Amérique et en Afrique.

Mais Charleville-Mézières reste un des grands centres mondiaux du marionnettisme et j'y retourne toujours avec beaucoup de plaisir, surtout à l'occasion du Festival Mondial des Théâtres de Marionnettes. Pendant plus de dix jours, 250 compagnies venues des cinq continents se réunissent dans cette ville pour présenter leurs créations à plus de 100 000 spectateurs, eux aussi venus du monde entier! Ce festival, qui a été créé en 1961, a lieu (takes place) tous les trois ans. C'est aussi en 1961, et à Charleville-Mézières, que l'Institut International de la Marionnette a été créé sous le patronage du Ministère de la Culture. Et c'est dans cette même ville que l'École Nationale Supérieure des Arts de la Marionnette est née en 1987. Vous voyez donc que j'ai beaucoup de bonnes raisons de rester très attachée à cette région!

Avez-vous compris? Answer the following questions with information from the text.

1. Dans quelle ville du nord de la France Isabelle a-t-elle fait ses études?

_____

2. Pourquoi ce choix a-t-il eu une importance considérable dans sa vie?

_____

3. Pourquoi Isabelle dit-elle qu'elle se sent chez elle partout où il y a des enfants?

_____

4. Nommez quelques types d'endroits où Isabelle et sa troupe présentent leur spectacle.

_____

5. Pourquoi Isabelle retourne-t-elle toujours avec beaucoup de plaisir à Charleville-Mézières?

_____

6. Nommez trois raisons pour lesquelles cette ville est un des grands centres mondiaux du marionnettisme.

_____

_____

Ⓑ À vous de lire: Édith Piaf. The following article describes the continuing appeal of the legendary French singer Édith Piaf (1915–1963). Before you read the article, jot down answers to the questions that follow. Next read the article, comparing the details concerning Piaf with the ideas you jotted down. Finally, answer the questions after the article in French.

In your opinion, what makes a good singer?

_____

What do you like and dislike about certain performers and their music?

_____

Where do songwriters get the ideas for their songs?

_____

Elle n'a pas été remplacée. Le public attend toujours une nouvelle Piaf. Beaucoup de chanteuses ont essayé de l'imiter mais elles n'ont pas réussi. C'est pourquoi les disques de Piaf continuent à avoir un grand succès. Même aujourd'hui, longtemps après sa mort, on éprouve une émotion profonde en écoutant sa belle voix émouvante. Pourquoi cette place privilégiée dans le cœur du public est-elle restée vide?

Piaf était capable d'émouvoir et d'enthousiasmer le public parce qu'elle n'était pas un produit fabriqué. Ses colères comme ses tendresses, ses haines comme ses amours, ses chagrins comme ses joies sont les témoins de son authenticité. Elle était impulsive, c'est vrai, mais elle était sincère. Et c'est cette sincérité qui a gagné l'affection et l'indulgence du public. La nature avait donné à Piaf une voix capable d'exprimer le sublime, le pathétique. Mais une voix n'est rien si elle n'a rien à dire, si elle n'est pas nourrie d'une sensibilité venant de l'expérience de la vie, si elle n'est pas l'objet d'un travail constant.

Ce sont là les principales raisons qui séparent Piaf des autres chanteuses. Inconsciemment, Piaf a divisé sa vie en deux actes. Dans le premier acte, elle s'abandonnait à ses sentiments, à ses excès. Après avoir accumulé les souvenirs et les expériences, elle les transformait en chansons. C'était le deuxième acte.

Piaf a chanté l'amour admirablement, mais elle l'a rarement connu. Elle a surtout connu les déceptions, la solitude et la maladie. Après une déception amoureuse, elle passait des semaines et des mois dans un état de dépression totale. Et puis, un jour, elle décidait de se remettre au travail.

Si les chansons de Piaf étaient émouvantes, c'est parce qu'elles exprimaient des expériences et des sentiments réels. Les compositeurs qui travaillaient pour elle composaient des chansons qui étaient le reflet de ces expériences.

La préparation d'un spectacle demandait beaucoup de temps. Quelquefois Piaf aimait la musique d'une chanson mais non le texte. Alors, elle demandait aux compositeurs de changer ce qu'elle n'aimait pas. Ils l'écoutaient parce que Piaf connaissait bien son public et elle se trompait rarement. Après avoir choisi les chansons, Piaf préparait son concert. Elle le préparait pendant deux ou trois mois en y travaillant dix à douze heures par jour.

Puis, le soir de la première arrivait et elle triomphait. Elle était heureuse de son succès. Mais jamais pour très longtemps. Après un certain temps, elle commençait à s'ennuyer. Elle était prête pour un nouvel amour et un nouveau chagrin. Une nouvelle moisson de chansons était en train de naître.

1. En général, quelle est la réaction des gens en écoutant chanter Édith Piaf?

_____

2. Pourquoi le public aimait-il tant *(so much)* Piaf?

_____

3. En quoi consistaient les deux actes qui se sont répétés bien des fois au cours de sa vie?

_____

4. Est-ce que Piaf a eu une vie très heureuse? Expliquez votre réponse.

_____

5. Pourquoi les chansons de Piaf étaient-elles particulièrement émouvantes?

_____

6. Est-ce qu'elle restait satisfaite de son succès pendant très longtemps? Pourquoi ou pourquoi pas?

_____

_____

C **À vous d'écrire: Les Américains et la musique.** How would you describe American music or the music that Americans like to introduce to their French friends? Follow these four steps to prepare your description.

1. Préparation

The questions that follow give you ideas about different topics you can include in your description. Read through these questions and check off five (or more) that you can use in your discussion, then jot down notes about those questions. The lines at the end invite you to add topics or ideas not included in this list.

☐ Est-ce qu'il y a un genre de musique que les étudiants américains aiment particulièrement?

_____

_____

☐ Est-ce qu'on enseigne la musique dans les lycées américains? Et dans les universités?

_____

_____

☐ À quelles activités musicales les étudiants peuvent-ils participer?

_____

_____

☐ Quelles sont les chansons qu'on chante pour les différentes fêtes, surtout pour les fêtes de fin d'année?

_____

_____

☐ Y a-t-il des chansons que la plupart des enfants américains apprennent pendant leur enfance? Si oui, quelles chansons? Vous souvenez-vous des paroles *(words)* de ces chansons?

_____

_____

☐ Qu'est-ce que les Américains aiment faire en écoutant de la musique?

_____

_____

☐ Y a-t-il des chansons qu'on vous chantait quand vous étiez petit(e)?

_____

_____

☐ Y a-t-il certains genres de musique qui sont typiques des différentes régions des États-Unis? Décrivez quelques-uns de ces genres.

_____

_____

☐ Quelles sont les chansons qui sont particulièrement populaires en ce moment?

_____

_____

☐ Si on vous demandait de choisir quelques chanteurs ou chanteuses pour représenter la musique américaine, qui choisiriez-vous et pourquoi?

_____

_____

Autres idées:

_____

_____

_____

2. Brouillon

Use your answers to these questions and vocabulary you know to write a description of at least 200 words and three or four paragraphs. Write this first draft on a separate sheet of paper. Vary your sentences as much as possible. Remember that you're giving a general idea of Americans' musical tastes, not those of a particular group of individuals. As you have done in previous chapters, find an interesting way to introduce your reader to the topic, organize your points into logical paragraphs, and then end your description with an effective concluding statement. Remember also to have a lead-in sentence for each paragraph.

3. Révision

Now that you have finished writing your draft, read through what you have written and check the following.

- Did you answer adequately the questions you selected in **Préparation**? If not, what else could you say?
- Does your description provide an overview of Americans' musical tastes, or have you concentrated too much on one particular group of people?
- Reread your introductory sentence: Does it grab the reader's attention? Does it make the reader want to read more? If not, how could you change the introductory sentence?
- Is your conclusion effective? If not, how could you modify it?

4. Rédaction

Write the final draft of your description of American taste in music in the space provided here. Make the corrections and insert the additions you noted in step #3. Then reread your description to be sure you are satisfied with it.

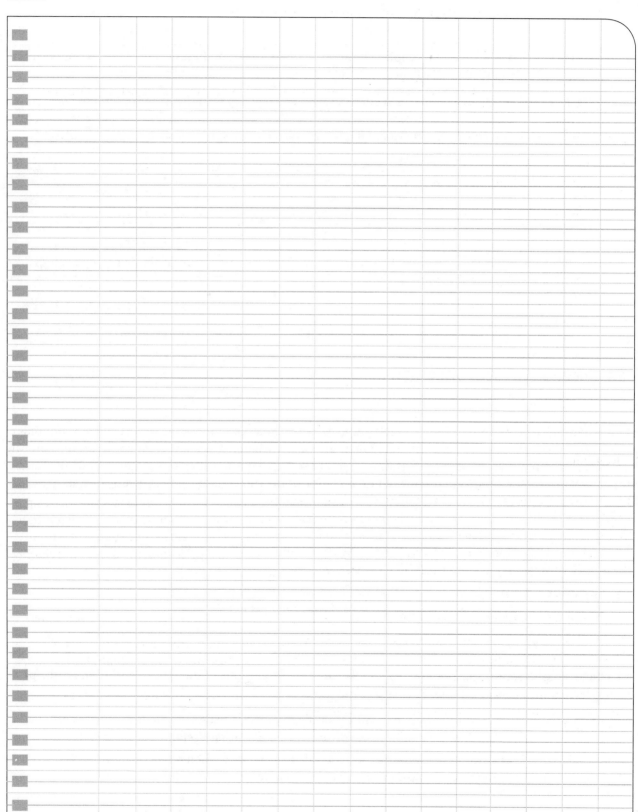

PARTIE ORALE

Point de départ

CD6, Track 19

15.1 Préférences artistiques. Several people are discussing their artistic and musical preferences. Jot down in English each person's comment. You will hear each item twice.

> **EXEMPLE** You hear: J'aime bien l'opéra, mais j'ai beaucoup de difficulté à comprendre ce qu'on dit.
> You jot down: *likes opera but has trouble understanding what is said*

1. _____
2. _____
3. _____
4. _____
5. _____
6. _____

Les pronoms démonstratifs

CD6, Track 20

***15.2 Situation: Tu n'y connais rien!** (p. 439) Françoise and Christophe are having some trouble communicating. The conversation concerns certain reproductions. But which ones? Listen to their conversation. You will hear the conversation twice. Listen the first time as you hear it read, paying attention to intonation, tone, and pronunciation. During the second reading, repeat each line of the conversation after it is read to you.

CD6, Track 21

***15.3 Contradictions.** (p. 439 A) Your tastes are very different from those of your friend Julie. Each time she gives her opinion about something, you say the opposite.

> **EXEMPLE** You hear: Cette reproduction est très jolie.
> You say: **Ah non, celle-ci est beaucoup plus jolie.**

CD6, Track 22

***15.4 La nostalgie du bon vieux temps.** (p. 440 B) Honoré Regret is one of those people who thinks the past was better than the present. What does he say?

> **EXEMPLES** You hear: Je n'aime pas ma nouvelle maison. (la maison où nous habitions autrefois)
> You say: **J'aimais mieux celle où nous habitions autrefois.**
>
> You hear: Je n'aime pas ma nouvelle maison. (la maison de mes parents)
> You say: **J'aimais mieux celle de mes parents.**

CD6, Track 23

15.5 Au musée d'Orsay. Amélie and her friends are talking about their trip to the **musée d'Orsay** in Paris. As you listen to what they say, decide whether a demonstrative pronoun is used each time. If you hear a demonstrative pronoun, write both the pronoun you hear and what it refers to; if you don't hear one, write **non.** You will hear each item twice.

EXEMPLE You hear: Celui qui pourrait nous parler intelligemment des impressionnistes, c'est Monsieur Laroche.
You write: *celui, Monsieur Laroche*

1. _____
2. _____
3. _____
4. _____
5. _____
6. _____
7. _____
8. _____

Le plus-que-parfait et le conditionnel passé

CD6, Track 24

*15.6 Situation: Je te l'avais bien dit! (p. 442) Monsieur and Madame Clément decided to go to a concert. Monsieur Clément was supposed to buy the tickets, but he forgot. Listen to their conversation at the ticket window. You will hear the conversation twice. Listen the first time as you hear it read, paying attention to intonation, tone, and pronunciation. During the second reading, repeat each line of the conversation after it is read to you.

CD6, Track 25

*15.7 Tant pis pour vous! (p. 442 A) You were invited to the home of some friends, but you arrived much too late.

EXEMPLE You hear: ils / manger
You say: *Ils avaient déjà mangé.*

CD6, Track 26

*15.8 Si j'avais été à votre place. (p. 443 C) You have a friend who never hesitates to say what he would have done if he were in your shoes. This time, he's criticizing what you did last weekend. What does he say?

EXEMPLE You hear: ne pas assister à ce concert
You say: *À ta place, je n'aurais pas assisté à ce concert.*

CD6, Track 27

15.9 Des regrets? Some friends are talking about how their lives could have been different. Based on the comments you hear, decide whether each person is happy and mark the appropriate column. You will hear each item twice.

> **EXEMPLE**   You hear: Si je n'étais pas allé à l'université, je n'aurais jamais fait la connaissance de mon meilleur ami.
>
> You mark: *oui*

	oui	non			oui	non
1.	☐	☐		5.	☐	☐
2.	☐	☐		6.	☐	☐
3.	☐	☐		7.	☐	☐
4.	☐	☐		8.	☐	☐

Le participe présent et l'infinitif

CD6, Track 28

*15.10 Situation: C'est plutôt bizarre… (p. 446) Mylène has broken her arm. Her friend Anne-Sophie is rather surprised when Mylène explains how it happened. Listen to their conversation. You will hear the conversation twice. Listen the first time as you hear it read, paying attention to intonation, tone, and pronunciation. During the second reading, repeat each line of the conversation after it is read to you.

CD6, Track 29

*15.11 Avant, pendant ou après? (p. 448 D) Your friends have very different habits. Laurent likes to listen to music while doing something else. Colette prefers to finish her work so she can concentrate better. As for Nadine, she is too impatient to wait. When do Laurent, Colette, and Nadine listen to music?

> **EXEMPLE**   You hear: faire ses devoirs
>
> You say: *Nadine écoute de la musique avant de faire ses devoirs.*
> *Laurent écoute de la musique en faisant ses devoirs.*
> *Colette écoute de la musique après avoir fait ses devoirs.*

CD6, Track 30

15.12 Quand? People are talking about when they do certain things. Decide whether each person's idea is plausible and check the appropriate box. You will hear each statement twice.

> **EXEMPLE**   You hear: Je me brosse les dents après m'être couché.
>
> You mark: *non*

	oui	non			oui	non
1.	☐	☐		5.	☐	☐
2.	☐	☐		6.	☐	☐
3.	☐	☐		7.	☐	☐
4.	☐	☐		8.	☐	☐

Intégration et perspectives

CD6, Track 31

15.13 Un fou de musique. You are going to hear about the musical interests of Monsieur Clément. Before you listen, read the questions to help you anticipate the ideas presented in the passage. After you listen, answer the questions. You will hear the passage twice.

1. Qu'est-ce que Monsieur Clément va faire ce soir après son travail?

_____

2. Combien de chanteurs y a-t-il dans sa chorale?

_____

3. Qu'est-ce que la musique lui permet d'oublier?

_____

4. Quelle est la profession de Monsieur Clément?

_____

5. D'après le texte, est-ce que l'intérêt pour la musique classique est en train de diminuer ou en train d'augmenter?

_____

CD6, Track 32

15.14 Suggestion. Samira had wanted her friend Sabine to accompany her to an art exhibit, but things didn't work out. During the pauses provided, write in French what she says. You will hear each line twice, then the entire passage will be read once again so that you can check your work.

1. _____

2. _____

3. _____

4. _____

CD6, Track 33

*15.15 Bien prononcer: Comment lire la poésie classique. (p. 458)

In general, where more formal language is expected, a greater number of **liaisons** will be made, and, conversely, there will be fewer elisions of the mute **e** (/ə/). In classical poetry, these rules become even more formalized because each line (**un vers**) contains a set number of syllables (**une syllabe**). An **alexandrin,** for example, is a verse of 12 syllables. As seen earlier, elision of the /ə/ can reduce the number of syllables, and **liaisons** can increase it. Therefore, the writing of poetry is based on fairly rigid conventions as to which sounds should be pronounced. The reading of poetry, in turn, must observe these same rules in order not to destroy the carefully crafted rhythm intended by the poet. To illustrate these rules, consider the following lines from a poem by Charles Baudelaire.

1. In French, the tendency is to have open syllables, i.e., syllables ending with a vowel sound, whereas English tends to have closed syllables, i.e., ending in a consonant sound. Thus, the word *temple* in "a Roman temple" has two closed syllables in English whereas in French, **un temple romain** has two open syllables.

2. If a word ends in a consonant sound and the next word starts with a vowel, the consonant is linked to that vowel and forms the start of the next syllable **(un enchaînement).** For instance, **La nature est un temple…** should be divided into syllables as follows: /la na ty rɛ tœ̃ tɑ̃pl/

3. The new consonant sound introduced in a **liaison** also goes with the next vowel sound (for example, in **…est un temple** /ɛ tœ̃ tɑ̃pl/).

4. A mute /ə/ followed by a consonant sound must be pronounced. However, if /ə/ is followed by a vowel sound or comes at the end of the verse, it is not pronounced. In **La nature est un temple…,** the /ə/ at the end of **nature** is not pronounced because it is followed by a vowel. But in **laissent parfois sortir de confuses paroles,** all the mute **e** in the verse are pronounced except for the **e** in **paroles,** because it is at the end of the verse.

Now practice saying the following two stanzas of Baudelaire's poem entitled *Correspondances.*

Text/Realia Credits